Soccer
FOR
DUMMIES®
2ND EDITION

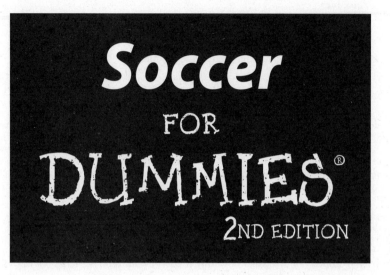

Soccer
FOR
DUMMIES®
2ND EDITION

by Tom Dunmore and Scott Murray

WILEY

John Wiley & Sons, Inc.

Soccer For Dummies®, 2nd Edition

Published by
John Wiley & Sons, Inc.
111 River St.
Hoboken, NJ 07030-5774
www.wiley.com

Copyright © 2013 by John Wiley & Sons, Inc., Indianapolis, Indiana

Published by John Wiley & Sons, Inc., Indianapolis, Indiana

Published simultaneously in Canada

For general information on our other products and services, please contact our Customer Care Department within the U.S. at 877-762-2974, outside the U.S. at 317-572-3993, or fax 317-572-4002.

For technical support, please visit www.wiley.com/techsupport.

Wiley also publishes its books in a variety of electronic formats and by print-on-demand. Some content that appears in standard print versions of this book may not be available in other formats. For more information about Wiley products, visit us at www.wiley.com.

Library of Congress Control Number: 2012956403

ISBN 978-1-118-51066-7 (pbk); ISBN 978-1-118-51065-0 (ebk); ISBN 978-1-118-51067-4 (ebk); ISBN 978-1-118-51069-8 (ebk)

Manufactured in the United States of America

10 9 8 7 6 5 4 3 2

WILEY

About the Authors

Tom Dunmore is an editor of *XI*, a North American soccer quarterly. He is the author of a *Historical Dictionary of Soccer* and is a former chairman of Section 8 Chicago, the Independent Supporters' Association for the Chicago Fire Soccer Club. Tom was born in Brighton, England, and remains an avid long-distance fan of Brighton and Hove Albion. He likes playing soccer for his recreational team the Seawolves and greatly enjoys living in the best city in the whole wide world, Chicago.

Scott Murray is a freelance writer and former sports editor of guardian. co.uk. He writes regularly for guardian.co.uk, the *Guardian*, the *Fiver*, and *FourFourTwo*. He also has written for the *Observer*, *GQ*, *Men's Health*, *GQ Sport*, *Shortlist*, the *Evening Standard*, and *Arena*. He is co-author of the football miscellany *Day Of The Match: A History Of Football In 365 Days*, and an upcoming biography of Maurice Flitcroft, the world's worst golfer, *Phantom Of The Open*. The club he supports has won quite a lot of trophies, but then he also has to follow Scotland, so it all balances out.

Dedication

This book is dedicated to all those who have built soccer in the United States, often against the odds, out of the sheer love of the game. I'd like to personally thank those who have supported the sport in my current hometown, Chicago, especially Peter Wilt, who built the club I support here, the Chicago Fire. Without that I may never have met my wife Monika, to whom I owe everything else.

Authors' Acknowledgments

From Tom:

I'd like to thank all those at Wiley who made this book possible, especially Michael Lewis and Susan Hobbs for their help on the project. I'd also like to thank technical editor Vic Baker for his thoughtful comments and queries. This book is a revision of an English version, Football For Dummies, and is built off that superb framework written by Scott Murray.

From Scott:

I would like to thank everyone at Wiley, especially Simon Bell for his help and never-ending patience, especially upon being quizzed about the managerial merits of Frankie Gray. I would also like to thank Annabel Merullo and Tom Williams at PFD.

Publisher's Acknowledgments

We're proud of this book; please send us your comments at http://dummies.custhelp.com. For other comments, please contact our Customer Care Department within the U.S. at 877-762-2974, outside the U.S. at 317-572-3993, or fax 317-572-4002.

Some of the people who helped bring this book to market include the following:

Acquisitions, Editorial, and Media Development

Project Editor: Susan Hobbs
(*previous edition Simon Bell*)

Acquisitions Editor: Mike Lewis
(*previous edition Wejdan Ismail*)

Copy Editor: Susan Hobbs
(*previous edition Charlie Wilson*)

Assistant Editor: David Lutton

Editorial Program Coordinator: Joe Niesen

Technical Editor: Vic Baker

Editorial Manager: Carmen Krikorian

Editorial Assistant: Rachelle Amick

Art Coordinator: Alicia B. South

Cover Photos: © narin sapaisarn /
iStockphoto.com

Cartoons: Rich Tennant (www.the5thwave.com)

Composition Services

Project Coordinator: Patrick Redmond

Layout and Graphics: Jennifer Creasey,
Joyce Haughey

Proofreaders: Melissa Cossell,
John Greenough, Judith Q. McMullen

Indexer: Riverside Indexes, Inc.

Publishing and Editorial for Consumer Dummies

Kathleen Nebenhaus, Vice President and Executive Publisher

Ensley Eikenburg, Associate Publisher, Travel

Kelly Regan, Editorial Director, Travel

Publishing for Technology Dummies

Andy Cummings, Vice President and Publisher

Composition Services

Debbie Stailey, Director of Composition Services

Contents at a Glance

Table of Contents

Introduction

. . . .

Congratulations! You have a copy of *Soccer For Dummies,* 2nd Edition, in your hands. This book has been written specially for people who want to know all they can about the greatest and most popular sport on the planet: Association Football, whose name is usually shortened in the United States to *soccer* (avoiding confusion with that other sport of football). *Soccer For Dummies,* 2nd Edition, aims to satisfy your curiosity, help you to understand the basics of how to play the game, arm you with knowledge so you can enjoy watching it to the fullest extent possible, and show you a whole world of soccer to explore. There's a reason why soccer has taken off all around the globe and is becoming increasingly popular in the United States.

Soccer is the simplest of sports in principle — in the final analysis, all you need to know is that to win, one team has to score more goals than the other. Nevertheless, a plethora of rules, tactics, and skills exist that can easily flummox the beginner.

That's where this book comes in. I wrote it so that anyone who wants to enjoy soccer — whether by playing it, coaching it or watching it — can come to grips with the sport quickly and easily, without feeling overwhelmed or intimidated. And I promise it won't be long before you've become something of an expert on the most talked-about sporting pastime in the world. You'll never look back!

About This Book

The simple aim of this book is to provide you with all the basic skills and every scrap of crucial knowledge that you need to become a proper fan of the game. All the information you need is between the covers of this book. But although it's all crammed in here, don't feel daunted: You certainly don't have to read every word, from start to finish, to get the most from the book.

Each chapter covers a separate topic about soccer, so you can easily dip into the chapters to find out about something you don't quite understand. Say you're watching a World Cup game on television, but don't really know much about the history of the competition; just turn to the chapter that talks about the competition and this book fills the gaps in your knowledge.

If you're motivated to get up off the couch and play for or help to run a team yourself, this book explains how you can get involved. The book offers plenty of handy hints and practical skills you can develop. Maybe you'd even like to become a referee. Well, that's no problem. I even help you find a whistle.

And even if you're not an absolute beginner, I'm confident that *Soccer For Dummies* can still help you discover plenty that's new and fascinating from the long history of soccer.

Getting Started

Don't worry if you feel you know absolutely nothing about soccer. Chances are you already know more than you think, and this book helps you gain confidence in your knowledge.

But even if you don't have a scrap of understanding about the game to start off with, don't worry! This book soon gets you up to speed. And remember: Even folks who think they know everything about the game have some gaps in their knowledge. Soon enough, I'm confident the information you glean from this book will make an expert of you.

At the moment you may ask:

- ✔ Why do some teams kick the ball up in the air but others pass it around the floor?
- ✔ Why are there two people running up and down the side of the field waving flags?
- ✔ Why is there an offside rule, and how does it work?
- ✔ Who was the greatest soccer player ever?

This book answers those questions — and many, many more. My only assumption is that you know nothing about the game to start with. I take it from there, and it won't be long before you understand all there is to know about soccer.

How This Book Is Organized

This book is organized into six distinct parts. Each section focuses on a different — but important — part of the world of soccer.

Part I: Kicking Off

If you're a complete beginner, this part gives you a basic grounding in what soccer is all about. This part describes what soccer is and why people love playing and watching the game so much. It tells the history of the sport, from its early days in China to the modern game that's showcased in stadiums and on televisions all across the globe. And I show you how to get ready to join in, whether you'll be getting yourself onto the field or just watching from the stands!

Part II: Playing the Game

I don't waste any time getting to the nitty-gritty here. The first chapter in this part explains the rules of the game — which are the same whether you're playing a recreational game in a local league or playing in the World Cup final! The other chapters in this book explain what each player on the field is expected to do, the tactics they're told to employ, and the skills they need to play. Tips on coaching, how to keep fit, and where you can put it all into practice on the field are also included.

Part III: Exploring The World of Soccer

Soccer is the biggest sport in the world, and this part explores everything about the professional game. I explain all about the biggest show on earth — the FIFA World Cup — and other international tournaments such as the European Championships, Copa America and the CONCACAF Gold Cup. The part also explains how club soccer is organized across the world, from the English Premier League to Major League Soccer in the U.S. I run down all the important international and club teams, so you know your Brazils from your Barcelonas and your Argentinas from your Arsenals. Plus there's an in-depth look at women's soccer — a fast-growing sport in its own right.

Part IV: The Fans' Enclosure: Following the Game

If you love watching the game, this is the part for you. The chapters here explain what you can expect to find when you attend a professional soccer game, as well as point you in the right direction to find soccer on television and websites, and in newspapers, magazines, books, movies, and DVDs. I even explain what to do if you want to enjoy controlling a virtual game on your video-game console.

Part V: The Part of Tens

The part without which no *For Dummies* book would be complete. This part is packed full of nuggets of information you can squirrel away for use later, when you need to impress someone with your soccer knowledge. Who was the most controversial soccer player of all time? The answer's here — along with many other facts that are in turns funny, illuminating, tragic, and interesting.

Icons Used in This Book

To help you navigate through this book, keep an eye out for these icons, the little pictures that sit in the margin. They help you spot particular snippets of information. This list tells you what the icons mean.

This highlights small pieces of advice that can help you become a better player or a more knowledgeable soccer expert.

This information is especially useful to remember. If you only remember one thing from each page, make sure this is it!

Hopefully, this won't come up too much — but when it does, take heed, because the information accompanying it ensures you'll be prepared.

The great thing about soccer is the amount of random trivia it generates. There's lots of trivia in this book, and you'll quickly become an expert if you commit all these facts to memory.

Where to Go from Here

So here you are, ready for kickoff. Exactly what you get out of this book depends on your needs. If you're a complete beginner, the book gets you up and running. If you already know a bit about the game, the book soon fills in the gaps in your knowledge. And even if you think you may be something of an expert, well, everyone's still learning, so hopefully you'll find something new and fascinating in here, too.

But although I'd advise beginners to start at the beginning, even they don't have to. This book is designed for you to dip in and out of — so if you want to find out about the world's most famous clubs first, turn to that chapter. You can always turn to a different chapter to bone up on the rules of the game. Or its history. Or its most famous games. Or the hardest tricks to pull off to impress your team mates. Or . . .

Part I
Kicking Off

In this part . . .

To break you in gently to the great game of soccer, this part provides an introduction to the game, covering how it began, and what it is all about. Those of you who are new to soccer receive a comprehensive rundown of the whys and wherefores of the game right here.

In this part of the book, I describe how soccer has become the most widely played and watched team sport on the globe. I explain the basic aims of the game, the field on which the game is played, and, last but not least, what gear you need to have to play it.

Chapter 1

Introducing Planet Soccer

In This Chapter

▶ Understanding why soccer is the simplest game

▶ Learning how to play: The basic aims and rules

▶ Playing and watching

▶ Explaining why people love soccer so much

Association Football — soccer, as it's known in the United States — is the most popular sport in the world. It's referred to by many different names around the world: *football, footy, soccer, fitba, fútbol, calcio, futebol, voetbol, le foot, foci, sakka,* or *bong da.* Whatever it's called, the game remains the same: two teams of 11 players, each team trying to kick a spherical ball into a goal more times than the other.

Soccer is fiendishly addictive, whether you watch, compete, or do both. Across the planet more supporters and spectators follow the professional game than any other sport, and at grass-roots level more amateur participants enjoy the game than any other athletic pastime. Though its growth has been slower in America than elsewhere, it's become one of the most popular participation sports in the United States. As a spectator sport, millions now attend games and tune in to international soccer games via television or the Internet, and the top professional league in North America — Major League Soccer — is growing fast and thriving.

Soccer arouses passion in spectators and players like no other game in the world — and perhaps like nothing else known to humankind. It has done so ever since some English rule-makers formalized the pastime of kicking a ball around into a sport during the late 1850s and early 1860s. (That's 150 years and counting, *and it's still getting more popular by the day.*) But why have billions of men and women, boys and girls, adults and children been enthralled by this simplest of sports for such a long time? What makes soccer so special? Read on for some ideas.

Nothing as Simple as Soccer

John Charles Thring was spot on the money when, in 1862 in Uppingham, England, he wrote a set of draft rules for the game that later became known as Association Football. With the sport yet to be christened, Thring decided to entitle his rules "The Simplest Game."

Thring's rules were tweaked before being ratified by the newly founded Football Association in England the following year, but the new sport of Association Football remained *the simplest game*. Because no game (with the possible exception of running in a straight line, and that's not really a game, is it?) is less complicated than soccer.

The basic aim: It really is that simple!

The object of the game is simple: for a team of 11 players to guide a ball into a goal and do it more times than the opposition team can manage.

That's it!

So why is soccer so popular around the world?

Pop psychologists have written more words attempting to explain why soccer is so popular than on any other subject (except organized religion, maybe, although some soccer fans will tell you that's pretty much the same thing).

The truth is, nobody's ever been able to quite put their finger on why the game is so popular, so I'm not going to pretend to give you a definitive answer. There simply isn't one. The best I can do is offer you the following three suggestions:

- ✔ **Its simplicity makes it readily accessible.** You only have to watch a couple of minutes' worth of action to work out what the teams are trying to do.

- ✔ **Goals have a rarity value and are at a premium.** Basketball involves scoring tons of points, and a tennis player may win a point every 30 seconds. But you can watch 90 minutes of soccer and not see a single goal scored by either team. Some skeptics say this makes the game boring, but its massive popularity around the world suggests that the rarity value of goals only increases the excitement of soccer for many, many people.

> ✔ **The teams belong to the people.** Despite its origins in British private schools, organized soccer quickly became a working-class sport, a release from the tedium of everyday life all around the world. Results really began to matter. Following a team became tribal, with a sense of belonging and a commitment to a cause.

Having said that, thousands of other, better reasons may exist. After you've watched a few games, or played soccer yourself, you no doubt have a few theories of your own. Actually, that's another great thing about soccer: Everyone's got an opinion about it — often a strong one!

Where do people play soccer?

Everywhere, basically. The game, in a very basic form, is thought to have started out in China over 2,000 years ago, with the ancient Greeks, the Romans, and indigenous Australians playing variations on a theme over the centuries.

It wasn't until the mid-1800s that the game as you know it today developed in England, but by 1900 it had spread all over Europe and to South America. Fast-forward another 110 years and every country and continent in the world is now playing the game. That includes the United States, a country that has long favored other sports such as baseball and its own version of football, but now has a well-established professional men's league, a very successful women's national team, and a huge level of participation in youth soccer.

Soccer: Not an Americanism

One of the great myths in the sport is the origin of the word *soccer.* It's generally considered to have been coined in the United States — where the game commonly known as *football* in the United Kingdom is indeed called *soccer.* But in fact, the word is a creation of the English elite.

In British universities and elite private schools, well-spoken students had the habit of abbreviating nouns and then appending them with the suffix *-er,* to create a new informal word. For example, someone with the surname Johnson would be known as *Johnners.* Similarly, the game of rugby union was called *rugger.*

According to legend, in the mid-1880s, someone asked an Oxford student named Charles Wreford-Brown whether he wanted to play a game of rugger. Preferring to play football, he shortened the *association* of *association football* to *soc* and tacked on the usual colloquial suffix — quipping back that he'd rather have a game of *soccer.*

This tale may well be apocryphal, but what's definitely true is that Wreford-Brown went on to captain the England national football — sorry, soccer — team.

Explaining a Few Rules

So how does this team of 11 players actually go about playing the game and scoring these elusive goals? I go into further detail about the laws of the game in Chapter 4, but first here's a brief overview of how you play a soccer game.

The field

You usually play soccer on grass, occasionally on artificial surfaces, but always on a field no bigger than 80 yards wide and 120 yards long. Figure 1-1 shows you how the field looks.

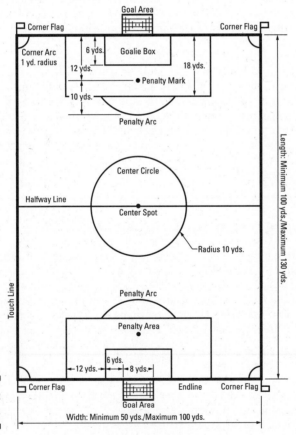

Figure 1-1:
The field.

Each end of the field has a goal, composed of two upright posts 24 feet apart and 8 feet high, topped with a horizontal crossbar. One team tries to score in one goal, and the other team tries to score in the other goal. While both teams are trying to score, they are also trying to stop the other team from scoring.

The ball isn't allowed to leave the field. If a player in one team kicks the ball off the field, then a player in the opposing team must throw or kick the ball back in.

The players

Each team has 11 players. Ten of these players aren't allowed to touch the ball with their arms or hands. They're called *outfield players.* The other member of the team is called the *goalkeeper;* he can use his hands and arms in the penalty area around the goal he's tending.

Four basic positions exist:

- ✔ **Defender:** A defender's job is primarily to defend his goal and stop players from the opposing team scoring.

- ✔ **Forward:** A forward's role is to score goals or create them for other players.

- ✔ **Goalkeeper:** The goalkeeper's job is to stop the ball going in the net at all costs, thus ensuring the opposing team doesn't score a goal. He can do so by using any part of his body.

- ✔ **Midfielder:** Midfielders — usually the team's most adaptable players — cover a lot of ground and help the defenders defend and the forwards attack.

These players are arranged in different places around the field, and the variations on ways to do this are known as *formations.* The most common is 4-4-2: four defenders, four midfielders, and two forwards. An alternative is 4-3-3: four defenders, three midfielders, and three attackers, a more offensive lineup than a 4-4-2. You may notice both of those formations only add up to 10 players, not 11: That's because the goalkeeper isn't listed in the formation; his position is taken for granted. Find out more about the fun of formations in Chapter 5.

General behavior

A referee is on hand to officiate every game, and his decision is always final.

Players aren't allowed to shove each other away from the ball, kick each other, trip each other up, or obstruct each other. If they do, they give away a *foul* and the referee awards the other team a *free kick*. (See Chapter 4 for more on free kicks.)

If one team concedes a free kick close to the goal, the team awarded the kick has a fair chance of scoring directly. If a team concedes a free kick in the penalty box, the referee awards the opposition a *penalty* — a free shot from 12 yards out with only the goalkeeper, who must stay on the goal line until the ball is kicked, in the way.

Referees can send off (eject for the rest of the game) players who continually concede fouls. Find out more about free kicks, penalties, and obeying the laws of the game in Chapter 4.

Goal!

To score a goal the whole ball has to cross the whole goal line, going between both of the posts and under the crossbar.

Players are allowed to score by shooting with their feet or heading the ball into the goal. This sounds easier to achieve than it actually is, which is why goals are greeted with such unbridled joy by crowds.

Keeping score . . .

The scoring system in soccer is simple. If Team A has scored one goal and Team B hasn't scored any then the score is 1-0. If Team B then scores two goals the score is 1-2.

A game may end with neither team scoring a goal. This score is 0-0; this is usually known as a *nil nil* scoreline, not zero zero or nothing nothing.

. . . and keeping time

A game lasts 90 minutes, split into two 45-minute halves. The team with the most goals at the end of 90 minutes wins the game. If both teams have the same number of goals, the game is a tie (also called a *draw*). Depending on the rules of the competition the game is being played in, ties are sometimes settled by playing extra time or going to a decisive penalty shootout.

Playing the Game

The beauty of soccer as a sport is that anyone can play it, anywhere. That's something you can't say about horse racing or NASCAR.

You don't even really need any equipment, apart from a ball — and even then you can improvise. In fact, famous players like the Brazilian legend Pelé and Argentinian icon Diego Maradona both grew up in shanty towns and played with rolled-up newspapers.

Playing solo

Although soccer's a team sport, you don't even need anyone else to play it with. Soccer is a game you can have just as much fun practicing alone. Bobby Charlton, who won the 1966 World Cup with England and the 1968 European Cup with Manchester United, used to spend all his spare time as a little boy practicing with a tennis ball up against a wall. As well as keeping him fit and healthy, it honed the skills that turned him into one of the greatest players the world's ever seen.

Playing with others

It's easy to find people to play soccer with at parks all around the world. Join in a pickup game for some friendly competition and a chance to hone your skills in a (usually) relaxed setting.

But if you want a proper game, don't fret. There are thousands of organized teams that you can join, for all age groups and levels of ability. And who knows: If you're good enough, you may one day get a try-out for a professional team. And then . . . well, we're not promising anything, but *somebody's* got to be the next Pelé, don't they?

Even simpler soccer

Sometimes you may only have a few friends to play with at your local park, but it's still easy to have fun playing games in lieu of a proper game of 11 on 11.

✔ **Headers and volleys.** One player's the goalkeeper, with the other players trying to score, but only with headers and volleys. Players get a point for a goal scored but have to go in goal if their attempts are caught in the air by the keeper.

✔ **Knockout.** The best street soccer game, bar none. You have only one goalkeeper. Everyone else pairs up. Each pair tries to score; whenever they're in possession all the other pairs try to stop them. Upon scoring, a pair qualifies for the next round. Each round sees the last pair to score dropping out.

Watching Soccer and Supporting a Team

Professional soccer is the most popular spectator sport in the world. Billions of people follow the game by going to a stadium to witness the action in the flesh or watching live coverage or edited highlights, either on television or over the Internet.

Following club and country

Most people follow the fortunes of two favorite teams: the club team closest to their heart and their international team that represents the country of their birth or that of a parent.

Fans choose club teams for different reasons. It can be the closest team to them growing up. Maybe their father or mother, or some other close family member, was a fan. Or it can be that a person watched a particular game and fell in love with the club immediately.

There can be other reasons. Their favorite player plays for the club They really like the color of the team jerseys. They visited the stadium once and especially enjoyed the atmosphere. Anything is possible when people are making emotional attachments.

Who you support is up to you, and you can't change what feels right. One warning, though: If you're a Manchester United fan from Chicago, some fans will accuse you of being a *glory hunter* (someone who follows a club just to associate themselves with its success) and ask why you aren't supporting the team from your home city as well or instead. You'll never win this argument, so don't bother getting involved in it. Remember, who you support is a personal decision; no right or wrong answer exists.

Remember, too, that supporting Team X means that you automatically dislike Team Y. (Think Portland/Seattle, Rangers/Celtic, Arsenal/Tottenham, Real Madrid/Barcelona.) These rivalries can generate a lot of pain, but a lot of joy as well. It may not be edifying, but it's an important part of the game.

Winning trophies: The be-all and end-all?

At a very basic level, professional soccer is about winning. Club teams compete to win league championships and cup competitions, and countries try to win the World Cup.

But it's not just about winning the big trophies, which is just as well because there aren't that many to go round — and it's always the top teams and perennially successful nations who land them anyway. Soccer is also about:

- **Beating your biggest rivals.** Your team can end the season without a trophy while your rivals walk away with the championship. But if you've beaten them over the season series — preferably convincingly — you still maintain the most important bragging rights that season. There's logic in there, albeit logic that's a bit twisted.

- **Registering an unexpected win.** Some weekends it's best to write off a result in advance, especially if you're going to the league leaders in full knowledge that they're miles better than you. It insulates you from the pain of defeat, and also makes it 100 times better when your team somehow comes away with a ludicrous 4-1 win.

- **Schadenfreude.** It's not necessarily an emotion to be proud of, but few feelings are better in soccer than letting rip a guttural guffaw after watching a painful defeat befall a club you dislike intensely.

- **Strategy and tactics.** Soccer isn't just a visceral thrill; it can be an intellectual pursuit, too. Working out how your team played, and why they won or lost, can be enlightening and frustrating in equal measure.

- **Having an opinion (and an argument).** Apart from the hard facts on the scoreboard, no absolute rights and wrongs exist in soccer. A heated discussion with fans of either your team or another club over the performance of various teams, refereeing, and the merits of different players can be one of the real joys of being a fan — and a pressure valve to let off steam and keep you sane.

✔ **The game's history.** Soccer is over 150 years old, and there are thousands of fascinating stories to be told. If you're bitten by the bug you may never be able to stop reading about old-school players and what they got up to.

✔ **A famous jaw-dropping moment.** Everyone remembers where they were when Zinedine Zidane headbutted Marco Materazzi in the 2006 World Cup final, or when Landon Donovan scored in the last minute against Algeria to send the United States through to the next round of the 2010 World Cup.

✔ **A personal jaw-dropping moment.** Nobody will remember this one apart from you. Maybe it was a moment spent watching the game as a youngster with your mom or dad, or the time you met your favorite player and he signed an autograph for you.

✔ **Watching the biggest games.** You may never see your team compete in one, but still nothing shares the pomp, ceremony, and sheer anticipation of the final of a major tournament.

✔ **The pain of defeat.** Because without it, you wouldn't appreciate the good times.

Chapter 2

Getting the Ball Rolling: A Brief History of Soccer

*W*herever you go in the world today you're doing well if you can avoid soccer for more than 24 hours. Since the late 19th century, the game has spread to every last nook and cranny on the planet — yes, even the United States — and can justifiably claim to be the number-one team sport in the world.

But how did soccer get so big? And when and where did it start? This chapter looks into the rich history of the sport, from its inauspicious beginnings to the multibillion dollar behemoth it is today.

Discovering the Ancestors of Modern Soccer

So did someone kick a ball in anger first? As you'd expect, both the Ancient Greeks and Ancient Romans played games that occasionally involved propelling a ball by hoofing it around with the foot. The Greeks played games called Episkyros and Phaininda, the Romans a sport called Harpastum. However, it seems these sports have more in common with rugby — or all-in wrestling — than anything you'd recognize as modern soccer.

Want some proof? Here's the Greek comic poet Antiphanes describing a game of Phaininda: "He seized the ball and passed it to a team-mate while dodging another and laughing. He pushed it out of the way of another. Another fellow player he raised to his feet. All the while the crowd resounded with shouts of 'Out of bounds! Too far! Right beside him! Over his head! On the ground! Up in the air! Too short! Pass it back in the scrum!'"

Luckily, other ancient civilizations were partaking in pastimes altogether more refined . . .

Anyone for Cuju?

Far across the seas, in China, the Han Dynasty (206 BC to 220 AD) had come up with a game remarkably similar to modern soccer. It was called *Cuju* — a literal Chinese translation of kick ball.

The aim of the game was simple. Two teams of up to 16 players tried to kick a ball through a goal — usually a hole in a silk sheet suspended between two bamboo posts. Players could use any part of the body apart from the hand. The game was remarkably similar to today's soccer, though huge melees occurred that would be more familiar to modern day rugby fans.

Over the centuries, the ball — which historians think was usually made out of leather stuffed with feathers — became more lightweight and finally filled with air. In turn the sport became more refined, less inclined to degenerate into rabbles running around chasing the ball. As the later section "Inventing Modern Soccer: How It All Began in England" explains, this wasn't the last time the sport morphed from a free for all into a more skill-based pastime.

But Cuju fell out of fashion during the Ming Dynasty, from the 14th century onwards, and quickly became obsolete.

Kemari, Marn Gook, and Calcio Fiorentino

Cuju isn't the only ancient sport with similarities to modern soccer. In Japan, during the sixth century, an extremely hectic pastime called Kemari became very popular. Possibly more group exercise than sport, the idea was to keep an air-filled ball made of deerskin up in the air using only the feet. All players interacted with each other in order to achieve this goal.

On the other side of the planet, indigenous Australians were partaking in a hobby known as Marn Gook (it means "game ball"). Marn Gook is easily as old as Cuju — it was played well into the 1800s and had been around for at least 2,000 years.

Accounts suggest there was little intrinsic point to the games, which featured up to 50 players. Keeping the ball off the ground and showing off elaborate skills while doing so seemed to be the order of the day. Foot skills earned larger applause, so they became the focus of the game.

A similar free-for-all developed in Italy in the 16th century. Calcio Fiorentino — or Florentine Kick Game — was basically a psychotic version of soccer played on the beach. The game was set in a huge sandpit, and players kicked the ball toward designated goals — though they were also allowed to catch, throw, punch, elbow, headbutt, and choke. Kicks to the head were outlawed, though.

Many other old, ball-kicking sports existed, from games between Native Americans in deserts to ice-based games between Inuits in Greenland. Other communities in the north of France, Ireland, and the Shetlands played kick-and-chase games, whole villages often joining in a massive melee. But it was only when players in England slowly got themselves organized in the 1850s that the sport of Association Football, or soccer as we call it in the United States, really began to develop.

Inventing Modern Soccer: How It All Began in England

The English have played a form of soccer for nearly a thousand years. The earliest record of a game (of sorts) being played in the country is in 1175, when schoolboys in London staged a game in the city streets. There were few rules save trying to punt the ball to a predetermined point at one end of the street or the other. It was a dangerous pastime indeed, so much so that over the next few centuries the game was regularly declared illegal by royal decree (see the nearby sidebar "Red card! We've been banned!" for more).

The 1850s: Time to lay down some rules

The first soccer (known as football in the UK) teams in the world were set up in England during the mid-1800s. Elite private schools and universities in the south founded some; cricket clubs or businesses in the industrial north set up others. By 1860, historians estimate that at least 70 clubs existed across the country.

Everyone was playing to a different set of rules, and that was a problem; soccer as an organized sport struggled to take off. The first attempt to write standardized rules came in 1846, when scholars at Cambridge University cobbled some together.

Red card! We've been banned!

The ballyhoo caused by rowdy soccer games annoyed more than one king of England. In 1314 Edward II decided that anyone playing the sport was causing a breach of the peace. He declared, "Forasmuch as there is great noise in the city caused by hustling over large balls, from which many evils may arise, which God forbid; we command and forbid on behalf of the King, on pain of imprisonment, such game to be used in the city in future."

Yet people kept playing games. Richard II, Henry IV, James III, and Edward IV all made soccer illegal, one statute reading, "'No person shall practise any unlawful games such as . . . football . . . but that every strong and able-bodied person shall practise with the bow for the reason that the national defence depends on such bowmen!"

But archery was considered a duty, rather than a fun pastime, and ordinary folk kept on playing soccer, despite the sport being proscribed. The majority of the country could only afford soccer and were quite satisfied playing it anyway, despite Sir Thomas Elyot, writer and snooty social commentator, describing it in 1564 as "beastlike fury and extreme violence."

The masses kept on playing, even with many individuals getting fined or physically punished for doing so. By the 1800s the authorities seemed beyond caring, and the game had spread all across the country.

In 1857 the first-ever soccer-only club was founded in Sheffield. (Other soccer clubs existed already, but they were either linked to schools and universities, or cricket and rugby union clubs.) The men behind Sheffield FC (Football Club) laid down some rules of their own — the Sheffield Rules — and by 1860 even had another team to play, a new set of local rivals called Hallam.

Enter the FA

But while a burgeoning scene was developing in Sheffield, in 1863 several London-based clubs — mainly from local elite private schools — got together at a pub in Covent Garden, London, to pen the definitive set of rules. They formed the Football Association (FA), with the intention of governing the game right across the country.

Governance didn't happen immediately, and for the first decade of the FAs existence their rules coexisted alongside the Sheffield Rules, among many others. But the FA kept printing out their rulebook and sending it around to the nation's clubs. Eventually, their rules became the standard, as more and more clubs joined the association. (Of course, it also helped when, in 1871, the FA launched the first major soccer tournament in the world: the FA Cup.)

The FA also helped give the game its name — Association Football — which distinguished it from Rugby Football. That name was soon shortened to *soccer* from as**soc**iation, just as rugby was shortened to *ruggers*. So although many people think soccer is an American name for the game, it actually comes from the birthplace of the sport itself, England.

Step aside for the professionals!

The FA Cup — or to give it its full name, the Football Association Challenge Cup — was first held in the 1871–72 season. By this time the FA had 50 members, although only 15 clubs decided to compete. The first final of the first major soccer competition in history was won by founder members Forest-Leytonstone, who had been renamed Wanderers, and was the team of the FA secretary Charles Alcock! Hmm.

By 1883 over 100 teams were competing in the FA Cup. In the first 12 years of the tournament's existence a team of amateurs from the South won the cup every time. But in 1883, Blackburn Olympic won, backed by a local manufacturer who'd controversially paid for the players to take a week off in Blackpool ahead of the final in preparation. Professionalism was on its way.

Governing soccer nationally

The Football Association (FA) is the oldest national governing body in the world. This explains why there's no "English" in the title: Because it was the first, the founders felt no need to identify the country.

It was formed on October 26, 1863, when representatives of London public schools, civil service departments, and sporting clubs met in a pub in Covent Garden, central London, to agree on a single code for the sport.

Agreement on rules didn't come immediately — handling the ball, for example, wasn't outlawed for another three years (which explains why some of the founding members quickly dropped out to become rugby clubs, going on to form the sport of rugby union in 1871). The FA kept going, though, kicking challenges from several rival organizations aside to establish itself as English soccer's governing body.

The FA runs English soccer to this day, from the grass roots to the very top of the sport. All other countries have since followed England's lead by forming a national association to run soccer. In the United States, the governing body today is known as the United States Soccer Federation (US Soccer, or the USSF). It was founded in 1913 and oversees the entire sport, including the men's and women's national teams and Major League Soccer (MLS).

Dribbling or passing?

Why were the Scots so dominant in the early days of the Scotland/England internationals? It was all down to the different tactics they played.

The English liked to run with the ball and dribble it past opponents, but the Scots realized that passing it around among each other paid dividends. They still ran with the ball, too, but mixed up their play with short and long passes. This was called *combination play.*

As the British took the game around the world, many countries copied combination play, swiftly adapting it because most Europeans and South Americans were more interested in the skillful side of the game rather than the trademark British physicality.

Being professional in 1883 was, technically, against FA rules. But nobody complained until a team called Upton Park played the pros of Preston North End in 1884. Upton Park — old-school southern amateurs — protested to the FA that their northern industrial opponents had an unfair advantage. The FA banned Preston, along with several other clubs, from competing in the following year's FA Cup — so the teams (from the industrial North and Midlands) simply threatened to form a breakaway professional association.

The FA buckled, allowing professionalism to become legal. Professionalism meant players had to be paid, so regular games were needed to ensure revenue. William McGregor, the chairman of Aston Villa, suggested an amazing new idea: a league of teams playing each other once at home and once on the road, with the new "Football League" inaugurated in 1888.

Beyond domestic league play, international play had already begun. Scotland soon gained the upper hand in the early annual fixtures, recording 7-2, 6-1, and 5-1 wins during the first decade. English clubs, noting Scotland's dominance, enticed many Scottish players south of the border, and these players became a major factor in the legalization of professionalism.

Exporting Soccer Around The World

After the FA set down their rules in 1863, British sailors, soldiers, and bureaucrats started taking them round the world. Often packing a ball in their bag on their travels, they introduced the game first to mainland Europe and later South and North America.

The game takes over Europe . . .

The first club in mainland Europe predated the FA, though it still required a traveling Brit to set it up. The Lausanne Football and Cricket Club was founded in Switzerland in 1860.

In turn, Switzerland helped popularize soccer in Spain. It was a Swiss, Hans Gamper, who founded the famous FC Barcelona in 1899 — but not before British miners working in copper mines in Andalucia helped to set up Recreativo de Huelva, the oldest club in Spain, in 1889.

Meanwhile, British students had taken the game to Portugal, introducing Lisbon to the game in 1866; Belgium, setting up a club in Antwerp in 1880; Austria, forming two clubs in Vienna in 1890; Russia, where they played soccer in St Petersburg in the same year; and Germany, where a club in Berlin was formed in 1893.

Other countries discovered England's creation for themselves. The Dutch started their own FA in 1889, having witnessed British embassy staff at The Hague enjoying kickabouts. And traveling Italian textile worker Edoardo Bosio, after experiencing soccer in Nottingham and London, took a ball back to his native Turin and in 1891 formed Italy's original club, Internazionale Turino.

Bosio's club is not to be confused with the famous modern team Internazionale, who hail from Milan.

How Britain gave soccer to Brazil

Brazilian soccer may bear little relation to its more prosaic English cousin, but the game may never have taken off in the country were it not for an English schoolboy.

Charles Miller was the son of a wealthy Scottish diplomat who'd settled in Brazil. Miller was packed off back to Britain in his youth and became a skillful soccer player while at boarding school. Nicknamed "Nipper," his tricky dribbling skills won him an invitation to play for St Mary's, the club that later became Southampton FC.

St Mary's hoped Miller would stay and become a professional with them, but Miller returned to Brazil in 1894, taking with him two balls and the FA rulebook. Disembarking at São Paulo with his goodies, he soon won over the ex-pats in the country with the new game, and in 1901 helped form Brazil's first league.

Miller has a square named after him in São Paulo. Brazil is the most successful country in world soccer, having won five World Cups.

FIFA: The world governing body

By the turn of the 20th century people all over the world were playing soccer. The need for an all-encompassing governing body was imperative.

Because England had given the game to the world, the world looked to England for guidance. But it got none. Great Britain was an extremely inward-looking island, with a massive superiority complex, and saw little need to get *too* involved in the organization of the sport across the globe.

So instead the French took the lead, forming the Fédération Internationale de Football Association (FIFA) on May 21, 1904. FIFA — as it became colloquially known — drifted for a while. Few associations bothered joining in its early days, and even when membership increased, World War I got in the way of progress.

After the war, the British Nations — England, Scotland, Wales, and Ireland — withdrew from FIFA, citing an unwillingness to play against countries Britain had been at war with. They also fell out with FIFA over "broken time" payments to amateur players. (FIFA wanted to make sure players who missed work, or incurred expenses, were recompensed.)

In truth, though, the British simply saw international competition as beneath them, still regarding their teams as the best in the world. It was a ridiculous stance: They missed out on the first three editions of FIFA's new baby, the World Cup, and when they finally returned to the fold in 1950 they found themselves lagging behind the rest of the world — they lost at the 1950 World Cup to the United States, who had been a member of FIFA since 1913.

FIFA today is the international governing body of soccer. It organizes all of soccer's major worldwide tournaments — the jewel in the crown being the World Cup — and has 209 member associations. It's based in Zurich, Switzerland.

. . . *then South America* . . .

Many British emigrants already lived in South America due to long-established trading routes, so the game quickly caught on across the continent. Several British boarding schools in Buenos Aires began playing the game in the mid-1860s, not long after the FA was set up.

By 1867 the city had its first team — Buenos Aires FC — and by 1891 a league association had been set up. Outside of England and Scotland this was the oldest league in the world — although for the first few years of its existence it was primarily populated with British ex-pats and not locals.

The game reached Uruguay in 1891, when diplomats and businessmen formed the Montevideo Rowing Club, and Brazil in 1894, when Charles Miller, a former pupil of a Southampton boarding school, arrived in São Paulo with a couple of balls and the FA rulebook. (See the nearby sidebar, "How Britain gave soccer to Brazil," for more on Miller).

... and finally the world

It wasn't long before soccer became the global game. Although the Brits were the main players in spreading the word, French, German, and Portuguese colonialists ensured soccer made inroads into Africa. And after a rocky road, soccer is now established as a major sport in the United States.

The first officially recognized international game away from the United Kingdom was between Uruguay and Argentina in Montevideo, Uruguay, in 1902. Argentina won 6-0.

Becoming the World's Biggest Game

Soccer really began to take off in the middle of the 20th century. Domestic leagues in England, Scotland, Spain, Italy, Brazil, and Argentina were becoming huge news. FIFA added to soccer fever by launching the World Cup in 1930.

Massive crowds flocked to the games. In Scotland, crowds of over 100,000 were frequent; in 1937, 149,415 flocked to Hampden Park in Glasgow to witness the annual Scotland versus England game.

The story was the same the whole world over: A crowd in excess of 200,000 people watched the final game in the 1950 World Cup between Brazil and Uruguay in the Maracanã, Rio de Janeiro.

Television switches on

The popularity of soccer made it perfect for the new medium of television. (It was also easy for the cameras to cover.) By the mid-1950s live game were already a regular fixture on televisions across the globe, though not yet in the United States.

The first live game on TV was the 1938 England versus Scotland game. That same year the FA Cup final in London was televised for the first time.

With huge crowds turning up to stadiums, and TV further popularizing the game, people were making plenty of money, but players weren't necessarily seeing much of it. In Britain, for example, the clubs enforced a maximum salary, which saw some players venturing abroad in search of more money.

The problem wasn't solely a British one. In South America, many players felt poorly paid. At one point in the late 1940s and early 1950s, the Colombian league broke away from FIFA and paid players huge sums to play in a break-away league.

Players become stars

Soon enough, wage restrictions were stripped away. And with TV becoming ever more popular, players became global stars. Pelé — the 17-year-old prodigy in the 1958 Brazilian World Cup winning team — was arguably the game's first major star.

Others soon followed, and the concept of *superstar* players really began to take off in the 1960s. In Britain, people treated Manchester United's George Best — with his good looks, fashionable Beatles haircut, and silky skills — like a pop star. And he acted like one, spending as much time in nightclubs and driving around in flashy sports cars as he did in practice.

Players like Pelé started making large sums of money through endorsements and advertising. Soccer players became celebrities. It's a trend that has snowballed to the present day. Players such as Cristiano Ronaldo, Lionel Messi, and David Beckham are as recognizable as Hollywood stars in most places around the world.

As players became more powerful, so did the bigger clubs. Teams from the big cities — such as Manchester United, Milan, Juventus, Real Madrid, and Barcelona — naturally drew bigger support than teams from the provinces.

An imbalance was always bound to occur, though it took many years to become evident. Even as late as 1980 a relatively small provincial club like England's Nottingham Forest could win the European Cup. But times were about to change.

Television changed everything

With the advent of deregulated satellite television in the 1990s, the major European leagues were able to charge vast sums of money for television rights. The big clubs became vastly wealthy — and with increased worldwide exposure thanks to satellite television, new markets opened up for sales of merchandise such as replica jerseys. Soccer had become a massive industry.

The players now also became incredibly rich, thanks in no small part to a Belgian player called Jean-Marc Bosman, who took his club, RFC Liège, to the European courts in 1995 after they refused to trade him to another club when his contract had run out. Citing restriction of his free movement as a worker, Bosman won his case. His victory gave players more freedom to move between clubs, and therefore play hardball in contract negotiations.

From this point onwards, even an average top-flight player earned tens of thousands of dollars a week in the biggest European leagues, with the top stars earning well over $100,000 a week. No longer did they arrive at the stadium on the bus, or were they forced to take on extra jobs to make ends meet!

So is the game better for the changes? Opinions vary. Some miss the old-school innocence; others think the game is much improved as a spectacle because players earn their money by becoming fitter, faster, and more skillful. Some also express concerns that the vast sums of money gambled on players and salaries mean smaller clubs are in danger of going out of business.

All these views are valid. But one thing seems certain: Whether the game is in boom or bust, its worldwide popularity will grow and grow — just as it is doing in the United States.

Establishing Soccer in America

Soccer is now one of the most popular participation sports in America, with millions of adults and youngsters playing every week. An established professional league, Major League Soccer, is today nipping at the heels of baseball, football, and basketball as a major sport. But it has been a long and winding road for soccer to become a fixture on the American sporting scene.

An immigrant game

It's thought that native Americans played a ball game with their feet called Pasuckquakkohowog before Europeans arrived in North America, but the details are lost to history. Modern soccer was brought to America by immigrants from Great Britain in the 19th century. In the 1860s, the Oneidas of Boston became the first organized club, surviving only a few years. Soccer was played regularly in colleges on the East Coast, and as British immigrants also flooded there to work in mills and shipyards in the 1890s, the game quickly grew in towns like Kearny, New Jersey. (A century later, Kearny provided three of the United States' 1990 World Cup roster with John Harkes, Tony Meola, and Tab Ramos, all hailing from the area.)

In the early 20th century, the game began to be organized with a national governing body (now U.S. Soccer) formed in 1913, affiliating to FIFA that year. In the 1920s, the East Coast–based American Soccer League proved a popular attraction, and the United States sent a team to the 1930 World Cup, finishing in third place. But warring factions each trying to control the game destroyed soccer's chances in the 1930s, and soccer remained too dependent on British immigrants. Compared to baseball, a sport perceived as native to America, soccer seemed all-too-foreign for a country in an isolationist mood.

Shooting stars, the NASL-era

Despite one great result at the 1950 World Cup — the United States defeated England 1-0 in one of the shock scorelines of all time — soccer advanced little in the 1950s and early 1960s, with no national league established until the formation of the North American Soccer League (NASL) in 1968.

The NASL attracted some of the biggest stars in world soccer in the 1970s, although often in the twilights of their careers: Johan Cruyff played for the Washington Diplomats and Los Angeles Aztecs, while Franz Beckenbauer and, most famously, Pelé appeared for the league's best-known team, the New York Cosmos, who often drew enormous crowds.

The NASL, though, was not built to last — it expanded too fast, and other teams in the league could not compete with the mega-spending Cosmos. Soccer lacked a broad base of understanding, as most Americans struggled to follow the rules and flow of a game they had rarely played as children. This was about to change, though, as an explosion in the popularity of youth soccer in the 1970s and 1980s sowed the seeds for the future growth of soccer in the United States.

From indoor soccer to the 1994 World Cup

The outdoor NASL league folded in 1984, as the 1980s saw a curious phenomenon with Americans embracing a form of the sport rarely appreciated elsewhere in the world — indoor soccer. A mix of ice hockey and soccer, with the ball rebounding furiously off the boards, its showbiz razzmatazz briefly made indoor soccer the sport of the '80s.

But indoor soccer faded away, and the outdoor game regained its prominence, kick-started by the men's national team's qualification for the 1990 World Cup — its first appearance since 1950. The next year, the United States' women's national team won the inaugural Women's World Cup, and soccer bleeped strongly on the American sports' radar in 1994 when the United States hosted the World Cup, with record crowds of almost 4 million total fans drawn to the tournament. It was won by Brazil, who had beaten the American hosts in the second round.

A future built to last: MLS

Fulfilling a promise made to FIFA, U.S. Soccer founded Major League Soccer (MLS) in 1996, giving the United States a top-level professional league for the first time since the NASLs collapse in 1984. Meanwhile, youth soccer and women's soccer continued to boom, with the women's national team, led by Mia Hamm, winning the World Cup in 1999 on home turf — their second triumph in under a decade.

Though MLS lost two teams to contraction in 1999, it has flourished since with expansion to 19 teams today, and average crowds now surpass the NBA (although with fewer games played per season). MLS has attracted stars such as David Beckham, but it keeps in place a strict salary cap preventing teams from spending themselves out of existence as in the original NASL.

The U.S. men's team has yet to reach the final of a World Cup. Since 1990, the closest it has come was the quarter-final stage at the 2002 World Cup in Japan and South Korea. But growing numbers of American soccer players surely mean they will one day match the achievements of their female counterparts on the world stage.

Chapter 3

Getting Your Game On: The Gear You Need

- -

In This Chapter

▶ Rolling the ball — how it ended up round

▶ Finding the right gear for the game

▶ Training gear and other equipment

▶ Wearing it like the pros: Replica jerseys and other merchandise

- -

You need a set of clubs to play golf; a bat, ball, helmet, and bases for a game of baseball; and a whole bag of expensive tackle if you want to go fishing. The beauty of soccer, however, is in its basic simplicity. To start playing, all you need is a soccer ball — and as you see in this chapter, if push comes to shove you don't even need that!

Having said that, you can't have an organized game without the right equipment. So this chapter covers all the equipment you need to get you looking like a soccer player. And there's no more obvious place to start than with the thing you kick around.

Having a Ball

Most people agree that the greatest two players in the history of soccer are Pelé and Diego Maradona. Amazingly, neither man learned how to play the game using a real soccer ball. Brought up in extreme poverty in, respectively, the cities of Três Corações, Brazil, and Buenos Aires, Argentina, neither Pelé nor Maradona could afford a proper ball. Both children had to improvise if they wanted to play, using rolled-up socks, newspapers scrunched up and tied together with string, and even old grapefruits or melons.

How balls have rolled down the ages

The ball is round, but that hasn't always been the case. The oldest soccer ball known to still be in existence is over 450 years old. Made in Scotland, it was constructed by inflating a pig's bladder by blowing into it with a pipe, then pulling deerskin tightly around it and stitching the whole thing together. An innovative design, and one that no one improved on for centuries.

In the very early days of organized soccer — in the early 1800s when only students at British elite private schools and universities played the sport — the balls were crudely-stitched-together leather pouches, totally dependent on the shape of the pig's bladder and often almost boxlike in shape.

By the 1860s some bright spark had invented inflatable rubber bladders, and the ball literally began to take shape. For the best part of a century the design remained the same: a rubber bladder covered by 18 orange leather strips. One part of the casing had a large lace where the ball had been laced together. If players headed this they sometimes cut open their foreheads. The balls also got heavy in wet weather — it was often hard to kick the ball any meaningful distance in torrential weather. Many believe the heavy ball also tragically caused some players brain damage through repeated heading.

But in the 1960s new technology brought synthetic-leather balls. The balls became lighter and easier to play with in all conditions. A new 32-panel design replaced the old 18-strip leather cover, and the modern ball as you know it was here to stay.

Whether that helped their ball skills is a moot point, but what this irrefutably shows is this: You don't need the most expensive ball or the best pieces of gear to enjoy the game or become proficient at it.

You can buy all sorts of balls. Kids often play with softer sponge balls and then move up to kick around light, plastic air-filled balls of various sizes.

Playing with smaller balls, such as tennis balls, is a good way to improve your ball control and dribbling skills.

But if you're serious about playing, you eventually have to familiarize yourself with a proper soccer ball.

Modern balls are usually made of 32 panels of waterproofed leather (or sometimes rubber): 12 pentagonal, 20 hexagonal. When filled with air they blow out into an (almost) perfect sphere. However, manufacturers are always creating innovative designs: The ball used in the 2010 World Cup final, for example, had just eight curvy panels.

Still, a ball is a ball is a ball, and as long as it meets the official FIFA (Fédération Internationale de Football Association, or International Federation of Association Football in English) Laws of the Game, it'll do the job. A full-size ball must meet the following criteria:

✔ **Material:** The ball should have a leather covering or be covered by "other suitable material."

✔ **Pressure:** The ball must be inflated to a pressure of between 8.5 and 15.6 psi.

✔ **Size:** The ball should have a circumference of between 27 and 28 inches.

✔ **Shape:** The ball must be an air-filled sphere.

Size is important, too, especially in youth soccer. Three main sizes of ball exist:

✔ **Size 3 ball:** A small 10-ounce version recommended for children between four and nine years old. This is small enough for their small feet and allows them to dribble, shoot, and take throw-ins.

✔ **Size 4 ball:** A 12-ounce ball for children between 9 and 14 years old.

✔ **Size 5 ball:** The size of ball used by professionals and in most adult games. At 14 ounces minimum, players of 14 and up can use this ball.

Costs vary wildly depending on quality. You can get a perfectly serviceable leather ball to play and train with for between $10 and $20. Mid-range balls are priced anywhere between $20 and $75. A professional standard ball — a replica of the ones players use in the very highest-level games, such as Major League Soccer or the World Cup — could cost between $100 and $200.

The variations in price are often dependent on the quality of material and construction — perhaps the stitching or bonding of panels is stronger — and give you a rough idea how much life you can get from the ball. However, remember that you're also paying for aesthetic design and branding: A ball similar to the one used in the World Cup final is obviously of a higher quality, but you're also paying a premium for the official imprint.

It's certainly worth spending money on a good-quality ball for official games. But you don't need to spend so much on practice balls, or balls for everyday use. If you're buying a bag of balls for practice sessions, the cheaper sort will suffice.

Balls are usually predominantly white, although you can always find some more colorful designs. Additionally, all major clubs produce their own branded balls — and of course, a Chicago Fire one is likely to be red, a Seattle Sounders ball bright green.

If you play indoor soccer or futsal, you may need a bespoke (custom-made) indoor ball. If the field is small, you usually want a smaller one that is covered with softer felt rather than hard leather panels. A futsal ball is made of synthetic leather and is heavier than the traditional outdoor ball. This helps to absorb impact, making the ball bounce less — ideal because this means the ball runs out of bounds less often, putting an emphasis on good ball skills.

One of the most famous worldwide sayings in soccer is "the ball is round." It's an irrefutable fact, but the maxim (uttered by the 1954 World Cup winning coach, West Germany's Sepp Herberger) means "anything can happen in soccer," because a ball can roll in any direction.

Getting The Right Look

If you want to play in an organized game, certain gear is mandatory. The following sections take you through what you need.

Jerseys

All players on the same team, the goalkeeper apart, must wear identical jerseys. Players can decide individually whether they'd like their jerseys to have long or short sleeves, but all shirts must have a sleeve of some description.

Cameroon wore a sleeveless vest jersey in the 2004 Africa Cup of Nations. It was popular with players and fans, but later outlawed by FIFA, who refused to let them wear the jersey in the World Cup.

Jerseys are usually made of a lightweight polyester. Apparel manufacturers are constantly coming up with new materials that keep players' bodies as cool and dry as possible because they work up a sweat.

In the past, jerseys were made of thick cotton and sometimes even wool. They were handy for keeping players warm in cold climates, but often soaked up sweat and became very heavy during games, requiring players to put in more effort simply to run around.

You can buy jerseys in traditional, simple designs, or more contemporary fashionable ones. Cost often dictates choice: As a rule, the simpler and less elaborate a jersey's design is, the cheaper it is.

Simple jerseys in basic colors, suitable for pickup soccer, cost between $15 and $50, depending on style and manufacturer.

Remember first and foremost this is a sporting garment. It's important that you can move freely in it — so make sure your jersey isn't too tight, even though a slightly looser fit may not be fashionable or contemporary.

Shorts

Players on the same team, goalkeeper apart, must wear identical shorts. The design of shorts is usually quite basic, although there have been various changes in fashion. In the late 1800s and early 1900s, shorts were very long, often past the knee in Victorian times. Lengths gradually got shorter, a trend that continued until the 1980s at which point the garment's legs barely reached the top of the thigh. In the 1990s fashion swung back with longer shorts. Today shorts are somewhere in the middle, a happy compromise of style and function.

Shorts should neither be too short (they offer the legs little protection when slide tackling) nor too long (flapping material can hinder movement).

Unlike jerseys, which are highly visible and often designed for the purposes of fashion, shorts are functional items and as a result cheap to buy. You can usually pick up a pair in a sports retail outlet for less than $10. If you're buying for an entire team it pays to negotiate a bulk deal.

Make sure your shorts don't clash with your jerseys. Although it's not against the rules to wear hideously clashing colors, it could cause you problems when playing other teams — if you wear red shirts and blue shorts you'll almost certainly have to change at least one part of your outfit to avoid team-color confusion during games.

Cleats

It's vitally important to get the right footwear: Your shoes, after all, are the ultimate tools of your trade. If you're playing soccer on grass or outdoor turf, you need a shoe with studs on the bottom, known as *cleats* in the United States (and *boots* in Britain). These help you grip the ground, especially in wet, muddy conditions.

In the olden days, cleats were big, lumbering items, hard-leather clogs covering the ankle and a fair bit of the shin. Nowadays the designs are much lighter; the most expensive models slip onto your foot almost like a glove.

First things first: Above all, make sure the shoes fit snugly but aren't too tight. A snug-fitting shoe is preferred by most players because it allows them to feel both the ball and their feet on the ground.

A wide array of designs are available. Narrow down the options by deciding what's best for you. Are you a fast-sprinting striker? Some cleats are designed to be as light as possible, with speed and sharp movement in mind. Or are you a midfield enforcer? It may be best to choose cleats that offer maximum protection because of the larger number of tackles you make during every game.

You may also want to take the actual cleats themselves — the studs on the bottom of the shoe — into the equation. Most cleats have molded, plastic-studded soles — although some are metal, which are more suitable for muddy conditions. The length of the studs determine which field a pair is suitable for — longer studs are for softer grass, shorter studs for hard or firm surfaces.

Some designs are less performance-related, with an eye on fashion: Different colors from the usual black are popular. Some are priced higher simply because of their association with a high-profile player such as Cristiano Ronaldo, who is paid big bucks to wear a new look on his feet every season.

You can get a decent pair of leather cleats for around $50. The latest high-end designs can cost anything between $150 and $300.

There's no point buying an expensive pair of cleats if you don't play in games regularly or you're not a particularly proficient player — you simply won't reap the benefit. Many of the cheaper pairs are still very well made shoes that protect your feet and make your feet feel good. Remember that although the most expensive cleats are obviously of high quality, you're also paying a premium for design, manufacturer name, and recommendations by famous players. If you're buying for a child still growing, don't waste a lot of money on something that won't fit in six months to a year.

Turf shoes

When you're not playing in games, you want a pair of shoes to wear for practice, especially if you're regularly practicing on firm, artificial turf surfaces or indoors. Turf shoes have a sole covered in small rubber studs, giving good traction on hard surfaces — but they are less useful on wet or soft surfaces, because you may slip.

India has qualified for the World Cup only once, in 1950, but withdrew after several of their players said they'd only play barefoot, which was against FIFA rules.

Shin guards

Shin guards — also known as shin pads — are compulsory in any official game. They drastically reduce a player's chance of serious leg injury. Two types of shin guards exist: a hard plastic guard, padded on one side, which fits down the front of your sock and in front of your shin; or a tightly fitting fabric tube, pulled onto the leg, with a guard sewn either into or onto the front, protecting the shin and also supporting the leg muscles.

The more basic, old-fashioned plastic guards cost around $10 for a pair, whereas the tight-fitting tubular pads cost between $15 and $30 for a pair.

Goalkeeping gear

Goalkeepers are a breed apart, and they need to look different on the field as well. This section tells you what you need to know about ensuring your goalkeeper has the right gear.

Jerseys and shorts

Goalkeepers must wear a different-colored jersey than the rest of their team for purposes of instant identification. Green or black are the traditionally preferred colors, although any color is permitted as long as players can easily distinguish it from the rest of the players.

Goalkeeping jerseys are made with protection of the upper body in mind because the keeper has to dive around during the game. They offer more padding than a normal soccer jersey, especially on the elbows.

You can also purchase elbow pads to wear beneath the goalkeeping jersey for extra protection.

Goalkeeping jerseys are usually priced between $30 and $75.

Goalkeeping shorts and long pants should have padding down the sides of the legs and, in the case of pants, on the knees. Shorts cost marginally more than outfield pairs, at around $15 to $20, and pants can cost between $20 and $40.

Don't skimp on quality for goalkeeping gear: Make sure all items have sufficient padding in order to remain injury free!

Gloves

Keepers wear gloves to protect their hands from blisters, cuts, ripped nails, and other impact injuries, as well as to cushion the force of the ball. They cost between $30 and $100, and a decent set will probably set you back at least $60.

Just like shoes on an outfield player, picking the right pair of gloves is a personal issue. Some keepers want extra padding; others may want extra feel. It's worth trying on a few different pairs to find the pair that fit like, well, a glove!

The referee

The referee's gear is supplied by the league or organization that is running the competition. If you're refereeing in an informal game, then you don't need any special kit, providing your jersey and shorts don't clash with either side and you have a pocket for your cards and whistle. Even so, you can buy gear especially designed for referees: Jerseys usually cost around $50, with shorts and socks $10 apiece.

Remember that a referee requires other tools of the trade:

- **Notebook, pencil and cards:** You need, at the very least, a scrap of paper and a pencil in order to record any yellow or red cards you issue (see Chapter 4 for card stuff). You can buy made-to-order referee sets for around $5 and wallets for between $10 and $20.

- **Stopwatch:** Referees need to time each half — 45 minutes exactly — and may have to pause the clock for lengthy stoppages such as injuries. You can buy a sports timer at around $10; models with more features may cost between $30 and $60.

- **Touchline flags:** A set of two flags for the assistant referees costs around $20.

- **Whistle:** A simple plastic whistle costs around $3. You can pick up a more hard-wearing metal whistle for around $7.

Additional garments

Although not required by the Laws of the Game (see Chapter 4 for these), other useful items include:

- **Baseball cap:** Outfield players aren't permitted to wear headgear, but the goalkeeper can wear a peaked cap to help him see long balls coming through the air when the sun is in his eyes.

- **Gloves (other than for the goalkeeper):** These come in handy on particularly cold days.

- **Undergarments:** If your team's jerseys are short-sleeved, you can wear a long-sleeved undergarment to keep your arms warm. You can also wear lira under shorts. These items should be the same colors as the jersey or shorts worn above.

- **Sports bra:** Female players should wear a supportive bra while playing, to reduce the risk of damage to ligaments in the chest.

✔ **Track pants or leggings:** You must always wear shorts over them, but if it's cold you're usually permitted to wear track pants or some form of leggings. These are also recommended if you're playing on an artificial turf surface, where slide tackling can lead to blisters and friction burns. Goalkeepers are allowed to swap their shorts for track pants.

✔ **Practice pinny:** A *pinny* is a small and lightweight colored vest that you can wear over a jersey. You use them in training sessions, when the coach divides a group of players into teams for practice games; one team wears the colored pinnys to distinguish it from the other team.

Approaching Equipment

The ball isn't the only piece of equipment you need to stage a proper soccer game.

Goals and nets

If you're just having an informal kick around in the park, then throwing down a couple of backpacks or sweatshirts for goalposts will do. But if you're embarking on a serious practice session, or a full-blown game, you need proper goals. Goals, nets, and corner flags are nearly always provided as part of the field rental fee or by the league you play in for official games, and will already be there for you.

If you need to purchase small-sized goals for practice or pick-up purposes, it will cost you between $50 and $200 for a pop-up set, depending on the size and quality that you want.

First-aid kits

You should always have a first-aid kit at a game or training session. You can cobble one together yourself, but it's often easier (and not particularly more expensive) to buy a sports first-aid kit. Basic kits start at around $20, with bigger kits costing between $30 and $50. Single-use ice or heat packs can help treat injuries; they cost around $1 each, but you can buy more cheaply in bulk packs.

Practice aids

A wide range of practice equipment is available. The following are the most basic and common practice aids:

- **Hurdles:** Useful for fitness drills and stride technique, different heights cost between $6 and $9 per hurdle.
- **Marker cones:** Perhaps the most essential training aid, you can pick up a set of 50 flat-disc plastic markers for around $15.
- **Passing arc:** Loops through which you pass balls, they cost around $10 per arc.
- **Slalom poles:** Used to improve dribbling technique, these spiked poles cost around $5 apiece.
- **Traffic cones:** More visible than marker cones, these usually stand a foot high and have a reinforced base. Five cost between $10 and $15.

Other gear and equipment

You can buy a few other items that you may consider useful:

- **Ball bag.** A nylon carrying bag for up to 20 balls usually costs around $20. Unless you're a juggler as well as a soccer player, this makes your life a whole lot easier if you have more than two balls to carry.
- **Ball pump.** Essential if your soccer ball loses pressure, which it will. Sizes are usually universal, but make sure the nozzle fits your ball or that you have an adaptor to make it fit. A pump costs around $5 to $10, but if you have a lot of balls you may require an electric pump costing around $100.

  You need a ball pressure needle to measure the air pressure of the ball after it's been inflated. Soccer balls that exceed the recommended amount of pressure could result in injury.
- **Drink bottles.** A plastic drink bottle costs around $5. You can buy them in sets with carriers.
- **Tactic board.** You can buy magnetic wipe-clean whiteboards with numbered counters in a set, usually costing around $40 to $60.

Meeting Up with Merchandise

Soccer merchandising is now a global industry responsible for raising many millions of dollars annually for the world's bigger professional clubs. An amazing range of merchandise is on offer for the discerning — and not so discerning — fan.

Replica jerseys

You don't have to wear soccer jerseys only when you play. Whereas fans once went to the games displaying their allegiance with a scarf bearing the club colors, nowadays they also wear the team's latest jersey. All clubs sell replicas of their current jersey. Many Major League Soccer teams have a store at their stadium selling jerseys, or you can order online, where you can also purchase jerseys from your favorite club overseas.

Up until the 1970s, teams rarely changed their jerseys, perhaps updating their look once a decade with the then slow-moving vagaries of fashion. (For example, v-necked collars were in vogue during the 1950s and round collars defined the 1960s.) Many clubs didn't even have a team logo on their jerseys. But during the 1970s, jerseys began to carry distinctive embellishments and striking logos.

As a rough rule, clubs change the design of their primary jerseys once every couple of years. The primary kit almost always features the club's traditional colors but has enough significant changes in the design to make the previous version look dated, thus encouraging a new purchase. Teams also always have a secondary jersey, and sometimes a third design as well.

Replica jerseys cost between $60 and $80 when they're released, whereas authentic jerseys — identical to those the players wear — can cost double that. Replica shorts and socks are also on sale, though these are usually only popular in children's sizes.

Don't throw away your old jersey after you get the latest one. Even if it's out of fashion now, tastes are cyclical — in 10 or 20 years' time it'll be a retro classic and possibly even worth some money to collectors! Check out the section "Retro jerseys" for more on the appeal of old-style looks.

Soccer fans usually buy the jerseys of the teams they support, although some companies do a brisk trade in selling replicas of classic teams from around the world, especially if the design — or even the team — is considered fashionable and successful. Notice an uptick in the number of Brazil jerseys you see players wearing at pick-up games the next time they win the World Cup.

Numbering and lettering

You can get the name and roster number of your favorite player printed on the back of your replica or authentic jersey at either your local soccer store or online. Most stores usually charge a dollar or two per letter. You can also ask the store to put your own name and number on the back of the jersey.

Retro jerseys

Some fans eschew the modern in favor of classic jerseys of yesteryear. Retro jersey manufacturers such as Toffs (www.toffs.com) offer a huge range of jerseys from all around the world, replicating designs from as far back as the 1800s. Supporters often buy jerseys that are synonymous with a certain period of success for their club, that fans consider to be the one true "classic" design of their club's look, that are fashionable, or that have some retro-kitsch appeal. Retro jerseys cost between $50 and $75.

Some retro jerseys never go out of fashion, such as those that are iconic for the achievements of the team that wore the originals, and because the design is simple enough to pass as fashionable in any era. Brazil's World Cup 1970 jersey — all yellow, green trim — will always be considered a classic design.

Rightly or wrongly, many fans see retro jerseys — whether newly manufactured to old design specifications or old, original replica shirts — as a badge of honor because they either show knowledge of a club's history or prove that the wearer has been a fan of the club for years.

Scarves

In the days before replica jerseys became the norm, it was de rigueur to wear a long woolen scarf with your club colors on it. (If you supported Arsenal in London, for example, your scarf may be colored red, or more likely striped red and white.) Scarf-wearing is still popular, even though it's not always an ideal garment for what is primarily a summer sport in the United States.

Scarf designs usually bear the club name in large print. Some scarves even bear the name of two clubs that usually commemorate big games between the two teams or countries who rarely play each other.

You can buy a variety of scarves from soccer stores, supporter groups, online soccer outlets, and at stadiums during games. They cost between $20 and $30.

Other official merchandise

Clubs are happy to put their branding on just about anything, from bedding to bottles of cheap red wine. Some of the less tenuous merchandise offered by soccer clubs today includes caps and hats, branded casual wear such as polo shirts and track jackets, sports training gear . . . and (of all crazy things . . .) soccer balls.

Knowing Where to Get It All

Most cities have at least one sports retail store. Many boast several, including larger warehouse-sized hangars usually located at shopping malls.

You can likely find a wide range of practice equipment — but if you want some very specific gear, you may have to go to a more specialist retailer or hunt the products down online. You can find just about everything on the Internet: Google is your best friend here.

For club-specific merchandise, the club store at your team's stadium is the best place to visit if you are local. Most clubs also have an online store, which you can find through their official website, whereas general online retailers carry branded gear from most of the biggest clubs around the world.

Part II
Playing the Game

The 5th Wave   By Rich Tennant

"Okay – who told the goalie she could use her trampoline?"

In this part . . .

In this part, I start off by explaining the Laws of the Game (that's Laws, not rules: it's a serious business). I also talk you through the different playing positions, and the various tactical formations that have been used through the history of soccer, and the ones that continue to be used to this day. I also explain in detail the skills you need to acquire in order to excel on the field.

Getting and staying physically fit for soccer is important, and I give you advice both on how to stay in the game for the full 90 minutes, and how to avoid and deal with injury. And if you who want to be a coach, or even set up your own team, this part describes the steps you need to take.

Chapter 4

Laying Down the Laws

· ·

· ·

The Laws of the Game — as the rules of soccer are officially known — may seem daunting to the beginner. The official FIFA (Fédération Internationale de Football Association, or International Federation of Association Football; the world governing body) handbook runs to 140 pages!

Official competitions such as Major League Soccer follow the laws outlined by FIFA to the letter, but competitions at different levels do sometimes vary from the laws outlined in this chapter. Don't worry too much, though, because the game is ultimately as basic as they come. The object of soccer is beautifully simple: to send a ball by foot, or any other part of the body except for the hands and arms, into your opponent's goal. And that's it!

Well, okay, not quite . . . but the rest is easy to pick up, I promise. Even the offside rule!

Living by the Laws

Under the auspices of FIFA, the International Football Association Board writes the Laws of the Game. The Board consists of members from the English, Scottish, Welsh, and Northern Irish Football Associations, plus representatives of FIFA.

Every season the Board makes changes to the rules. Sometimes they're major changes, such as when it outlawed back passes to the goalkeeper in 1990. And sometimes they're minor alterations; for example, referees are often asked to crack down on a particular rule, such as time-wasting or feigning injury.

The simplest game

Here are the original rules of soccer, from which today's Laws of the Game are descended. They were written by a J. C. Thring in 1862, and adapted by England's nascent Football Association a year later.

The rules were for a sport called The Simplest Game:

A goal is scored whenever the ball is forced through the goal and under the bar, except it be thrown by hand.

Hands may be used only to stop a ball and place it on the ground before the feet.

Kicks must be aimed only at the ball.

A player may not kick the ball whilst in the air.

No tripping up or heel kicking allowed.

Whenever a ball is kicked beyond the side flags, it must be returned by the player who kicked it, from the spot it passed the flag line, in a straight line towards the middle of the ground.

When a ball is kicked behind the line of goal, it shall be kicked off from that line by one of the team whose goal it is.

No player may stand within six paces of the kicker when he is kicking off.

A player is out of play immediately he is in front of the ball, and must return behind the ball as soon as possible. If the ball is kicked by his own team past a player, he may not touch or kick it, or advance, until one of the other team has first kicked it, or one of his own team has been able to kick it on a level with, or in front of him.

No charging allowed when a player is out of play; that is, immediately the ball is behind him.

Much has changed since 1862, but the aim remains the same — to score more goals than the other team.

The press, websites, and television always highlight any changes before the start of a season or major tournament, so keep your eyes peeled.

Law 1: The field of play

The field of play is usually known in North America as *the field,* though you may also hear it called *the pitch,* the British name used for the field of play in soccer and other sports.

The surface

You can play soccer games on natural surfaces, such as grass, or artificial ones, such as Astroturf (depending on the rules of the tournament).

The color of any artificial surface must always be green.

Size, shape, and markings

The *field of play* (the green bit in the middle) must always be rectangular, marked out with boundary lines. Check out Figure 1-1 in Chapter 1 for what the playing surface looks like.

The two longer lines down the sides are called *touchlines.* The shorter ones (on which the goals stand) are the *goal lines.*

The touchlines must be a minimum of 100 yards long, with a maximum length of 130 yards. The goal lines must be a minimum of 50 yards wide, with a maximum width of 100 yards.

For international games, the size of the field of play is more rigidly defined: a minimum and maximum length of 110 yards and 120 yards; and a minimum and maximum width of 70 yards and 80 yards.

In youth soccer, the field is often smaller than for adult games. Sizes vary by age group — for children under 10, the field is typically a maximum of 80 yards long by 40 yards wide.

The field of play is divided into two halves by the *halfway line,* which joins the middle of both touchlines. In the middle of this halfway line is the *center mark* commonly referred to as the *center spot.* Around it is marked a circle with a 10-yard radius.

The *penalty area* surrounds the goal. Lines are marked starting out from the goal line, 18 yards either side of each post, and extending 18 yards into the field of play. These lines are joined by a line parallel to the goal line.

A *penalty mark* is drawn 12 yards from the goal, on an imaginary line drawn exactly between the two goalposts.

Flags are placed on each corner of the field, and at either side of the halfway line, not less than 1 yard outside the touchline.

The goal

The goal must be placed on the center of each goal line. It consists of two upright posts, joined by a horizontal crossbar at the top.

The goal must be 8 yards wide, and 8 feet tall. A net must be attached behind the goal.

A *6-yard box* is marked by lines extending six yards from the goal line. There are no special rules for play in this box, though the goalkeeper restarts play from a goal kick by placing the ball inside the box for a kick (see Law 16 below for more on goal kicks).

Law 2: The ball

Think any old ball will do? If you're playing an official game, please think again.

Properties

The ball, it surely goes without saying, must be spherical. It has to be made of leather or a similar suitable material, have a circumference no bigger than 28 inches and no smaller than 27 inches, weigh between 14 and 16 ounces, and maintain a pressure of between 8.5 and 15.6 psi.

What if it bursts?

If the ball becomes defective in any way, the referee must immediately stop the game and issue a replacement ball. Play is restarted either with a dropped ball, for which both teams can compete, or with a set piece or throw in if the ball was out of play.

Nobody can change the ball without the referee's say-so.

Law 3: The number of players

Two teams play in a game. Each team consists of a maximum of 11 players, one of whom is the goalkeeper. Teams must have at least seven players or they can't play in the game.

Teams rarely field fewer than the full 11 players from the outset. Should a team's roster be legitimately decimated by illness or injury, or some other extreme circumstance, a postponement of the game is usually agreed. Teams often have fewer than 11 by the end of a game, though: Players can be sent off for foul play, and injuries may outnumber the substitutes allowed.

Teams can make three *substitutions* during a game. A substitution occurs when a team brings a nominated substitute player into the game to replace one who was already playing. Teams can name between three and seven possible substitutes at the start of a game, depending on tournament rules.

To substitute a player, the assistant referee must inform the referee. This usually happens with the assistant referee signaling to the referee by holding his flag at both ends over his head. (For more on the roles of game officials check out the sections "Law 5: The referee" and "Law 6: The assistant referees," later in this chapter. Figure 4-1 shows the signal the assistant referee makes.)

Before the team can make a substitution, the referee must give the okay in a break in play — the team can't substitute when play is continuing.

Figure 4-1:
An assistant
referee
signaling an
imminent
substitution.

Substitution

The substitute — usually called the *sub,* for short — can come onto the field of play only after the player he's replacing has left it.

The player who's been substituted can no longer take any part in the game. It's possible to substitute the substitute.

Players are allowed to swap places with the goalkeeper, but only if the team informs the referee, makes the change during a natural stoppage in the game, and the new keeper wears the keeper's jersey.

Any attempt to substitute a player without the referee's say-so results in a caution for that player. Should a team play more than 11 players then the referee cautions the extra player(s) and then asks them to leave the field of play — a sending off.

Not everyone plays by all of FIFAs rules. For example, in college soccer an unlimited number of substitutions can be made, though no player can reenter a game during the same half in which he left.

Law 4: The players' equipment

Players must wear the following basic uniform:

- ✔ Footwear: cleats or turf shoes
- ✔ Shin guards (which must be covered by the socks)
- ✔ Jersey with sleeves
- ✔ Shorts
- ✔ Socks

Colors

To avoid confusion, the two teams must wear colors that are easily distinguished. They must also not clash with the referee's uniform.

Goalkeepers must wear separate colors that distinguish them from both their team mates and the opposition (and the referees).

Safety first

Players must not wear, or use, equipment that could cause harm to themselves or any other player on the field. This means no jewelry — in other words, players must remove all bling. However, players can continue to wear items such as earrings or wedding rings, providing they cover these with medical tape.

Argentina's infamously thuggish Estudiantes team of the late 1960s used to take paper clips and small blades onto the field of play and poke them into opponents during breaks in play.

Law 5: The referee

Every game is controlled by a *referee,* a man or woman who has the power to enforce all rules of the game.

It's irrelevant whether players think a referee has made a right or wrong decision: The ref's decision can't be changed. The Laws of the Game state, "The decisions of the referee regarding facts connected with play are final." In other words, even if the ref's wrong, he's right.

If you're playing, don't bother arguing with the referee's decision. A referee has yet to be born who's changed his mind, and you only end up receiving a caution if you argue too much.

Playing to the whistle

The referee is armed with a whistle, a stopwatch, yellow and red cards, and a book and pencil. A blast on the whistle means the referee's made a decision, and play must stop (or restart). Referees whistle to start and stop the game, call fouls, award free kicks and penalties, caution or send off/red card players (the book and pencil), or pause the game so that an injured player can be treated.

The referee also usually acts as official timekeeper for the game, hence the stopwatch. In high school and college soccer, this rule is modified with timekeeping usually kept via a running clock with the game ending when it counts down to zero.

Referees may look as though they're running around like headless chickens, but they usually jog diagonally across the field, hopefully covering all angles with the help of their assistant referees.

As I said, referees are always right, even if they're wrong. But sometimes they can be very, very wrong. In the 2006 World Cup, English referee Graham Poll showed two yellow cards to Croatian defender Josip Simunic in a game against Australia, but failed to send him off! Simunic got his marching orders only when Poll issued him with a *third* yellow. Oops.

Changing his mind

A referee can only change a decision he's decided is incorrect — usually as a result of intervention by one of the assistant referees — if the game has yet to be restarted. If play has continued, the decision has to stand.

Law 6: The assistant referees

Assistant referees, formerly known as *linesmen* or *lineswomen,* run down the touchlines with flags in their hands, following the path of the ball. They provide the referee, also known as *the man in the middle,* with invaluable assistance.

Assistant referees can help the referee by ensuring the game is played in accordance with all of the Laws of the Game outlined in this chapter. In particular, the assistance referee plays a key role in indicating

- ✔ **When the ball has left the field of play:** In doing so they show which team has won a corner, goal kick, or throw in. See the later section "Law 9: The ball in and out of play" for the definition of *out of play.*

- ✔ **When a player is offside:** See the later section "Law 11: Offside" for the intricacies of this thorny subject.

- ✔ **When a player is to be substituted:** See the earlier section "Law 3: The number of players" for more on substitutions.

- ✔ **When they've spotted a foul:** Especially if the referee appears to have missed it.

Although not required as part of the Laws of the Game, many games now have a *fourth official.* They take over many of the sideline duties from the assistant referees (such as substitutions), allowing them to concentrate on the action. They also take over from the referee or an assistant referee should they be unable to continue with their duties.

Law 7: The duration of the game

Soccer games are split into two equal halves, lasting 45 minutes apiece.

Although professional games are always 45 minutes per half, games at other levels — such as high school and college — are often shorter.

The half-time interval

All games have one; otherwise, you wouldn't get two halves. The interval must be no longer than 15 minutes.

Half-times used to be ten minutes maximum, but over the years they were lengthened, primarily to allow television to show plenty of commercials during the interval. This continues to be the subject of much speculation — constant rumors abound that intervals may grow to 20 minutes in length for commercial purposes.

At the end of the day . . .

After the 90 minutes are up the referee should bring play to a halt; however, he makes allowances for substitutions, injuries, and time-wasting, allowing added time.

On average, referees add on 30 seconds of time for each major incident. So if there have been three substitutions, one player treated for injury on the field, another carried off, and one incident of time-wasting, the referee will add three additional minutes of play (6×30 seconds).

In knockout competitions, such as the World Cup, a game that requires a definitive result may end tied after 90 minutes. Should this happen, the game either goes to 30 minutes of extra time — played in two 15 minute halves — or straight to a penalty shootout.

Law 8: The start and restart of play

Although the 90 minutes start with a blast of the referee's whistle and a first prod of the ball, the very first act of a game is the coin toss.

The winner has the option of either kicking off or deciding which way to kick in the first half. In the second half the teams change ends and kick in the opposite direction.

Kicking off

Kickoffs start the game at the beginning of both halves. They are taken from the center spot. They also restart play after a team scores a goal; the team that's conceded the goal takes the kickoff. All players must be in their own half when the player takes the kick. Defending players must also be outside the semicircle surrounding the center spot.

The player may score a goal directly from kickoff, though this has never happened in the professional game. It's illegal to kick the ball a second time without another player touching it — so don't dribble away with the ball from the kickoff!

Weather conditions can play a part in deciding which way to kick in the first half. If it's windy, teams may prefer to play against the wind in the first half, getting the hard part out of the way first. Dazzling sun can also play a part: Defenders and goalkeepers hate to look into it because they can lose the flight of the ball, giving the attacking team an advantage.

The dropped ball

If the referee decides to halt the game while the ball is still in play, play can only be restarted with a dropped ball. This takes place at the exact point the ball was when play was stopped. The referee allows the ball to fall to the ground from shoulder height. When it hits the floor it's back in play.

Usually, one team agrees to pass the ball back to the team that was in possession when play was stopped, but occasionally dropped balls are contested. When they are, it's usually each team's hardest tackler who goes in hard, hoping to come out with possession!

Law 9: The ball in and out of play

Rules don't get much simpler than this: The ball is out of play if the *whole ball* crosses either the goal line or the touchline, whether rolling along the ground or flying through the air.

If *any part* of the ball, no matter how small, is level with the goal line or touchline, the ball is still in play; for example, the whole ball must cross all of the line.

The ball remains in play if it rebounds off a post, crossbar, or corner flag. It's also still live if it hits the referee (or one of the referee's assistants should they be on the field of play at the time).

Law 10: The method of scoring

This is what soccer is all about. A player scores a goal when the entire ball crosses over the goal line, between the goalposts, under the crossbar, and into the net, whether in the air or on the ground.

The principle is the same as Law 9: If *any part* of the ball fails to cross the line, no matter how small, the player hasn't scored a goal.

Whoever scores more goals wins. If the teams score an equal number of goals, or no goals, it's a tie. In certain knockout tournaments the game may then be decided by the away goals rule (in a series of two games), extra time, and/or penalty kicks. Check out the section "Noting Other Points" at the end of this chapter, for more on these means of settling games.

Some of the most controversial decisions in soccer come when the referee has to determine whether a ball crossed the goal line or not. Technology is coming to the rescue to help referees decide this — various systems are being tested that automatically indicate whether a ball crossed the line or not. This would have helped in the 1966 World Cup final: With the scores level between England and West Germany in extra time, English striker Geoff Hurst swept a shot onto the underside of the crossbar. The ball bounced down, onto the line, and away, only for the linesman to signal a goal. Replays proved the whole ball never crossed the line.

Law 11: Offside

Here's a guaranteed few minutes' worth of fun: Go up and ask any soccer fan to explain the offside law to you. No matter how long they've been watching the game, I guarantee they'll tie themselves up in knots and then change the subject.

It's possibly the most misunderstood law in the sport, but a bit of careful explanation clarifies this tricky rule.

Why do you need an offside law?

If the offside law didn't exist, players could just hang around by the goals, waiting for the ball to be punted up to them.

So when is a player offside?

A player is caught offside if he's nearer to the opponents' goal than both the ball and the second-last opponent when his team mate plays the ball forward. In other words, a player can't receive a ball played forward from a team mate unless there are at least two defending players either level with him or between him and the goal. The goalkeeper can count as one of the two players. Figure 4-2 illustrates the offside law.

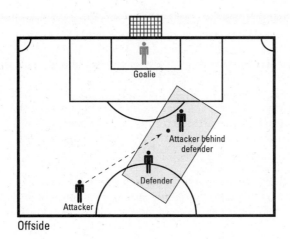

Offside

Figure 4-2:
Explaining
offside.

Onside

It's not an offense in itself to be offside. A player is only penalized for being offside if he is deemed to be involved in active play, so a player can be called offside only if he is:

- In the opposition's half.
- Interfering with play (that is, he's part of the attacking move).
- Interfering with an opponent (that is, he's preventing the opponent from defending against the attacking move).
- Gaining any advantage by being in that position.

A player also cannot be offside from a goal kick, throw in, or corner.

When calling an offside, the assistant referee holds his flag upright and then straight ahead of him. The referee awards an indirect free kick to the defending team from the place the offside occurred. Check out the next section, "Law 13: Free kicks," for the differences between direct and indirect free kicks.

The crucial phrase in this rule is "when his team mate plays the ball." The key to beating the offside trap is to time the run forward properly so that when a team mate passes the ball forward the runner is still onside — but by the time the runner receives it he's running clear of the last line of defense.

In recent years the Laws of the Game have encouraged referees and their assistants to give the attacking team the benefit of the doubt. If any doubt exists, the referee won't whistle for offside. So referees often let marginal cases — players are sometimes inches offside — go without punishment.

Law 13: Free kicks

Hold on . . . what happened to Law 12? Don't worry, it's coming up next. But first, we're going to explain the difference between direct and indirect free kicks because they're extremely relevant to Law 12 and the awarding of fouls.

Types of free kick

You need to know one thing about free kicks above all else: They're either *direct,* or *indirect;* it's all in the name. If a player kicks a direct free kick straight into the opponent's goal, it's a goal. And an indirect free kick? For a goal to be scored, the ball has to touch another player before it enters the goal. You can achieve this by either passing it to a team mate and allowing him to have a shot, or by a deflection, however slim, either off a team mate or an opponent.

Here's a fact not widely known: If a team kicks either a direct or indirect free kick straight into their own goal, the referee doesn't award the opposition with a goal. Instead, the opposition gets a corner.

Upon being awarded a free kick . . .

After whistling for a foul, a referee signals for a direct free kick by holding his arm out perpendicular to his body. See Figure 4-3 for how it's done. The referee signals an indirect free kick by holding his arm above his head, as in Figure 4-4. The rules to bear in mind are:

✔ The player must take the free kick from the exact spot the foul was committed. The player must wait for the referee to whistle again before taking the kick.

✔ The ball must be standing still before the player takes a free kick. After taking the kick, a player can't touch the ball again until another player touches it.

✔ A direct free kick awarded to the attacking team in the opposition's penalty area results in a penalty kick (see the later section "Law 14: The penalty kick").

Figure 4-3:
Referee
signaling
for a direct
free kick.

Direct free kick

Figure 4-4:
Referee
signaling for
an indirect
free kick.

Indirect free kick

If a referee awards a free kick against a team, all that team's players must stand at least 10 yards away from the ball until it's kicked. The section "Law 14: The penalty kick" tells you where to stand if the referee awards a penalty against you.

Law 12: Fouls and misconduct

There are many types of fouls but only two types of recompense for the victim: a direct free kick (or penalty, if it's in the penalty box) or an indirect free kick. I deal with penalty kicks (actually a type of direct free kick) in the next section, "Law 14: The penalty kick."

Offenses resulting in a direct free kick

The referee awards a direct free kick for violent, aggressive, or serious offenses, such as when a player — either deliberately or clumsily — kicks, trips, charges, jumps at, strikes, holds, or spits at an opponent, or handles the ball with his hand or arm.

The player takes a direct free kick from the exact position the offense occurred. If the referee awards a direct free kick in the aggressor's own penalty area, the team gets a penalty kick.

Offenses resulting in an indirect free kick

The referee awards an indirect free kick for more technical offenses, such as goalkeeping handling errors — goalkeepers aren't allowed to pick up or handle back passes from their own team mates, or hold onto the ball for more than six seconds — or *obstructions* (when a player deliberately impedes the progress of another with no challenge for the ball).

The player takes an indirect free kick from the exact position the offense occurred. It makes no difference if the referee awards an indirect free kick inside the penalty area; it's still only an indirect free kick and the referee doesn't award a penalty kick.

Yellow and red cards

If a referee thinks a foul is worthy of punishing a player more than by simply awarding a free kick against his team, the referee has the option to caution or send off the player.

The referee awards a *caution* — also known as a *booking* — by showing the player a *yellow card.* This tells everyone playing and watching that the player has been cautioned. Figure 4-5 shows how this is done.

Figure 4-5:
Referee
issuing a
yellow card.

Issuing a yellow card

Players pick up yellows for unsportsmanlike behavior, dissent, persistent minor fouling, time-wasting, encroaching at free kicks, corners, or throw ins, or entering or leaving the field of play without the referee's permission.

If a referee shows a player two yellow cards (during the same game, he then shows him a red card and sends the player off. A player who's shown a *red card* is automatically sent off. He must leave the field and can't return to the game; he also can't be replaced by a substitute.

The referee shows a player a red card if he commits one of the following seven offenses:

✔ Deliberate handball to deny the opposition a chance to score

✔ Fouling to deny the opposition a chance to score

✔ Serious foul play

✔ Spitting at another person

✔ Using offensive or abusive language or gestures

✔ Violent conduct

✔ Receiving a second caution in the same game

Play on!

Just because a player commits a foul doesn't mean the referee will definitely blow his whistle and award a free kick. Referees can *wave play on,* gesturing for play to continue if they think the attacking team will gain an advantage by doing so. Figure 4-6 shows a referee waving play on.

Figure 4-6:
Referee waving play on.

Play on

If the referee waves play on, he makes an ostentatious sweeping movement with both hands. This shows he recognizes a foul has been committed, but that he'll deal with it later.

If a referee waves play on after a foul he may well award a yellow or red card when a natural break occurs in play. This can happen several minutes after the foul, depending on how long the game continues without the ball going out of play.

A team doesn't necessarily gain an advantage if a referee awards them a free kick for a foul. For example, a player may be hacked down but one of his team mates may be able to pick up the ball and burst through on goal. Should the referee whistle for a free kick, the defending team will have time to get players back and organize their defense — and the chance will be gone.

Some players can go through their entire career without ever picking up a caution. The former England striker Gary Lineker played over 500 games for club and country without a referee ever showing him a yellow card.

On the other hand, many players have appalling disciplinary records: In Scotland, a referee once sent off the Aberdeen midfielder Dean Windass three times in one game for separate offenses upon leaving the field *after* picking up his first red card.

Law 14: The penalty kick

A referee awards a *penalty kick* — usually referred to simply as a *penalty* — when a direct free kick is awarded against a team in its own penalty area. The main points to remember about a penalty are:

- ✔ A player may score a goal directly from it.
- ✔ The ball is placed on the penalty spot by a player who's identified to all as the intended taker.
- ✔ The goalkeeper must stay on his line until the ball is kicked, though the keeper can move along the line beforehand.
- ✔ All other players must remain outside the penalty area and behind the penalty spot (on either side of the box). They may not enter the area until the player has taken the kick.

After the referee blows his whistle the penalty taker can — wait for it — take the penalty. The player must kick the ball forward and can't kick it again until another player has touched it.

Obviously, the plan is to score directly from the kick. More often than not, that happens. But if the keeper saves the shot, the player — or any other on the field — is permitted to play the ball again, either in an attempt to score or to clear the ball.

If the ball comes back off the post or crossbar, the penalty taker can't play the ball again until another player has touched it. A team mate, of course, is allowed to follow up and play it himself.

Players don't necessarily have to go for goal directly from a penalty. Dutch giants Ajax Amsterdam scored one of the most famous penalties of all time in 1982. Johan Cruyff, the taker, surprised everyone by rolling the ball to the left of the spot. As the shocked keeper ran out to claim it, Cruyff's team mate Jesper Olsen rushed into the box and passed the ball back to Cruyff in the middle, who rolled the ball into the empty net.

Law 15: The throw in

The referee awards a throw-in when the ball leaves the field of play, crossing the touchline. Whoever put the ball out cedes possession; the opposing team gets to throw the ball back in.

The thrower must have at least part of both his feet touching the floor, either outside the field of play or on the touchline. He must throw the ball in using both hands, delivering it from behind and over his head. He must throw the ball in at the point it left the field of play. A player can't throw the ball onto the field and then play it himself — it has to touch another player before he can touch the ball again.

You can't score a goal directly from a throw-in.

It's crucial to throw the ball in correctly because players don't get a second chance. A foul throw concedes possession, and the opposition gets to throw the ball back in instead.

Law 16: The goal kick

The referee awards a goal kick when the ball runs out of play over the goal line and the attacking team were last to touch it.

Either the goalkeeper or a team mate takes the kick from anywhere within the goal area — the six-yard box in front of the goal in the penalty area. The ball must leave the penalty area before another player can touch it. No players, other than the kicker, are allowed in the area when the kick is taken.

If your keeper doesn't have a big or accurate kick, it's best to let one of the defenders take the goal kick instead.

You can score a goal directly from a goal kick, though this almost never happens.

Law 17: The corner kick

The referee awards a corner kick when the ball runs out of play over the goal line and the defending team were last to touch it.

The kicker must place the ball in the corner arc nearest the point where the ball crossed the goal line. The kicker isn't allowed to move the corner flag, and can't play the ball once kicked until another player has touched the ball. Opposing players are not allowed within 10 yards of the corner arc until the ball is kicked.

Players can score goals directly from corners, and this happens occasionally.

Noting Other Points

So those are the 17 laws of soccer. But there are one or two other minor points to note.

Extra time

In the section "Law 7: The duration of the game," I mentioned that games last 90 minutes and either end in a win for one team or a tie. But in some tournaments a result must be decided one way or the other.

Should a game finish level after 90 minutes, the referee may add on extra time. Extra time usually consists of two periods of 15 minutes. At the end of extra time, whoever is ahead on goals wins. If the scores are still tied, a sudden-death penalty competition may take place.

American soccer leagues have often tried to introduce tiebreakers so that even in regular season league play, games don't end without a winner. For the first four seasons of Major League Soccer (MLS) play between 1996 and 1999, a shootout was held if the score was tied at the end of regulation time. In this case, the shootouts saw players attempting to score by running in from 35 yards out and trying to beat the goalkeeper in a one-on-one contest for five seconds, with each team receiving five efforts each. Shootouts were scrapped in 2000 as MLS aligned itself with the international convention of accepting that ties happen during the regular season.

Penalty shootouts

A penalty competition can settle games requiring a winner that end in a tie or a tie after extra time.

Each team has five penalty kicks. Any player, including the goalkeeper, can take the kicks, providing he was on the field of play at the end of the game. Teams can't make substitutions after the final whistle.

The team who scores more penalties from their five kicks wins. If the scores are level, the teams take sudden death kicks, each team getting one kick apiece. The teams continue to get one kick apiece until one team scores and the other misses.

 Teams don't always have to take all the initial five penalty kicks. For example, if Team A score their first three kicks and Team B miss their first three, it's impossible for Team B to win because they only have two kicks left and are 3-0 down.

Away goals

Teams sometimes play a series of two games, with one at each team's home. Should the aggregate score — the total of all goals in both games — be level after the second game, *away goals* may count as double according to tournament rules. So if a team draws 1-1 at home but drew 2-2 on the road, scoring more away goals than their opponent, they win the tie.

The technical area

In major — usually professional — games, a designated area where coaches and their assistants can sit or stand is marked out.

Coaches aren't allowed to leave the technical area or encroach on the field of play. This is principally to ensure they don't get involved in unseemly arguments with the referee.

Common sense

Referees are technically required to follow the letter of the law, but sometimes they turn a blind eye if it's for the greater good. Say a team is losing 5-0, there are two minutes to go, and a player already on a yellow card commits a needless foul. A second yellow — and a sending off — is technically right, but the referee may not issue the card.

Some argue that the referee should still pursue a hardline policy to achieve consistency, and perhaps they're right. But don't be surprised to see refs sometimes showing mercy on already-defeated players.

Chapter 5

Players, Positions, and Tactics

*F*our basic positions exist in soccer: goalkeeper, defender, midfielder, and forward. Each has a specific duty to perform, although during the course of a game they all have to take on the responsibility of another position at some point. In this chapter I look at each position in detail and see what players in those positions have to do and how they interact with each other.

Because the tactical approach of a team determines much of what a player is expected to do, I also look at how different tactics and playing styles affect the way in which games develop.

Perusing Positions

Nothing in soccer is set in stone. Depending on how a game pans out, a player picked as a striker may end the game dropping back to defend a lead, and the losing team's goalkeeper can sometimes be found in the dying minutes of a game going up to contest a corner in desperation.

But as a rule, players concentrate on their specific duties first and foremost. From back to front, the four basic positions are the goalkeeper and the outfield positions of defender, midfielder, and forward. You can play each outfield position in many different ways.

The goalkeeper

The goalkeeper (often shortened to *keeper*) is the last line of defense. His job is to protect the goal and make sure the ball doesn't enter it. Each team has only one goalkeeper.

The goalkeeper holds a unique position in that he's the only player on a team who can handle the ball. He's allowed to handle the ball only inside his penalty area. If he does so outside the area, he runs the risk of receiving a red card. See Chapter 4 for more on red cards.

Goalkeepers aren't allowed to handle the ball in their own area if it's been passed back to them by a team mate who's used his feet to do so. If a goalkeeper does handle such a pass, the other team is awarded an indirect free kick. The keeper can, however, pick up a headed pass or one played off any part of his team mate's body above the knee, and do so without penalty.

Goalkeepers are allowed to play the ball with their feet, either on the floor anywhere on the field or with a drop kick from inside their area. They can run anywhere on the field, but rarely make excursions because this would leave the goal unattended, making it easy for the opposition to score. They're also permitted, like any other player on the field, to score goals.

A goalkeeper has the following main responsibilities:

- ✔ Keep goal and stop any shots from going in.
- ✔ Constantly organize and motivate the team's defenders, giving them tactical advice during play (because the keeper, playing at the back, has the advantage of seeing the whole field of play).
- ✔ Organize the team in the defense of free kicks and corners.
- ✔ Collect crosses and passes forward before opposition players can get to them.
- ✔ Take goal kicks and free kicks from inside his own area (or often anywhere in his own half of the field).
- ✔ Distribute the ball to team mates quickly and efficiently, by either throwing or kicking the ball, in the hope of setting his team on an instant counterattack.

Keepers effectively have three means of stopping the opposing team scoring a goal: use their hands to stop the shot — parrying it back out into play, tipping it away from goal or holding onto it; hack it clear with their feet; or somehow block it with any other part of their body, usually by spreading themselves as big as possible.

The back-pass rule

In days gone by, defenders were allowed to pass the ball back to their goalkeeper, whereupon the keeper was allowed to pick up the ball. Not only did this lead to some strange additional rules — keepers were then required to bounce the ball on the ground every four steps if they wanted to walk around their area with it in their hands — but it also produced negative soccer. If a team was under pressure at the back, they'd simply give the ball back to their keeper and the danger would be over.

After the 1990 World Cup, which many regarded as the dullest of all time, FIFA (Fédération Internationale de Football Association, or the International Federation of Association Football) decided to speed up the game by introducing the back-pass rule in 1992. This meant goalkeepers can no longer pick up back passes from their own defenders. If the ball is rolled back to them by a team mate using his feet, goalkeepers now have to play it with their feet or give away an indirect free kick close to goal if they pick it up.

As a result, keepers have had to become far more adept with their feet than goal custodians of generations past. To this day, most keepers choose to take no chances upon receiving a back pass, punting the ball high up the field, turning defense into attack, or into the stands, allowing the defense time to regroup. Some keepers take pride in their foot skills, however, and crowds always enjoy seeing their keeper roam from his box and outfox an opposition striker.

Keepers must wear distinctive clothing that distinguishes them from their team mates, all opposition players, and the referee. They can wear padded gloves and are allowed to wear peaked caps — to keep out the sun, making it easier to claim balls dropping from the sky — or padded headguards.

Teams must field a goalkeeper at all times. So if a goalkeeper is unable to continue through injury or is sent off, he must be replaced by a substitute goalkeeper (who'd either replace an injured keeper or outfield player in the case of the original keeper being sent off). However, if a team has no substitutions left, then one of the team's outfield players has to stand in goal.

In general, keepers consider safety first, and as a basic rule position themselves in the middle of the goal, in front of the net. However, while their own team is attacking and the ball is in the other half of the field, they often wander around their area, sometimes even venturing outside it.

Goalkeepers need to keep their concentration. They can conceivably spend the majority of the game doing absolutely nothing, only to find the opposition suddenly attacking strongly.

Sometimes, if the opposition breaks quickly upfield after a deep pass is played, leaving defenders in their wake, a goalkeeper rushes out from his area to punt the ball clear before any opposition player can get to it. He is effectively acting as a last-ditch defender, one example of when a player helps out a team mate in another position.

A numbers game

All players on the field have to wear a numbered jersey to enable the referee — and at professional level, spectators — to identify them.

The methods of numbering have changed over the years since the legendary Arsenal coach Herbert Chapman and his friend and Chelsea counterpart David Calderhead introduced them in 1928. On August 25 that year, the Arsenal and Chelsea pair persuaded the teams they were up against — Sheffield Wednesday and Swansea Town, respectively — that the players should run out in jerseys numbered 1 to 22.

The Football League ordered the teams to stop the practice immediately, considering numbers on the back of jerseys a desecration of club colors. But the idea caught on: At the 1933 FA Cup final between Everton and Manchester City, the idea was given another run-out, in order to help BBC radio commentators. Everton wore 1 to 11, City 12 to 22.

Eventually, after World War II, a new system of numbering — 1 to 11 for each team — was introduced across the board. Because teams were printed in game-day handouts on a diagram according to their positions on the field, numbers were assigned so they read logically across the field: 1 - goalkeeper; 2 and 3 - fullbacks; 4, 5, and 6 - halfbacks; 7, 8, 9, 10, and 11 - forwards.

As tactics changed, the numbers switched around gradually, but the principle remained the same. It all changed with the advent of the English Premier League in 1992, when roster numbers were introduced along with the players' surnames on the backs of their jerseys.

Although size isn't always a determining factor in picking a goalkeeper, it's rare to see a team fielding a keeper under 6 feet tall. In fact, even 6 feet is now seen as an under-average height for a keeper, with many of the top teams fielding players of 6 foot 4 inches and above. However, there's one disadvantage of being too tall — it takes a split second longer to get down for low shots.

As the last line of defense, a mistake by a goalkeeper usually ends up with the opposing team scoring a goal. This means the stakes for goalkeepers are high, as are the levels of criticism when things go awry. As a result, keepers have to grow a thick skin and have the sort of mental strength that allows them to put mistakes firmly in the past. This is easier said than done, even at the top level of soccer, where a single mistake in one game has defined many great professional goalkeepers' entire careers.

The United States has developed a tradition of very good goalkeepers since the 1990s, including Tony Meola, Kasey Keller, Brad Friedal, Tim Howard, and Hope Solo.

Defenders

The job of a defender is to play in front of the goalkeeper and put a stop to attacks from the other team. If the defender can't stop the attack altogether, then his next responsibility is to at least slow down the attack, giving team mates time to come back and assist.

Over the years defenders have become more and more important to the game. In soccer's infancy a century ago, teams usually fielded seven attackers, with only three outfield players stationed in defense and midfield. Nowadays much has changed, with teams rarely fielding fewer than four defenders (who are undoubtedly supported by at least one defensive midfielder — see the later section "Midfielders" for more).

A defender usually has a specialist position, although he's often able to play in any position along the back line. Primarily, two types of defenders exist: *central defenders* and *fullbacks*.

Usually, a team picks four defenders — a left-sided fullback (known as a *left back*), two central defenders, and a right-sided fullback (the *right back*). Broadly speaking, central defenders concentrate on defending the area directly in front of the goal, whereas the fullbacks deal with attacks down their respective flanks. Teams may play tactical variations on this theme — usually an extra central defender as part of a back five (or a back three if the fullbacks are then instructed to push farther forward) — but more often than not in modern soccer, teams place four across the back.

Defenders either play a *man-to-man marking* game or a *zonal defense*. The former technique sees him follow a particular player closely, tracking him during the game. The latter technique sees defenders pick up players when they come into the particular area, or zone, they're patrolling.

Both tactics have pros and cons. Man-to-man marking keeps things simple, but depending on the opposition, mismatches of speed, strength, height, talent, or experience can occur, putting the defender at a disadvantage. Zonal marking takes such pressure off individuals, but requires greater concentration and communication — if two players go for the same opponent, another may be left free to score.

Central defenders

The central defender's job is to patrol the central areas of the defensive third, attempting to stop opposition attacks. He can do this by tackling opposition players, harrying them into making mistakes, winning headers, or intercepting passes.

The central defender usually plays as one half of a two-player central defensive partnership. Both central defenders have essentially the same remit, although the two players usually have slightly different skills that complement each other.

Often one of the two central defenders is dominant in terms of height and strength and the other is a more assured ballplayer and is perhaps a quicker and more mobile runner. This combination theoretically covers all bases: The partnership won't be outmuscled by a tall, strong, bustling striker, and neither will it be caught flat-footed by a quicker and more wily opponent.

For example, the central defensive partnership at Manchester United in their 2008 Champions League winning season was between Rio Ferdinand and Nemanja Vidić. Vidić had a reputation for being totally dominant in the air, able to head the ball clear easily and strong in the tackle. Ferdinand's game, meanwhile, was more cerebral, dependent on clever positioning. Ferdinand was also the pacier player, able to cope with fast attacks, and a confident passer of the ball, skilled enough to set his team off on counterattacks of their own. Because they're usually some of the tallest players on the field — indeed, the very tallest — you often see central defenders heading into the opposition penalty area to contest corners or free kicks, with a hope of scoring. Central defenders can amass a decent tally of goals per season doing this, the very best often scoring ten goals or more per season.

Fullbacks

A defensive line usually features two fullbacks, one on either side of the central defensive partnership. The one on the left is known as the *left back* and the one patrolling the right wing is known as the *right back*.

Their roles are to defend the respective flanks of the field from attack. As a broad and basic rule, fullbacks don't move from their flanks, though in practice they often cut inside to assist their central defenders should they be pulled out of position.

Fullbacks are also increasingly asked to assist in attacks, working in tandem with the midfielder or winger ahead of them on the field. They push upfield, offering support to their team mates and making runs ahead of them down the wing, giving the attackers another passing option. This is known as *overlapping*.

Fullbacks who overlap many times during a game may have been given a more attacking remit, and are often referred to as *wing backs*. When fullbacks or wing backs are given scope to roam up field, teams often compensate by adding a third central defender, either as part of a back five or 3-5-2 formation (two of the five midfielders, the wing backs, drop back into defense when required).

Perhaps the most effective attacking fullback of recent years has been Paolo Maldini, who patrolled the right flank for both AC Milan and Italy between 1985 and 2009. He holds the record for the quickest ever goal scored in a European Cup final — 51 seconds against Liverpool in 2005.

Sweeper

A sweeper is effectively a third central defender, though one with a free-floating remit. The two other central defenders may cover either particular opponents or areas of the field, but the sweeper is allowed to roam as he sees fit — *sweeping up* any loose balls and dealing with any difficult situations. To do this, he plays just behind the central defensive pairing, where he can see all the play unfold in front of him.

Extremely talented sweepers possess such good passing skills, dribbling ability, and tactical awareness that they're the star players in their team, dictating the way a team plays. In effect, they end up taking the role of playmaker — historically a midfield or attacking role. So difficult is this combination, however, that it doesn't happen very often.

Two of the best exponents of this art were both German internationals. Franz Beckenbauer had the ability to saunter straight down the middle of the field almost at will, winning the 1974 World Cup with West Germany and three European Cups with Bayern Munich. Matthias Sammer reprised the role for Germany at Euro 96, where he ran the show from the back of the field and was unquestionably the player of the tournament.

The captain

All teams name one player as captain. The role of captain carries official responsibilities: He must participate in the coin toss at the start of the game to decide who kicks off and choose ends, and any coin toss prior to a penalty shootout.

Captains also communicate with the referee during a game: Should a team regularly break the Laws of the Game in some respect, a referee will have a word with the captain, asking him to sort out the behavior of his team.

The captain should be the strongest willed, most dominant player on a team. He's expected to encourage or chastise his team mates when necessary, perhaps even making minor tactical changes while play is running.

More often than not, captains are either defenders or midfielders, because players in these positions can see what's going on around them and control it directly. However, well-respected attackers and goalkeepers have been known to captain teams — 40-year-old goalkeeper Dino Zoff captained Italy's 1982 World Cup winning team.

Captains are usually also among the more popular players with the crowd, allowing a bond to develop between the supporters and the team.

Midfielders

Midfield is the most important area on the field, where games are effectively won and lost. Lose control of the midfield and your defense will be overrun. Win the midfield battles and your team will have a platform from which to launch attack after attack and dominate the game, or shut down opposition attacks, frustrating their attempts to score while you run out time.

Several different types of midfield players exist, and not all of them can play together in the same midfield. Midfielders can attack or defend, create or destroy, play near the front or the back, on either flank, or with a floating role.

Usually — but by no means exclusively — a team fields between three to five midfielders. A general rule of thumb is that a team with three midfielders plays them all in the central area; a team with four plays two in the center and one on each flank; and a team with five plays as a team with four, but with an extra free-floating player.

Central midfielder

The central midfielders are often the most crucial players on the park. Their remit is to attempt to control the game, helping out the defense when required, and the attack where possible. The most fit and active central midfielders, who are able to run all around the field for 90 minutes without tiring, contributing to both attack and defense, are known as *box-to-box midfielders* because they run so frequently from one penalty area (the box) to the other. Top-quality box-to-box midfielders are as adept at executing a crunching tackle as they are playing a sweet 40-yard pass.

Most central midfielders, however, concentrate on one job above all else. They often operate as a partnership with at least one more central defender: Usually there's a defensive central midfielder and a more attack-minded partner.

The defensive midfielder patrols the area just in front of his defense, acting as a stopper. He breaks up opposition attacks, harries and hounds opponents, and does anything it takes to win the ball before giving it to a more creatively minded team mate, often his central midfield partner.

The attacking central midfielder dictates the pace and direction of play, instigating attacks by either passing the ball around to better-positioned team mates or making runs forward with the ball. He's likely to be a frequent goal-scorer and a good free-kick taker, and is confident at running with the ball.

Attacking central midfielders are often known as *playmakers* for their ability to change the shape of a game. However, the definition of a playmaker is fairly loose: Deep-lying forwards are also often referred to as playmakers, with the line between both positions blurred.

Playmakers (or Number 10s, or *fantasisti* . . .)

They can be central midfielders, attacking midfielders, even sometimes wingers or strikers, but playmakers are always one thing: head and shoulders above the rest of their team in terms of ability.

Playmakers are the ones, through their passing and dribbling skills and tactical vision, who can dictate how a game develops. They're the focal point of their team and are usually so dominant that when they have a poor day their entire team plays badly. On the other hand, when they play well they can drag any old rabble to victory (as Diego Maradona proved with a very average Argentina team at the 1986 World Cup).

Playmakers are often known as Number 10s, even if, in the days of roster numbering, they may not actually wear that number. That's because nearly all of the great playmakers have worn 10 on their backs. Here are ten great Number 10s: Diego Maradona, Pelé, Ferenc Puskás, Gianni Rivera, Sandro Mazzola, Michel Platini, Roberto Baggio, Dennis Bergkamp, Zinedine Zidane . . . and the only one on this list currently playing today, the Brazilian women's star Marta.

Wingers (or left- and right-sided midfielders)

In the old days, on either side of the field in midfield, teams deployed *wingers.* Their job was to take up the ball in the middle of the field, race down the touchline, and, with a combination of tricky ball skills and pace, beat the fullback and send a dangerous cross into the box. They had little or no defensive responsibilities whatsoever.

However, in the modern game even the most talented wingers, such as Portugal's Cristiano Ronaldo, require other strings to their bows. Players positioned on the left and right wings still need to try to beat their man, but they must also be able to link up with their central midfielders, interchanging with them as play unfolds. They also have to track back and assist their fullbacks in defensive duties.

Midfielders are usually the fittest players on the field because their workloads are, in theory, greater than anyone else's.

Midfielders of all persuasion — but especially central attacking midfielders — are increasingly expected to chip in with a large number of goals, taking some scoring responsibility off the shoulders of the strikers. Spain illustrated this to an extreme at the 2012 European Championship, often playing without a recognized striker at all and instead relying on midfielders such as Cesc Fàbregas and Xabi Alonso to chip in frequently with goals.

Strikers

The job of a striker — or a forward — is to either score goals or help their team mates score. Modern teams usually field between one and three strikers, with two the most common number but one becoming increasingly common.

Strikers usually work best in a partnership. Teams can field any attacking combinations of center-forward, deep-lying forward, attacking midfielder, or winger.

If a team fields one striker, their remit is usually to hold the ball up for midfield runners to come and join in the attack. The striker obviously also looks to score himself, but it's increasingly less important for him to do so — providing the midfield runners score enough goals.

Center-forward

The center-forward — also known as a *target man* — spearheads the attack. This player receives forward passes, wins headers and keeps possession of the ball — called *holding the ball up* — in order to bring team mates into play.

Center-forwards are usually tall and/or physically strong (though exceptions to this rule exist). A top-quality center-forward expects to score around one goal every other game; however, increasingly a center-forward's first responsibility is to keep attacks going, bringing other players into the game. This kind of forward should still notch a healthy number of goals, but providing the team is scoring and the center-forward is an integral part of that, modern coaches are less concerned about a striker's personal tally. (Fans, however, don't always see it that way and can give nonscoring strikers vocal abuse.)

Center-forwards usually work best with a partner. Often the most effective partnerships consist of players with contrasting abilities: tall and small, powerful and mobile, direct and tricky. At other times, players who seem to be similar can work very well together, such as the nimble and diminutive forward pairing of Romario and Bebeto for Brazil at the 1994 World Cup.

Deep-lying (or second) striker

A deep-lying striker isn't expected to hold the ball up, but drops back, either into central midfield, onto the wings, or into what's known as *the hole* between the opposition's defense and their midfield. This *hole* is difficult to define in practice, but in theory is the part of the field where opposition defenders and midfielders are either unsure or unwilling to follow attackers. This gives the deep-lying striker time and space in which to make dangerous passes or take shots on goal. He's sometimes known as a *false 9*, because he lines up as a forward but actually drops back into midfield much of the time.

Total football

In the late 1960s a new approach to soccer was born in the Netherlands — one which meant that no player (other than the goalkeeper) had a fixed role to play. It became known as *total football,* because players could interchange positions across the whole field.

The theory was simple: A team would set out with ten outfield players in their respective positions, but after one moved out of position as the game unfolded, another in the team would immediately replace him. This would move all along the chain: The player who'd moved into the first player's position would in turn be replaced by another . . . and so on. The system requires top-quality players throughout the team because each must have the ability to play in several different positions comfortably.

The Dutch national team who reached the 1974 and 1978 World Cup finals played total football, as did the Ajax unit who won three consecutive European Cups in the early 1970s. Johan Cruyff was the star man in both teams.

Hungary's famous 6-3 win over England in 1953 graphically illustrated the benefits of playing in the hole. Seen as a seminal moment in English soccer — when England realized they'd fallen behind the rest of the world — the game saw Hungarian striker Nándor Hidegkuti dropping between the English defensive line and midfield. With nobody tracking him, he was allowed to run riot.

One of the most effective deep-lying strikers of modern years has been Francisco Totti of Roma, although Lionel Messi of Barcelona has at times also played that role to marvelous effect.

Tactics: Linking It All Up

It's all well and good putting 11 players out on the field and giving them fancy job titles, but if they don't interact with each other there's little point in anyone getting out of bed in the morning.

Dribbling: The first tactic

When organized soccer began in England during the 1860s, the emphasis was firmly on individual play. Most teams sent their players out to *dribble* (run with the ball at their feet) around the field, each player attempting to work themselves into position to shoot at goal. With up to eight forwards on each team — they gave little thought or effort to defense — the game would ebb and flow up and down the field, players taking turns to embark on long, lazy dribbles.

But in the 1870s a new tactic began to evolve in Scotland. Instead of attempting to beat opponents by dribbling around them, players simply cut them out by passing the ball to a team mate standing in space elsewhere and then moved on. What seems obvious now was highly controversial at the time — some English teams thought it unsporting — but when the Scottish teams started to repeatedly thrash the English teams it became clear there was no going back: Out-thinking your opponents was almost as important as beating them with the ball.

The main styles of play

At the risk of over-simplifying a game most coaches would have you believe is incredibly technical and complex, three basic styles of play exist. These are *possession soccer, counter-attacking soccer,* and the *direct game.*

Possession soccer

The possession game is the hardest approach to take because it requires, by definition, keeping hold of the ball for lengthy periods of play. You achieve this by a high level of technical skill: impressive close ball control, accurate passing between players, and good movement off the ball into empty space to give other players good passing options.

Possession soccer isn't necessarily the most physically demanding style of play, because if executed properly the opposition players have to expend more energy chasing around for the ball and making challenges. Providing players from a team playing the possession game keep it simple — playing low-risk passes to team mates in safe positions — the theory is that eventually a chance to launch an attack will open up because the tiring opposition makes mistakes.

Most fans consider this style to be the most attractive to watch. A team playing top-drawer possession soccer may end up scoring a goal after a sequence of ten or more passes. A famous example of superb possession soccer was the goal scored by Esteban Cambiasso at the 2006 World Cup for Argentina against Serbia and Montenegro. Cambiasso applied the finishing touch to a stunning 24-pass move that became an instant YouTube classic.

Counter-attacking soccer

The counter-attacking game is played by teams with confidence in their defensive abilities and pace in their attack. The idea is to either soak up attacking pressure from the opposition or harass them in midfield. After the opposition has committed players into attack, but has lost the ball, the counter-attacking team springs forward as quickly as possible, exploiting gaps left by the attacking team at the back.

The man who ruined football?

At 3.50 p.m. on March 18, 1950, a former British Royal Air Force wing commander named Charles Reep took a pencil and pad from the pocket of his overcoat and effectively gave birth to the long-ball game. For it was then — at half-time during a game between Swindon Town and Bristol Rovers — that he decided to undertake a statistical analysis of how goals are scored.

He soon found out that 85 percent of goals tend to be scored from passing sequences that involve a small number of passes, usually three or less. He argued that teams should adjust their styles of play accordingly, because this analysis proved that possession soccer was a waste of time.

Instead, Reep suggested teams should play *reacher passes* — a *reacher* being a "single pass from the defensive third into the attacking third." In other words, a long punt.

Teams used Reep's methods over the years to varying degrees of success. Wolverhampton Wanderers picked them up in the mid-to-late 1950s, winning three titles in six seasons, although no long-ball team has won the English league since. Norway used the long-ball game in the early 1990s and reached two World Cup tournaments, at one point beating reigning champions Brazil twice in two meetings. Then again, England used a watered-down version of Reep's tactics at the same time, and failed to qualify for the 1994 World Cup finals. And the present day success of Barcelona and Spain, who often keep the ball for over 60 percent of a game, suggests possession soccer can be a highly effective route to winning.

Counter-attacking teams aren't necessarily the prettiest to watch because they spend long periods attempting to break up play. Having said that, when in full flight a counter-attack can be exhilarating to watch as the ball is swept swiftly upfield.

 Just because a team takes a counter-attacking approach, it doesn't necessarily mean they'll spend the game punting long balls upfield. They're as likely to pass the ball quickly up the field with a sequence of short passes as they are to take a more basic approach. One of the top counter-attacking teams of recent times was Arsenal, who'd use the outrageously skillful Thierry Henry as an outlet to break up the field at speed.

The direct, or long-ball, game

Upon winning possession of the ball, teams playing a direct game quickly launch it upfield. Players pump long balls either directly into the opposing penalty box, where they hope the center-forward will win the ball or cause mayhem, or into the far corners of the field, causing opposition defenders to turn and chase the ball, putting them on the back foot as attacking midfielders put the pressure on.

The direct game is based on power rather than technique, and can be tedious to watch. However, those who justify the style argue that it's successful — the method allowed Jack Charlton to lead the Republic of Ireland to their first-ever major finals at Euro 88. Supporters of the direct game also point out that teams of limited skill can implement this style, and that not every team is able to afford the sort of players with the technical ability to execute a possession game.

The long ball game has always been reviled by soccer's more romantic figures. Brian Clough, the former Derby and Nottingham Forest manager, always tried to implement a pleasing-on-the-eye passing game, famously insisting that "if God had meant us to play football in the sky, he'd have put grass up there."

Formations

The term *formation* describes the way a team lines up on the field. Formations are usually indicated by a string of numbers giving the number of players in any roughly defined area of the field. So a 4-4-2 formation has four defenders, four midfielders, and two forwards. The goalkeeper is never included.

1-2-7 (1870s)

This is thought to be the first formation in soccer history because before this was used, players simply dribbled up and down the field in a very haphazard fashion. Three players stayed towards the back — one three-quarters back in the center and two halfbacks either side of him slightly farther up the field — although their role wasn't particularly defensive minded because they were charged with firing long balls up the field to the front seven.

Those front seven players were divided into three groups — two wingers patrolling each flank with three center-forwards in the middle. They fired short passes between each other in the hope of creating goal-scoring opportunities. The 1-2-7 formation is shown in Figure 5-1.

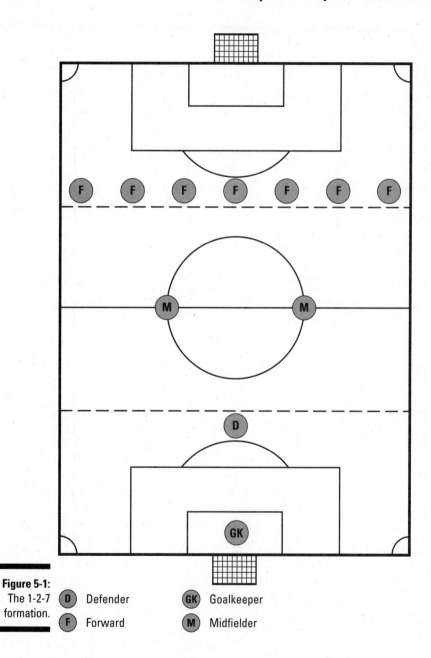

Figure 5-1:
The 1-2-7
formation.

(D) Defender   (GK) Goalkeeper

(F) Forward   (M) Midfielder

2-3-5 (late 1880s)

The better teams were beginning to run up large numbers of goals thanks to the advent of short passing, so eventually this system, shown in Figure 5-2, was introduced to counter it. Right at the back, two fullbacks covered the defensive duties, assisted when required by two halfbacks and a center-back just ahead of them.

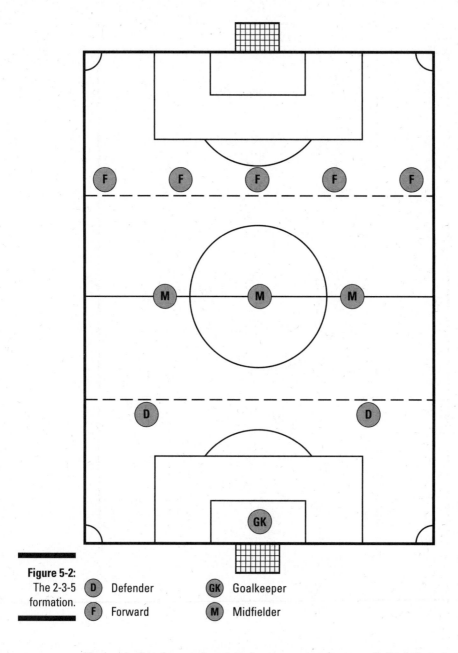

Figure 5-2:
The 2-3-5
formation.

D Defender		**GK** Goalkeeper	
F Forward		**M** Midfielder	

Now only five forwards existed — one winger on each flank, two inside-forwards, and one center-forward — though the halfbacks and center-backs were allowed to move upfield to bolster the attack when required.

M-W (mid-1920s)

In 1925 the offside rule changed, which meant only two defending players had to be between the attacker and the goal, rather than three. This caused an immediate glut of goals, so teams countered by withdrawing more players into defensive positions as shown in Figure 5-3.

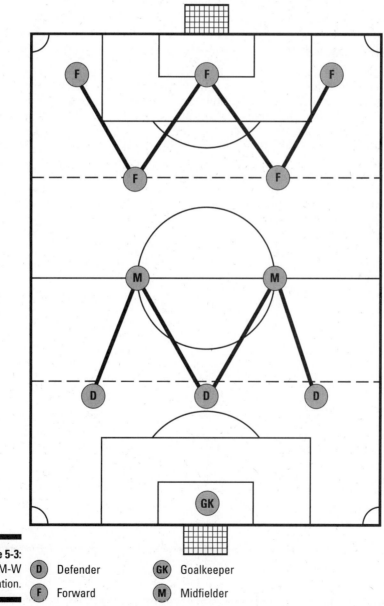

Figure 5-3:
The M-W
formation.

(D) Defender   (GK) Goalkeeper

(F) Forward   (M) Midfielder

The M-W — so called because of its shape — saw a back line of two full-backs and a center-back man mark the opposition forward and wingers. Wing-halves patrolled the space directly in front of the fullbacks, and the inside-forwards dropped back from the very front line into a more withdrawn position, bolstering the midfield.

Herbert Chapman's Arsenal team in the mid-1920s popularized this tactic, with help from star striker Charles Buchan. Arsenal went on to be the dominant force in English soccer during the 1930s.

M-U (early 1950s)

The famous Hungarian team of the early 1950s, who won the 1952 Olympics and reached the World Cup final two years later, made a simple, subtle change to the MW. They pulled the center-forward back into a withdrawn position, causing opposing defenses no end of confusion. While the center-forward pulled the strings from the hole between midfield and attack, the inside-forwards waited to advance into the space left by the withdrawn center-forward.

Inside-forwards were previously expected to track back to help their defense when required. Now they were ordered to stay upfield, giving the team options to launch speedy counterattacks. The M-U formation is shown in Figure 5-4.

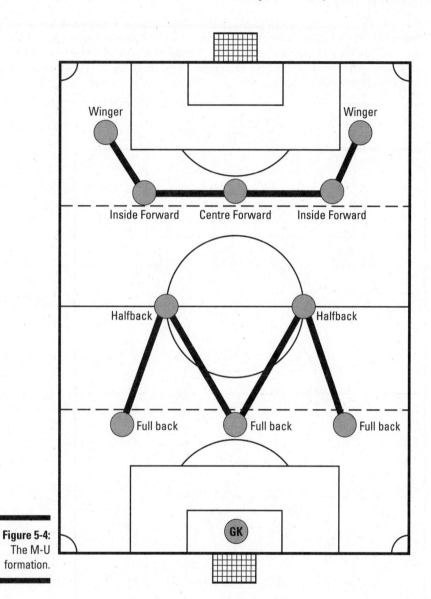

Winger   Winger

Inside Forward   Centre Forward   Inside Forward

Halfback   Halfback

Full back   Full back   Full back

GK

Figure 5-4:
The M-U
formation.

4-2-4 (late 1950s)

The M-U wasn't dominant for long. The flat back four was invented to deal with the spaces created by deep-lying center-forwards and rampaging inside-forwards. The two central defenders marked the areas the inside-forwards were looking to attack and were able to track the withdrawn center-forward along with the help of their two team mates in central midfield.

Meanwhile both fullbacks were able to move up the field when required, in order to bolster the midfield and, occasionally, the attack, where four players, two wingers and two center-forwards, plied their trade. This formation can be seen in Figure 5-5.

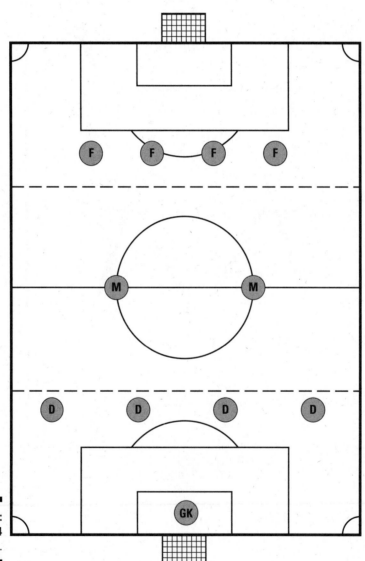

Figure 5-5:
The 4-2-4 formation.

1-4-3-2 (early 1960s)

The 4-2-4 was an attacking response to the M-U problem, but Italy had found a different solution. *Catenaccio* — literally meaning *padlock* — reigned for the best part of two decades. A flat back four was assisted by a sweeper, who patrolled just behind them, ready to snuff out any attacks. Three players in midfield were always on hand to drop back and further smother any opposition attack.

The team was prepared to mobilize quickly in order to launch counterattacks, but when a lead had been established the padlock snapped shut: 1-0 wins were the norm in Italy for years.

Catenaccio was first developed in Switzerland in the 1930s by the Swiss national coach Karl Rappan, although it was known as *verrou* — literally *the bolt*. Internazionale coach Helenio Herrera refined the tactic over two decades later, his team winning back-to-back European Cups in 1963 and 1964.

4-4-2 (mid-1960s)

In the 1960s a more defensive mindset was developing, and England became the first team to win the World Cup with a safety-first attitude. Alf Ramsey's *wingless wonders* played four across the back with the defensive midfielder Nobby Stiles patrolling in front of them. The left- and right-sided midfielders also worked hard to track back defensively, leaving the attacking to the single offensive central midfielder Bobby Charlton and two center-forwards.

The 4-4-2 (as shown in Figure 5-6) became the classic formation for the next three decades, and despite the current penchant for 4-5-1 (and variations thereof) is still the most widely used tactic today. Its popularity lies in its simplicity and solidity: It's easy for players to understand and execute.

4-4-2 (1980s)

Arrigo Sacchi's Milan team of the late 1980s dominated Europe with a variation on the 4-4-2. The back four operated as a line right across the field, pushing high up the field to catch opponents offside. With less space for the opposition attack to unfold in, the rest of the team then played a high-tempo pressing game, hunting down the ball and winning it back while expending as little energy as possible.

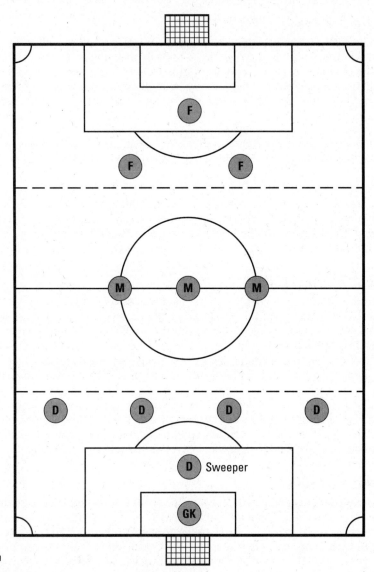

Figure 5-6:
The 4-4-2
formation.

Sweeper

D Defender   **GK** Goalkeeper

F Forward   **M** Midfielder

3-5-2 (1990s)

The 3-5-2 (as shown in Figure 5-7) was an attacking philosophy that became briefly popular in the 1990s and early 2000s. Teams set out with three central defenders at the back whom, it was hoped, would be able to deal with two forwards of a team playing the predominant defensive 4-4-2.

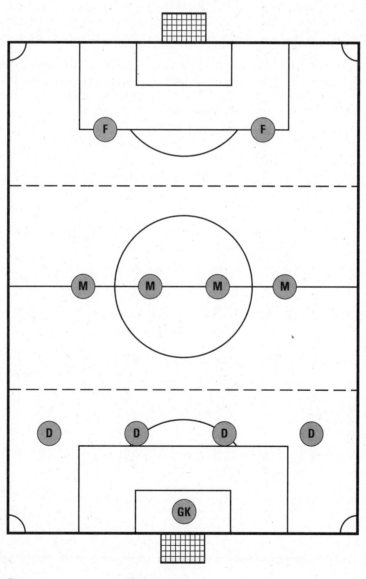

Figure 5-7:
The 3-5-2
formation.

D	Defender	GK	Goalkeeper
F	Forward	M	Midfielder

Should they require help, two attacking wing backs, effectively playing as wingers in a five-man midfield, dropped back to help. A defensive midfielder in the center, playing just behind two more attack-minded central midfielders, was also on hand.

4-4-1-1 (2000s)

This formation, or variations on its theme, is arguably the most popular formation in use today. Essentially a more flexible version of 4-4-2, it was initially used to position a striker in the hole between defense and a one-man attack.

Increasingly, the player in the hole is an attack-minded goal-scoring midfielder, feeding off the knockdowns from the lone attacker. Occasionally, this formation has even morphed into a 4-6-0, with no recognized striker lining up at all. The 4-4-1-1 formation is shown in Figure 5-8.

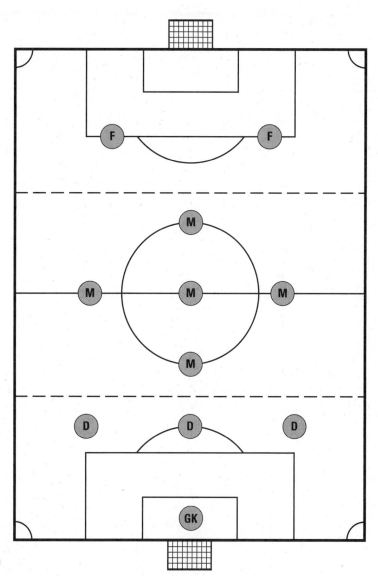

Figure 5-8:
The 4-4-1-1 formation.

 D Defender   GK Goalkeeper

F Forward   M Midfielder

Chapter 6

Honing Your Skills

● ●

In This Chapter

▶ Starting with the fundamentals of soccer

▶ Advancing your defending techniques

▶ Refining some attacking moves

▶ Goalkeeping for greats

● ●

Soccer is the simplest of games to play: Just put a ball on the ground, swing your leg at it, and you're ready to go. Like anything else, if you want to be proficient at the sport, you've got to put the hours in, first learning the basics and then embellishing the fundamentals with a few additional techniques. Remember, even Pelé had to spend hours every day practicing his art in the street with a ball of scrunched-up newspaper — and if it was good enough for the young Edison Arantes do Nascimento, it's good enough for you.

So in this chapter I take a look at some of the basic skills you need to become a competent player, plus a few extra skills to make you well rounded on the field. I can't promise to turn you into the next Cristiano Ronaldo, but even if you don't get to the very top you'll be able to enjoy playing the game for fun.

Mastering the Basics

It doesn't take long to acquire the basic soccer skills of running with the ball, passing, receiving the ball, shooting, and heading. If you concentrate on building a solid technique for each skill, you at the very least are able to join in real games or pickup play without feeling embarrassed or out of your depth. And when you've gained the confidence to do that, the world's your oyster.

When soccer was in its infancy back in the mid-1800s, there was only one way to play the game — take possession of the ball and dribble with it. Dribbling — another name for ball handling, ball skills, or close control — is still the most important skill in the game. So where better to start than at the beginning?

Up until 1872, when teams from Scotland worked out that passing the ball around saved a lot of time and energy, players would always dribble with the ball. Some teams fielded up to nine players up front, with only one man defending.

Dribbling

Ball control — the ability to run with the ball at your feet — is one of the most important skills in soccer.

It's initially a tricky skill to learn. As you likely found out as a toddler, don't try to run before you can walk. To become acquainted with moving along with the ball at your feet, try the skill at walking pace first, as described in these steps.

1. **Walk slowly along while bumping the ball forward with your instep — preferably using both feet if you can, one after the other. Keep knocking the ball about a foot ahead of you each time, roughly the distance of one or two paces.**

2. **When you're comfortable with Step 1, try nudging the ball along with other areas of your feet as well, the insides and outsides.**

3. **When you are happy with Step 2, pick up speed gradually. First walk briskly with the ball at your feet, working your way up to a light jog, then eventually a run. Never attempt to run faster than you can control the ball.**

While you're practicing this drill, try to keep your head up. Don't look down at your feet and/or the ball if you can help it. When you dribble in a real game you need to keep your head up to look around the field for team mates to pass to, as well as keep an eye out for opposing defenders.

If you have an open area of the field to run into, you can kick the ball farther ahead of you. This allows you to sprint more quickly. Conversely, if any opposing players are approaching, you need to keep a closer rein on the ball. The closer an opposing player is, the closer you should keep the ball to your body.

Basic passing skills

Dribbling has never gone out of fashion in soccer — some of the greatest players in the modern era, from Diego Maradona in the 1980s to Lionel Messi today, have utilized superlative close skills in order to outfox opponents.

But dribbling did quickly go out of fashion as soccer's premier tactic. In the 1870s, teams from Scotland worked out that it was quicker and easier to pass around an opponent with the help of a team mate than to beat the opponent with a dribble.

Ever since then, passing has become the most important basic skill in soccer. A short, simple pass is required to keep a move going so your team can hold on to possession, and a longer pass is often the one that cracks open an opposing defense, sending a team mate through on goal. Both are essential skills to learn.

Short pass

The short pass, delivered with the inside of the foot, is the most common technique for delivering a ball to a team mate. It's also called a *push pass* because players use a long follow-through as they push the ball, stroking it towards their intended team mate. You do it like this:

1. **Position the ball between yourself and the intended target.**

2. **Plant your nonkicking foot on the ground, approximately 5 inches to the side of the ball, pointing towards the intended target. So if you kick with your right foot, plant your left foot down to the left side of the ball, facing the player you're passing to. Make sure you slightly bend the knee: It shouldn't be locked.**

3. **Keep your kicking leg slightly bent. Take a short backswing and then make contact with the middle of the ball just below your ankle, along the inside of your foot at the arch.**

4. **Follow through with your leg pointing toward the intended target. The shape of your body naturally ensures that the inside of the foot ends up facing the intended target of the pass.**

Long pass

A longer pass works on the same principles as the short pass, but you use the following steps:

1. **Plant your nonkicking foot slightly behind the ball, as well as to the side.**

2. **Make sure your kicking foot makes contact with the bottom half of the ball. By kicking the underside of the ball, it lifts off the ground, into the air, and travels longer distances.**

It's important to practice the accuracy of your passing, as well as to make sure the ball travels the required distance. Players finding the ball missing to either side of the target may find they aren't following through properly but are stopping the kicking maneuver upon contact with the ball and *snatching* at the pass. Imagine a line drawn between you and the target with the ball in the middle — your leg should travel straight along this path. Figure 6-1 shows a short, inside-of-the-foot pass, whereas Figure 6-2 shows a longer pass.

Figure 6-1:
A short inside-of-the-foot pass.

Figure 6-2:
For longer
passes, kick
the ball with
your instep.

Receiving the ball

It's pointless knowing how to dribble and pass if you're not able to receive the ball and take up possession of it. You can use just about any part of the body to receive the ball, apart from the arms and hands.

The idea is to gain control of the ball — whether it's bouncing, rolling, or flying through the air, slowly or at speed — and keep it close to your body. The three most useful parts of your body are your feet, thighs, and chest — but you can also receive the ball with your head.

Great players are able to *kill the ball dead* — in other words, stop it from moving in whatever direction it was heading and take it immediately under their control. Delicacy of touch is the crucial thing here. A good way to conceptualize this is to imagine an egg or a water balloon being thrown at you — and you must keep it from breaking. You are a cushion, not a wall.

Foot

To receive a pass or loose ball using the foot, a player should use the following method:

1. **Position yourself in front of the ball.**

2. **Extend your leg and foot out before the ball arrives, a few inches off the ground (roughly about halfway up the ball when it gets to you).**

3. **Pull your leg back as the ball makes contact with your foot, to cushion it and retain possession. Think of it as catching the ball with the instep, almost as though it's nestling in the inside arch of the foot. Keep your foot relaxed because this can help to control the pass, especially if the ball is traveling at speed.**

The more experienced player can use all parts of the foot to receive the ball, though it's normal — and easier — to concentrate on the inside of the foot.

If the ball takes an unexpected hop, either off a divot on the field or as a result of an imperfect attempt to control it, the leg helps control the ball providing you've used the inside of the foot (because the ball is being played close to the ankle). Figure 6-3 shows you how to receive a ball with your foot.

Figure 6-3:
Receiving and stopping a ball with your foot is an important skill.

Thigh

The thigh is a very effective tool for controlling the ball when it is played to you above the ground because it offers a large contact area. A player using his thigh should do the following:

1. **Position yourself in front of the incoming ball.**

2. **Stand on one foot while raising the other knee and thigh to meet the ball. (It's easier to raise your preferred kicking leg, though good players can receive the ball easily with either.)**

3. **Cushion the impact of the ball as it hits your thigh, lowering the knee until the ball drops down to your feet. Swivel your hips to pull your thighs slightly backwards as they cushion the ball.**

Keep the thigh as parallel to the ground as possible in order to retain possession of the ball. If you fail to do this, and the leg is at an angle, the ball has a much smaller contact area to hit and may ping away from you. Figure 6-4 shows the right and wrong ways to receive a ball with your thigh.

Figure 6-4:
The right and wrong way to receive the ball with the thigh.

Right   Wrong

Chest

The chest is the hardest area of the body to receive the ball with, but after you have a solid technique it can be the most effective, pulling difficult passes and clearances out of the sky. Players must do the following to successfully receive the ball using the chest:

1. **Position yourself in front of, and square to, the approaching ball.**

2. **Puff out your chest just before meeting the ball.**

3. **Pull the ball backwards as it makes contact with your chest, cushioning the blow of impact. The ball should fall to your feet.**

Don't arch your back too much, because the ball can then rear up and bounce over your shoulder or head.

It will initially feel natural to bring your hands in front of your body, either to attempt to catch the ball or as part of an involuntary attempt to shield yourself from being hit by the ball. It's also tempting to use the upper arms to subtly cushion the ball. Both maneuvers are illegal and result in the referee awarding a handball foul against you. Figure 6-5 shows you how to receive the ball on your chest.

Right   Wrong

Figure 6-5: Receiving the ball with the chest is tricky. Don't be tempted to use your hands.

Head

If the ball is high in the air, you can bring it down using your head as follows:

1. **Make sure you are on the balls of your feet, able to either jump to meet the ball in flight or rise up on your feet toward it.**

2. **With your arms extended out to keep your balance, hit the ball gently on the hairline of your forehead, almost as though you're cushioning it.**

3. **Lean backward. The ball should drop to your feet, or onto your chest or thigh, where you can further control it.**

Heading the ball

When the ball is high in the air, you need to play it using your head. You can do this in order to retain control, pass to a team mate, make a defensive clearance, or attempt to score.

It's easy to execute a header incorrectly. The last thing you want is for the ball to either skim off the top of your head or smack you straight in the nose. To head the ball properly:

1. **Face the incoming ball.**

2. **Assess the flight of the ball and time your leap into the air so you are heading the ball at the highest part of your jump.**

3. **Keep your eyes open and fixed on the ball while keeping your mouth closed. Your eyes should never be closed before the point of impact.**

4. **Head the ball using the hairline of your forehead. Do this while stiffening your neck and chest muscles and thrusting your body forward from the waist up, driving the ball toward the intended target.**

The major principles of heading remain the same whether a player is crashing a header towards goal or cushioning a soft-headed pass to a team mate. Adjusting the power in your drive forward is the key.

Players attempting to head the ball toward the ground should head through the top half of the ball. Players hoping to make a clearance want to head the ball long and high into the air, so they should head below the middle of the ball. Figure 6-6 shows you how to head the ball correctly — and how not to.

Figure 6-6: Right and wrong ways to head the ball.

Right   Wrong

Shooting

Shooting is, without doubt, the most enjoyable aspect of playing soccer. The natural instinct when taking a shot is to hit it as hard as you can — and punt it with your toes. Sadly, the natural instinct isn't always the right one.

The rules of taking a shot using the most basic kick — the instep kick — are much the same as a short pass, and are as follows:

1. **Pick out a target. Decide where in the goal you want the ball to head.**

2. **Plant the nonkicking foot alongside the ball, pointing at the target.**

3. **Keep your head and eyes over the ball.**

4. **Hit the middle of the ball with the instep of your kicking foot.**

5. **Follow through towards the target.**

Power isn't always important — in certain circumstances good players choose to place their shots with care, sometimes rolling them delicately toward goal — but as a general rule, especially for beginners, some semblance of power is required in the shot.

It's easy for a player to forget two fundamentals that result in the loss of shooting power:

✔ **Keep your nonkicking foot planted right next to the ball.** When you do this you naturally approach the ball from a slight angle, and the resulting hip rotation when you kick, pivoting around your standing leg, generates extra power. If your standing foot is behind the ball you lose much of this power, and may even accidentally toe-punt the ball instead, which also loses shooting accuracy.

✔ **Remember to follow through when you've connected with the ball.** If you don't do this and you stop on impact, you've been decelerating before you even kick the ball, thus losing power.

Volleying

You don't take all shots with a stationary ball, or a ball that's rolling along the ground. You can also shoot a ball in the air before it touches the ground — this is called a *volley,* and it's the most spectacular way to score.

Volleying is technically an advanced skill, but one that's required so often in a game that you need to master it if at all possible. The following steps give you a brief lesson in volleying.

1. **Assess the flight and direction of the ball.**

2. **As the ball flies toward you, get the knee of your kicking foot over the ball, with your toes pointing down.**

3. **Take a short, sharp stroke at the ball. (You don't need to swing wildly because the speed of the flying ball supplies the power to the shot.)**

4. **Make contact just above the center of the ball. Hitting below the ball will cause it to balloon into the air.**

You can also use volleying to pass to your team mates, but this is an even more advanced technique that you should save for a later stage in your development.

Keeping It Tight at the Back

Defending is ultimately an act of destruction. Soccer is, when you boil the bones down, about scoring goals, and defenders try to stop that happening. However, you still require top skills to defend properly.

Although defense is less glamorous than attack, it's arguably more crucial. Teams with poor attacks have been known to win cups and titles, but teams with terrible defenses almost never do.

Marking

Marking, sometimes known as *guarding,* is when a defending player puts himself between the attacking player and his own goal. The object is to guard — or *mark* — an attacker, to prevent him from dribbling or passing the ball nearer to the goal, or shooting for goal. If you can't stop the attacker — by dispossessing him or forcing him to run out of play — then you must at least slow his progress.

You have to consider three points when marking an opponent:

- ✔ **Stay close.** The closer a defender is to an attacker, the harder it is for the attacker to use the ball constructively, whether he's trying to dribble, pass, or take a shot.

- ✔ **Be aware of the ball.** Being between an attacker and the goal is not useful if the defender has no idea where the ball is.

- ✔ **Notice the attacker's tendencies and foibles.** When you spot an attacker's favored techniques it's easier to mark them. If he always dribbles with his right foot, for example, a slight adjustment in your positioning may cause him difficulties. If he always plays to one side, you'll find it easier to intercept the ball.

Tackling

Being able to dispossess your opponent is crucial — if your team doesn't have the ball, you're going to find it very hard to avoid defeat. But remember, you aren't allowed to tackle your opponents by grabbing them as in American football — use one of the following techniques instead.

Block tackle

A defender uses this tackle to dispossess a player who's dribbling the ball toward you. To execute a successful block challenge, the defender moves directly toward the player and uses the weight of his entire body to tackle the opponent. The defender blocks the ball by applying steady and even pressure to it with the inside of his leg, the foot staying on the surface of the ball at all times.

Going into a block tackle, the player should plant one foot ahead of the tackling foot and then move in. He should be slightly crouched, enabling the player to react to any sideways movement the attacking dribbler may make. And it's important that the player concentrates on attacking the ball with his foot — ensuring the attacker isn't fouled but can't progress or keep hold of the ball. Figure 6-7 shows you how to execute a block tackle properly.

Figure 6-7: The block tackle.

a   b

Shoulder-to-shoulder tackle

A defender uses a shoulder tackle when he finds himself running alongside the player in possession. The idea is to use the weight of your shoulder to lean into the other player's shoulder, easing him off the ball.

Try to get slightly ahead of your opponent when making the challenge. This allows you to ease in front of him with your shoulder, forcing him behind you and off the ball. Figure 6-8 shows you a well-executed shoulder tackle.

Figure 6-8:
A well-executed shoulder-to-shoulder tackle.

a   b

Side tackle

Instead of using your shoulder to lever an opponent off the ball, you can also poke the ball away from him while running alongside him. The best time to make a move for the ball is when the attacker is about to pass or shoot, leaving space for the defender to nick the ball away.

After you've dispossessed the attacker, your work isn't necessarily over. If no other players are in the vicinity, make sure you react the quickest, going to fetch the ball you've just poked away. Otherwise the attacker may pick the ball up again himself, wasting the successful tackle.

Sliding

The sliding tackle is the most difficult tackle to execute and one that you usually only use as a last-ditch measure — when the attacker has worked his way into space and is about to either shoot or make a killer pass.

Sliding is a tricky skill to master. Here's a four-step guide:

1. **The approach. When a player is ahead of you with the ball, you have to catch up with and approach the attacker from the side. (Tackles from behind are illegal.) You must get up close to the attacker, or the opponent will be able to accelerate off when you begin to execute the slide.**

2. **The sliding leg. Drop your lower body and begin to slide along the ground with your leg closest to the attacker.**

3. **Top leg.** As your sliding leg makes contact with the ground it's bent and tucked underneath you and your top leg is extended out.

4. **The tackle.** Using the top leg, knock the ball away from the attacker's feet with as much force as you can possibly generate. This ensures the opponent can't simply pick up the ball again while you are still lying on the ground.

Figure 6-9 shows you how to get a sliding tackle right.

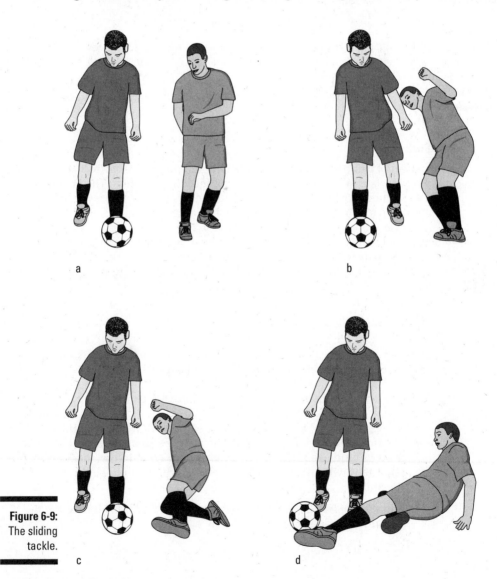

a

b

Figure 6-9:
The sliding
tackle.

c

d

It's important to execute a sliding tackle correctly. Reckless or overly aggressive tackles earn a red card and may cause the attacker serious injury.

Key defensive principles

It doesn't matter which defensive tactic the coach chooses, defenders must adhere to some principles at all times:

- **Don't lunge in.** If you mistime a tackle or challenge in a state of panic, wily attackers will find it easy to circumvent you and take you out of play.

- **Help out.** Just because a defender has been given one task to perform, it doesn't mean he has no responsibilities elsewhere. It's vital to assist and cover team mates who are in trouble. This doesn't just mean making last-ditch challenges to help — you may want to assist in double-marking a dangerous opponent, as a preemptive defensive measure.

- **Protect the 6-yard box.** The area directly in front of the net is where players score most goals. Keeping attacking players — and the ball — out of this zone drastically reduces the opposition's chances of scoring. (See Chapter 4 for more about the 6-yard box.)

Sharpening Your Skills Up Front

To put together dangerous attacks, players must have a variety of skills to ensure they keep hold of the ball and then confuse the defense into making mistakes. Here are some of the essential skills.

Shielding the ball

To either dribble effectively or give yourself time to pick out the killer pass, you need to keep hold of the ball under pressure from defensive opponents. In the following steps, you learn to achieve this by shielding the ball, which involves the attacker keeping his body between himself and the ball.

1. **Keep *side on*. By turning sideways you create more space between the ball and the defender, allowing you to take full control. It also opens up more of the field to you, giving you the options to pass or dribble away.**

2. **Try to avoid turning straight back.** As an attacking player it's natural sometimes for you to want to turn around if you see your route ahead is blocked by a defender. But unless you know an outlet exists behind you — a team mate who may be able to quickly switch play to another player in a more advantageous position, for example — it puts you at an immediate disadvantage. The defender will find it easier to tackle you as you turn, and after you've turned around all your team mates higher up the field are out of the game, and the attack is over.

Chip pass

A highly effective way to beat the last line of defense is to use the chip pass. Chipping over the opposition's defenders can allow a team mate, timing a run from deep, to break free on goal. Check out the following steps.

1. **Approach the ball from the side, and turn to strike it with the inside of your foot.**

2. **Snapping your knee while kicking forward at the ball, keep your ankle locked at contact, putting backspin on the ball.**

3. **Make contact with the side of your shoelaces (the upper side of the inside foot) just below the center of the ball. This chips the ball up into the air and sends it spinning back down quickly.**

You should feel like you're clipping the ball into the air. Try to visualize it as a golf shot — a crisp wedge chipped close to the flag, with the flag being your team mate and the defender a tree or bunker.

Outside of the foot pass

Using the outside of your foot as well as the inside gives you added passing options. It allows you to consider other angles without necessarily adjusting the entire shape of your body, sparing you crucial split seconds in getting your pass away. The following steps show you how to do this.

1. **Point your kicking foot down towards the ground and slightly inward, with your standing foot planted to the side of the ball and turned slightly away.**

2. **With a locked ankle, deliver the pass with the outside of your foot. When following through, make contact in the center of the ball with the little toe.**

Back heel

The back heel can look spectacular and tricky, but it's actually one of the simpler additions to an attacker's armory. Check out the following steps.

1. **Simply lift your kicking foot ahead over the front of the ball.**

2. **When your knee and foot are slightly ahead of the ball, snap your heel back onto the front face of the ball, sending it rolling off behind you.**

A deftly executed back heel can instantly wrong-foot a defender, who won't be expecting you to suddenly get rid of the ball — and in a different direction to the one you're facing. If you can direct your back heel immediately to a team mate, your team will be able to switch play quickly, leaving opponents in disarray.

Bending the ball

Being able to bend it like Beckham puts the attacker at a huge advantage because a whole new range of passing options open up. The ability to bend a ball correctly — a skill also sometimes referred to as a *banana shot* when going for goal — can take defenders totally out of the game. Check out the following:

1. **Approach from the side. When you kick the ball across the front, rather than straight on, you apply spin. Hitting it right to left makes the ball bend to the right (because you're setting the ball bending clockwise on the horizontal axis). Hitting it left to right makes it bend to the left.**

2. **Hit the ball below center. For the ball to curve, it has to fly in the air. You need to make contact with the ball at its bottom half.**

3. **Kick with the inside of the foot. Strike the ball with the inside of your shoe, above the big toe. Drive through the ball as hard as you can to impart maximum spin.**

You can apply principles of spin to the ball at all times. For example, you can bend spectacular volleyed passes by stroking across the face of a dropping ball, sending it arcing over long distances through the air. Bending the ball is one of the hardest techniques in the game, however.

Feinting

Feinting is the practice of faking an action in order to convince a defender you're about to do something you're not. It can be a devastatingly effective attacking ploy.

- **Feinting to shoot.** The attacker lifts his shooting foot, pulling the leg back as if to shoot. The defender, buying the *dummy,* goes to block — at which point the attacker can shift the ball round the committed player and into space.

- **Body feint.** Also known as *dropping a shoulder,* this involves leaning to one side in an exaggerated motion, as though the attacker is about to run that way. At the last nanosecond, with the defender ready to commit, the attacker quickly shifts his weight to the other side of his body and moves off in that direction. Caught on the hop, the defender can't shift his weight back in time before the attacker has run off.

Free kicks

Upon being awarded a free kick, it's important to agree with your team mates about who's going to take it. You have three main options:

- **Blast it towards goal.** Whoever has the strongest — and most accurate — shot should hit the ball as hard as he can. A well-struck shot into the top corner of the net can be almost impossible to save if hit at speed.

- **Dink it goalwards with finesse.** A player adept at either chipping or bending the ball may be able to find a route to goal using clever place-ment. Remember, you may have to get the ball up and over a defensive wall, making a direct blast at goal difficult, so sometimes this is a better option.

- **Pass it to a team mate.** Switching the play to a better-placed player can wrong-foot the opposition. Sometimes teams have worked out complex passing moves before the game on the practice field.

If the free kick is indirect, you should nudge the ball to a team mate before taking a direct shot. However, if the indirect free kick is at close range, one tactic is to blast the ball direct at goal anyway — if it takes the slightest deflec-tion off any player, attackers or defenders, before going in the net, the goal will be allowed to stand.

Taking penalties

A *penalty* is a free shot at goal from 12 yards out. In theory, it should be an easy skill to execute because the keeper has no time to save a well-struck and well-placed shot. However, nerves play a part because the attacker is expected to convert the chance.

A penalty taker must decide where he's going to place the ball and stick to that decision. Changing his mind as he runs up to take the kick is likely to lead to a scuffed shot, and a missed penalty. A player should simply concentrate on his shooting technique — it will hold up if he blocks out all other thoughts.

Remember to practice penalties before an elimination game because a penalty shootout competition can decide a tied game. Some teams have failed to do this in the past — infamously Italy in the 1994 World Cup final, when the team was defeated by Brazil in a penalty shootout.

Goalkeeping

The keeper is the last line of defense, the player with the greatest responsibility on the field: He has to stop the ball going into the net. The goalkeeper's ultimate aim is to let no goals in during a game — this is called *keeping a clean sheet.*

It's crucial for a goalkeeper to communicate with his defenders; it's the keeper's job to command the penalty area.

Keepers are the only players on the field who are allowed to use their hands to play the ball. Goalies either try to catch the ball or somehow divert it from going into the goal by punching, flicking, or parrying it away (see "Parrying and tipping," later in this chapter). The keeper also kicks the ball if necessary — in fact, he uses whatever part of his body it takes to stop a goal going past him.

As a general starting position, a keeper should stand in the center of the goal with his hands at his side, palms facing the ball. His center of gravity should be low, and his weight should be on the balls of his feet. He should have his knees slightly bent. This setup, in theory, gives the keeper the most options when reacting to a shot coming in on his goal.

Catching

If a goalkeeper catches the ball, the opposition is unable to score — simple as that. A good, clean catch immediately puts an end to an opposition attack and is the perfect way to avert danger. Here are some common methods of catching:

- **The chest catch.** If the shot is coming right at the keeper, this is the best option. Getting as much of his body behind the ball as he can, the keeper smothers the ball with his arms when it hits his chest, throwing his arms around it and keeping his elbows close together. The ball should be trapped safely against the chest.

- **The diamond, or W, catch.** The simplest catch to take, the keeper plucks the ball from the air when the shot is either wide of him or over his head. The keeper forms a *diamond* with his thumb and index finger, making a W shape with the fingers on both hands on either side of the ball, just behind its center. As an insurance policy it's important for a keeper to keep his body behind the ball, because should the shot slip through his hands, his body will be in the way to stop it.

- **The scoop catch.** The keeper picks up a shot trundling to the goal along the ground with a scoop catch. The keeper bends forward and places his hands on the ground, with palms facing up, gathering the rolling ball into his chest.

After a keeper catches the ball he should bring it close to his chest, so another player can't knock it out. In 1990, Nottingham Forest attacker Gary Crosby headed the ball out of the palm of Manchester City goalkeeper Andy Dibble, and rolled it into the empty net. The goal stood, much to Dibble's initial anger and subsequent embarrassment.

Diving

If the ball is heading for one of the far corners, just within range of the keeper's reach, the keeper must first take a stride towards the side of the goal the ball is heading. Then, with arms fully extended — and away from the face so the flight of the ball can clearly be seen — the keeper should dive and attempt to collect the ball using the diamond (or W) catch.

If the keeper is unable to catch the ball he should attempt to tip the ball around the post, averting the immediate danger. This is preferable to parrying the ball back out because the keeper will have dived onto the ground, leaving the goal open for a striker to knock any loose ball back into. (See "Parrying and tipping," later in this chapter for a description of parrying.)

One-on-one

This is the most dangerous save a keeper has to make, but it's the one that offers him the most glory, too. The object is to deny an opposition player who has broken clear of the defense — goalkeeper versus attacker, hence the name *one-on-one*.

When a player is advancing towards goal with the ball, the goalkeeper should stay on his feet as long as possible. This forces the striker to make the first decision — does he shoot low or high, attempt to lob the keeper, or dribble the ball around him? (Going to ground early helps the player make that decision — it would be easier to dribble around the keeper, or chip the ball over him, for example.)

The keeper should move forward toward the player with his hands low and palms facing the ball. If timed correctly, the keeper can dive toward the ball and smother it, with the striker yet to make his move. Should the striker shoot, the keeper is in position to make a close-range save, parrying the ball away to safety or even smothering the shot and catching it.

Going for crosses

A confident keeper comes off his line in order to claim crosses made by the opposition's wide players. Doing this helps relieve pressure on his defense because the central defenders don't have to battle with the attackers for the ball. In theory, a keeper should always have an advantage on every other player in the box because he can extend his arms higher while going up to take the catch.

The goalkeeper's communication is very important when taking the ball. Failing to communicate properly with your defenders can result in a mix-up.

To get the best possible jump, the keeper should leap off one leg and lift his other knee to add to the leap. When leaping in the air, your leading leg also offers protection from advancing attackers or defenders. When claiming the ball you should always take off using the leg nearest to the goal to generate lift because this acts as protection. Failing to do so can result in an attacker or defender pushing the goalkeeper in the direction of the goal. Moving forward toward the ball, the keeper should attempt a diamond (or W) catch, before returning to the ground and holding the ball tightly to his chest. Timing of the jump is essential: The keeper should meet the ball at the top of his leap.

If a catch isn't possible, the keeper should attempt to punch the ball away from the goal as far as he can.

It's crucial to hold the ball tightly upon landing, because the ball may otherwise squirm out of the keeper's grasp and back into play.

Goalkeepers often get the benefit of the doubt from referees if they go up for a cross and are knocked over in a challenge by an opposing striker — even if the striker has done nothing wrong. If there's a melee and the ball drops loose, the referee often rules that the keeper was fouled. When you're deciding whether to gamble going for a cross, this knowledge may help you play the percentages in a crowded area.

Punching

If the keeper can't catch the ball, his best option is to punch it clear of danger.

A goalkeeper should punch if he has any doubt over reaching the ball to claim a catch because a missed catch can be quite embarrassing, and often leads to a goal.

The keeper should leap as though he's about to claim the cross, but instead of attempting a catch he should make two fists, hold them together and punch the ball out of harm's way.

The aim of punching is to get the ball clear. Punch the ball just below the middle so that it travels upward as well as away from goal.

If the keeper is going for a ball at the very outer limit of his reach, he may have to extend one arm out on its own and punch away with one fist.

Parrying and tipping

If the keeper can't catch or punch the ball away from danger, parrying and tipping are two last-resort options.

Tipping the ball away from goal — round the post or over the crossbar — stops the opposition scoring a goal and allows your defense to regroup in order to defend a corner.

Parrying — blocking an effort on goal back into play — is equally effective in the first instance (it stops the opposition scoring a goal) but doesn't do a particularly good job of clearing the danger (because opposing players can pick up the loose ball and have another shot on goal immediately).

Parrying a shot back into play is very much the last resort because you'll be leaving the result to Lady Luck.

Positioning

A goalkeeper can save himself a lot of trouble with good positioning, and make life much harder for the opposition.

One of the most important weapons in a goalkeeper's armor is *narrowing the angles.* You do this by moving to the left of the net when the ball is to your left, and the right when it's to your right. This shows the attacker much less of the goal, giving him less space to aim his shot towards.

The near post (the post nearest the ball) is always the goalkeeper's responsibility. Keepers aren't expected to let shots in there. Moving towards the near post forces the attacker to consider shooting to the far side of the goal, a much harder proposition.

Although keepers should spend most of their time on their lines, they also need to venture off it in order to claim the ball, close down an angle, or put pressure on an onrushing attacker. But it's not a good idea to stray too far from the goal, because chip shots can then beat keepers. These shots are often difficult or impossible to recover; the keeper is left stranded.

Distribution

When a goalkeeper has the ball it's vital that he gives it to a team mate quickly and efficiently. Goalkeepers are increasingly asked to instigate immediate counterattacks upon receiving the ball. If distributed quickly and cleverly, the team that had been attacking can suddenly find themselves in danger.

According to the FIFA Laws of the Game, a goalkeeper must release the ball within six seconds of receiving it. Failure to do so results in the referee awarding an indirect free kick where the keeper was last standing (see Chapter 4 for more on how the Laws of the Game impact goalkeepers).

The goalkeeper has three options when distributing the ball:

✔ **Kicking the ball upfield:** By dropping the ball from his grasp and making a long pass up the field — this is called a *drop kick* — the keeper looks to find a team mate (usually one of the strikers) in the middle of the park. The hope is that, with the opposing team having committed players to attack, they will be short of players at the back and vulnerable to a scoring attempt. An accurate kick upfield sets a counterattacking move in motion very quickly.

✔ **Throwing or rolling the ball out:** A quick, accurate throw can start the team moving back up the field. Keepers usually roll the ball out to one of their defenders, but occasionally try long throws, lancing the ball upfield like a quarterback if a player is in space in midfield. An accurate long throw can be almost as devastatingly effective as a long drop kick.

✔ **Dribbling the ball upfield, or passing it out:** This isn't a good idea unless keepers have decent ball skills, though most professionals do since the backpass was outlawed in the early 1990s. A goalkeeper who can pass the ball confidently gives a team more options when looking to start new attacking moves from the back.

Saving penalties

When facing a penalty, a keeper is allowed to move anywhere along his goal line from left to right, but he's not permitted to advance towards the ball before the opposing player has taken his shot.

Goalkeepers are at an obvious disadvantage — though as the striker is expected to score with a free shot from 12 yards, the keeper, who isn't expected to save it, has nothing to lose. See Chapter 4 for the rules the goalkeeper has to follow during a penalty shootout.

Sometimes the weight of expectation puts the striker under pressure, so use this to your advantage. If there's any way of psyching the penalty-taker out before he takes his kick, do so. (Simply staring at some players makes them very nervous!)

Considering a few things may help you save the penalty. Is the taker right- or left-footed? Have you seen him take a penalty before — and if so, where did he put it? Are his eyes giving away where he intends to send the ball?

But, ultimately, it's down to luck. Wait until the very last second before choosing which way to dive — or whether to stand still for a cheeky penalty straight down the middle, the taker expecting you to dive out of the way. A goalkeeper doesn't look stupid if he dives the wrong way — but he appears very smart if he guesses correctly and saves the kick.

Chapter 7

Keeping in Shape for Soccer

. . . .

In This Chapter

▶ Warming up safely — before turning up the heat

▶ Reaching peak physical condition

▶ Eating and drinking well

▶ Preventing and treating injuries

. . . .

Soccer hasn't always been the healthiest of sports. Back in the 1950s, stars at the top English clubs regularly sat down ahead of a big game and dived into a large plate of steak and greasy fries. In the 1960s, Northern Irish star George Best used to turn up to practice most days with a stinking hangover. And in 1978, Ossie Ardiles was part of Argentina's World Cup winning roster, despite puffing on an average of 40 cigarettes a day.

These days, players simply can't get away with that sort of behavior. Soccer is now a fast, intense, and demanding game, and players need to commit to an athletic lifestyle — or they are simply wasting everyone's time.

It's not just about abstinence off the field. Putting the long yards in on the practice field is vital, because even if players live a life so clean and virtuous it would have put Mother Teresa to shame, they come off second best if they're not in peak physical condition.

The principle applies to any level of soccer: You can have all the natural talent in the world, but if the other player is miles fitter, you'll come out second best. On the other hand, if you've got the talent *and* you've done your training, the sky's the limit.

Keeping Fit

If your fitness level isn't close to 100 percent, it'll show very quickly on the field. Even the top professionals have to work hard to reach peak condition and stay there — if they take a week off from practice due to injury, the rule of thumb is that they then require a further two weeks to get back into top shape.

A decent level of aerobic fitness is essential, because a serious player runs on average anything from 3 to 7 miles in a 90-minute game. They also make several sprints during the game, so speed, power, and agility are vital.

Stretching those muscles

First things first: If you want to avoid pulling muscles when exercising, you need to give your legs a good stretch. A stretching session should last between 10 and 15 minutes.

The more stretches you do, the more flexible you become — and the less likely you are to pick up injuries.

Different players have their own personal stretching routines, depending on their physical makeup. A qualified fitness instructor can plan a customized regiment for you, but there's no need to worry if you can't do that because performing the following stretches should be more than satisfactory:

- ✔ **Quadriceps:** Stand by a wall. Bend one leg up behind you using one hand to steady yourself against the wall and the other to keep your leg in place by holding onto your foot. To make the stretch, gently pull your foot upwards. Figure 7-1 shows this exercise.

- ✔ **Hamstrings and lower calf:** Sit on the ground. With one foot extended out in front of you, extend your arm towards your foot. While sitting bolt upright, keeping your back straight, run your arm as far down your leg as you can. Figure 7-2 shows this stretch.

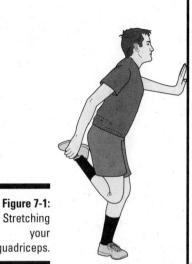

Figure 7-1:
Stretching
your
quadriceps.

Figure 7-2:
Working
on your
hamstrings
and lower
calves.

✔ **Groin:** Sit on the ground. Place the soles of both of your feet together so your knees are bent out to the side of your body. Then, while keeping your back straight, try to press both of your knees as close to the ground as possible. Push your chest out while you do this, as shown in Figure 7-3.

Figure 7-3:
Stretching
your groin.

✔ **Lower back:** Lie down on your back. Pull one or both of your knees towards your chest while keeping your shoulders and head on the ground. Figure 7-4 illustrates this stretch.

Figure 7-4:
Stretching
your lower
back.

✔ **Calf muscle and Achilles tendon:** Stand by a wall. Place one leg forward, bending it at the knee. Push forward against the wall, keeping your back foot flat on the ground. The forward leg stretches your Achilles tendon and the back leg stretches the calf muscle. Switch legs and repeat the stretch. Figure 7-5 illustrates this stretch.

Figure 7-5:
Stretching
your calves.

✔ **Hip flexor:** Get on one knee. Bend your rear leg so the knee is near the
ground while extending your front leg and your hands towards your
toes, as shown in Figure 7-6.

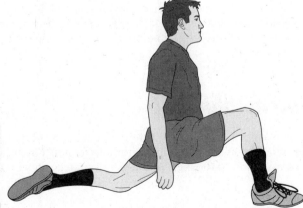

Figure 7-6:
Carrying out
a hip flexor
stretch.

Running

Some players run more than others. Former Manchester United midfielder Roy Keane, a *box-to-box player* (one who covers all the ground between the penalty boxes), would run up to 8 miles during a game, covering every blade of grass on the field. Equally influential on his team was Colombia's Carlos Valderrama — though he was rarely in great shape, he dictated the game with his passing skills rather than energetic drive. Both players were world-class. The moral? Running isn't the be-all and end-all. So don't worry if you're not a natural athlete — providing you have the skills, you can still make it.

Having said that, not being able to run well puts a player at an instant disadvantage in the fast-paced modern game. So it's worth putting in the extra work to get up to speed — literally.

Keep in shape by running regularly. You don't need to do too much: A 25-minute jog each day should suffice. It's important to keep your heart rate at a healthy level.

Long-distance running builds up your base levels of fitness and your endurance. Shorter sprinting practice is also vital because during games you need that extra burst of pace to explode past an opposing defender. It's much more beneficial to do drills over shorter distances — say between 5 to 30 yards — than longer sprints over 100 to 200 yards, distances you're not going to cover in a sprint during a game.

The first few steps in a sprint are vital — a mix of technique and power. Practice helps with technique; weight training with leg weights may help with power (though you don't want to bulk up too much).

Quickness as a player isn't just about sheer physical speed. Mental reactions are vital, too. A player who makes sure he keeps concentrating for every second of a game often gets to the ball before a faster opponent simply by being quicker off the mark.

Exercising aerobically

Aerobic exercise is essential if a player is to perform at a good level. Your heart and lungs must be in top condition; after all, the lungs fuel the heart, which pumps more blood to the legs. And legs are a soccer player's main tool of work.

Jogging is the simplest and most effective form of aerobic exercise for a soccer player. Tennis and basketball are also good, because both sports also feature the similar stop-start sudden changes of movement found in soccer. Swimming is also effective, although you use different muscles.

It's best to double-check with your coach as to what extra exercise you should take. Some coaches don't like their players using their "soccer" muscles for other pastimes, and so may prefer you to swim. If you're playing at a high level, the coach may also not want you to partake in other contact sports such as basketball, where you run added risks of injury.

In today's professional soccer world, clubs hire specialist strength and conditioning coaches to work on their players' health-related components of fitness.

Training with weights

Weight training can be useful to assist in the attainment of general fitness, core strength, and improved leg muscles. However, soccer players shouldn't be too bulky — mobility, flexibility, and agility are the watchwords.

So although you shouldn't neglect your upper body — players often use weights simply to keep their body toned or to recover from a specific injury — it isn't the most vital part of physical training.

If you want to train with weights in order to tone your muscles, repetition is more important than using large weights. Repetition tones; weight adds unwanted bulk.

Sorting out your stomach

Large amounts of running should be enough to keep your abdominal muscles in shape. But if you want to reach peak physical condition, a daily routine of sit-ups or stomach crunches will do no harm.

Cooling down

It's vitally important to cool down properly after practice or games. If a player has been performing at peak activity but then suddenly stops without cooling down, he runs the risk of cramps because the muscles are fully extended but no longer working.

Jogging slowly for a few minutes is a good way to cool down. You may also want to repeat some — or indeed all — of your pre-games stretches, although you don't need to spend 10 to 15 minutes on them.

By cooling down you not only avoid risking cramps, you are also much less sore the day after the game or practice session. Cooling-down exercises help relieve the buildup of lactic acid in the muscles that occurs during strenuous activity.

Professional teams cool down for anytime up to 45 minutes. If you hang around in the stadium long after the final whistle, you can sometimes see them out on the field performing their drills.

Balancing Your Diet

It's important to eat well at all times, but especially so if you're partaking in regular exercise. You're burning more calories and therefore require more energy for practice sessions and games.

A balanced diet is essential. A recommended balance for an active player is

- 60 percent of your daily calorific intake from carbohydrates
- 15 percent from protein
- 25 percent from fats

Carbohydrates are what keeps you going so you need to take on board a large amount. Foods containing a lot of carbs include pasta, bread, rice, potatoes, and cereals.

You find protein in milk, cheese, meat, poultry, and fish. Fats are found to varying degrees in butter, whole milk and whole cheeses, and meats like beef and bacon. Try to avoid saturated fats found in foodstuffs like chips and pastries, because they can raise your cholesterol to unhealthy levels. Saturated fats from foods such as nuts and olives are much better for you. For more information about maintaining a healthy diet, check out *Eating Clean For Dummies* by Jonathan Wright and Linda Johnson Larsen (Wiley).

Within one hour after a practice session or game try to drink two pints of fluid and take on board some carbohydrates. This is because the body replaces and stores energy more efficiently after exercise, when the muscles are still active.

Although it's important not to overeat, if you eat too little you'll be unable to keep up your energy levels during a game.

In the know about H$_2$O

Keep properly hydrated before, during, and after the game. Here are a few important tips to keeping well watered:

✔ Fluid intake varies per person, but most adults need between three to five pints of liquid per day. You need more if you're active, so make sure you're fully hydrated before the game. Do this by drinking a glass of water when you wake and taking regular drinks during the day.

✔ Remember that you start to feel thirsty only after you're already dehydrated, so make sure you take on water before you get thirsty.

✔ Always bring a bottle of water with you to games and practice. Don't assume water will be available — sometimes there's none, and you need to replenish yourself.

✔ Remember that water has no calories, so drink as much as you like.

✔ In addition to water, the body can get fluid from other drinks such as juice, tea and coffee — as well as fruit and vegetables.

Investigating Injuries

Soccer is a physically exerting pastime, and a contact sport to boot. Picking up injuries every now and then, whether big or small, is almost unavoidable, so it's important to know what to do when they occur.

Even so, prevention is better than cure — and it's worth remembering that if you prepare correctly, you significantly limit your chances of getting injured.

Preventing injuries

Follow these tips to decrease your chances of picking up an injury:

✔ **Check the condition of the field:** Adverse conditions can lead to injuries if you don't wear appropriate footwear. If you're playing on wet turf, be sure to wear shoes with long cleats to avoid slipping; a field that's full of holes and divots can easily cause injury, especially to the ankle or the knee.

✔ **Check the weather conditions:** An extremely hot day can lead to players suffering heat stroke. Make sure you have plenty of water handy.

✔ **Do your pre-game stretches:** As the earlier section "Stretching those muscles" outlines, a decent stretch of the leg muscles is mandatory. A full and thorough stretching session should last between 10 and 15 minutes, though providing you have at least stretched for a couple of minutes, the likelihood of pulling a muscle is slim. However, do remember that the longer and more often you stretch, the more flexible you become — and more flexible players are less prone to injuries.

✔ **Get checked up:** At the start of a season visit the doctor and get a medical. Your doctor can then address any minor health problems there and then, nipping them in the bud. A clean bill of health also gives you peace of mind — and with it, added confidence.

✔ **Make sure your shoes fit:** It may sound obvious, but do your soccer cleats and turf shoes fit properly? Footwear that's slightly too tight or too big for you causes blisters and other injuries — and can cause long-term damage to your feet. Get your shoes fitted properly by a professional when you buy them, and wear decent cotton socks that won't rub you the wrong way.

✔ **Remember your shin guards:** You always wear your shin guards in a game, but do you always wear them for practice sessions or during pickup? You wear them in games for a reason — they protect one of the most sensitive and endangered parts of a soccer player's body — so don't be blasé just because you're not playing an official game.

✔ **Stay in shape:** If you're out of condition your body can't cope with the rigors of exercise, let alone the trauma of possible heavy contact, as you clank around a soccer field. A fit player decreases his chances of injury. He's also able to bounce back from any knocks more quickly, and return from injury quicker than an unfit player.

Injury prevention isn't the only benefit of checking the state of the field. The 1954 World Cup final was played in wet conditions, but although the highly fancied Hungarian players were forced to wear their heavy-weather cleats with long cleats, the West German players were able to play in their normal footwear — because Adidas had designed their shoes with interchangeable screw-on cleats. The Germans won 3-2!

Treating injuries

Despite everyone's best efforts at prevention, somebody's bound to get injured at some point. It's important to know how to deal with any injuries should they occur.

First-aid kit

The basic essentials in a first-aid kit are as follows:

- ✔ **Antiseptic spray or antiseptic wipes:** To clean out cuts and grazes.

- ✔ **Bandages:** Assorted sizes, to cover cuts and wounds.

- ✔ **CPR mouth barrier:** For the unlikely event of performing mouth-to-mouth resuscitation.

- ✔ **Ice or ice packs:** Apply on a sprain immediately to reduce swelling.

- ✔ **Latex gloves:** To wear while tending to a bloody cut or wound.

- ✔ **Nail clippers:** For torn or ripped nails, especially if a goalkeeper isn't wearing any gloves in a practice session.

- ✔ **Scissors:** For cutting bandages and tape.

- ✔ **Sterile eyewash and eye pads:** For any injuries to the eye — mud, grass, and grit often get stuck in players' eyes.

- ✔ **Sunscreen:** Because playing 90 minutes under strong sun is harmful to the skin.

- ✔ **Tape:** For the application of bandages.

- ✔ **Tooth-preserving kit:** For the thousands of teeth that are accidentally knocked out each year on the field — this ensures dentists have a good chance of replanting the teeth of an unfortunate player.

- ✔ **Tweezers:** To remove any debris lodged in a player's skin.

Firstly, it's essential that at every game at least one person on the touchlines — *who's not playing and, therefore, has no chance of picking up an injury himself* — is able to administer simple medical attention to any players who get injured.

It's advisable that someone on your team has taken a course in first aid. Your local doctor's office can tell you where you can take such a course.

Should someone pick up an injury, whether small or serious, they need medical treatment as soon as possible. Players with serious injuries should be taken immediately to hospital.

If you're playing in an unfamiliar place, make sure you know where the nearest hospital is beforehand. Also, keep a cellphone handy in case you need to call for an ambulance.

It's also preferable that someone field-side knows CPR — cardio-pulmonary resuscitation — in the unlikely event a player's heart stops on the field.

No matter how fit a player appears, it's possible that he or she have a heart condition. Professional players such as Cameroon's Marc Vivien Foé and Sevilla's Antonio Puerta both collapsed and suffered fatal heart attacks on the field.

Treating injuries using RICE

Make sure that someone brings a quantity of ice to a game — packed, obviously, in an icebox or cooler. Ice is essential to treat many injuries because you use it to decrease the swelling of a bruise, after pulling or straining a muscle, spraining, or sometimes after breaking a bone.

You can remember the way to treat an injury with ice as follows:

1. **R:** Rest. Make sure that the player doesn't move at all.

2. **I:** Ice. To stop or limit blood flow and pain, place crushed ice in a plastic bag, a wet towel, or an ice bag, to make an ice pack. Keep the pack on the injury for 15 minutes every waking hour for the first 24 hours to three days, depending on the severity of the injury and how quickly the swelling dies down.

3. **C:** Compress. After the initial pressing of the ice pack, replace it with a tight bandage, preferably an elastic wrap. If you're wrapping a leg or arm, start at the place farthest from the heart, and work towards it in a crisscross pattern. Expose toes or fingers at the extremities so you can spot any skin discolorations.

4. **E:** Elevate. Raise the injured arm or leg to about the heart level for the first 24 hours to three days.

Figure 7-7 shows the RICE procedure in progress.

Figure 7-7:
The RICE
procedure.

Take a player to the hospital if the injury looks at all serious, if the swelling continues, or if you're in any doubt.

Knee injuries

Injured knees are quite common in soccer and can cause complications, even to the point of ending a player's career. They occur when a player has one leg planted on the ground, only for the leg to be hit hard by a sudden rotation of the body (which could be caused by a collision with another player, or simply by passing or running on his own).

The knee can bend through 150 degrees and is one of the most flexible joints in the body. This flexibility is crucial to a soccer player, who needs to change direction quickly. The knee has no muscles, but it does have three bones — the femur, tibia, and fibula — which are held together by ligaments.

Although knee injuries can occur in five places — ligaments, cartilage, muscles around the knee, kneecap, and tendons — it's the ligaments that are usually troublesome to soccer players. The most common injuries occur to the following four ligaments: the anterior cruciate, posterior, medial collateral, and lateral collateral.

A tear to the anterior cruciate ligament (ACL) is the worst knee injury. A player can damage their ACL by twisting or turning suddenly, being kicked just below the ligament, over-extending it, or slowing down too quickly. A player may hear a sickening loud pop or snap before he feels anything.

If an ACL injury is suspected, you should carry the player off the field and immediately apply ice to the knee. Seek medical assistance immediately. Reconstructive surgery could see a player out for at least a year.

Figure 7-8 shows an ACL injury.

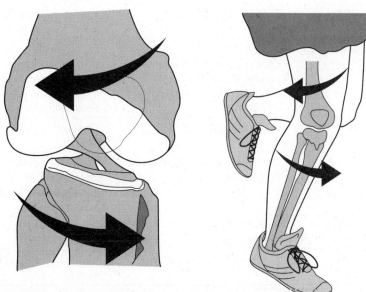

Figure 7-8:
ACL injury.

The most common knee injury is the medial cruciate ligament tear. It's the strongest ligament in the knee, and injuries to it shouldn't be serious. However, any player suspected of suffering such an injury should be immediately carried off the field, with ice applied to the knee. Happily, even severe tears should, with the help of a protective knee brace, see the player back in action within two months.

The degree of a knee injury tells you how much damage has been done. First-degree tears are mild, with only a slight swelling occurring and little loss of movement. A second-degree tear is a moderate tear that causes the player mild pain and requires rest. A third-degree tear is the worst and refers to a complete rupture of the ligament that may require a brace, cast, or corrective surgery.

Common injuries

Most injuries in soccer are, however, not too serious. Although players are known to break legs and arms, dislocate shoulders, and suffer head or neck injuries, these are thankfully quite rare — seek immediate medical attention in such an event.

Table 7-1 lists some of the more common ailments and how to treat them.

Table 7-1	Common Ailments	
Ailment	*Symptoms*	*Treatment*
Abrasion	Loss of skin	Cleanse with antiseptic and apply antibiotic ointment
Blister	Fluid buildup under skin	Have it drained by a doctor and clean the area with antiseptic
Concussion	Severe blow to the head that can cause dizziness, dull to severe headache, ringing in ears, disorientation, possible loss of consciousness	Substitute player immediately. Do not allow him to continue under any circumstances, even if he insists he's recovered. Seek medical attention.
Contusion	Bruised muscle or tendon	Treat with ice using RICE method.
Cramp	Involuntary and painful muscle contraction	Apply firm pressure on the muscle area, followed by gentle massage. Give the player water to rehydrate him.
Sprain	Injured ligaments	Treat with ice using RICE method.
Strain	Torn muscle or tendon	Treat with ice using RICE method.

Chapter 8

Coaching For Success

Soccer isn't just about the 11 players on the field: It's about one particular person standing on the sidelines, too, watching nervously as the game unfolds. That person is, of course, the team coach — also sometimes known as the manager.

In fact, there's a good case to be made that the coach is by far the most important person involved. Although the coach can't physically change what happens on the field as the game takes place, he's been responsible for picking the players, honing their skills in practice, and telling them exactly how to play.

With only a couple of notable exceptions, the personality and soccer philosophies of their coaches have shaped and defined all the great teams in history. This chapter explores how coaches have become successful in the professional game, and how you can succeed on the sidelines as well.

A Brief History of Coaching

Although the coach or manager is now the single most important figure of a team and/or club, that hasn't always been the case. The English national team, for example, played their first international in 1872, but didn't have a single boss in place until Walter Winterbottom was installed two years after World War II — 75 years later! And even then, Winterbottom was only permitted to train and advise the players. He wasn't allowed to pick the team — that was done by an executive panel of self-appointed Football Association *experts*.

It was only when Alf Ramsey took over in 1963 that the coach gained full control over the team. Ramsey agreed to take the England job only if he was given the all-reaching powers enjoyed by European legends like Vittorio Pozzo and Sepp Herberger — the former having won the World Cup with Italy in 1934 and 1938, the latter with West Germany in 1954. Within three years of Ramsey's appointment, England had a World Cup of their own, too.

Coaches like Pozzo, Herberger, and Ramsey were some of the first who became personalities in their own right. They may not necessarily have been born entertainers, but they imposed themselves and their soccer philosophies on their teams. Strong-willed coaches who run their clubs from top to bottom have ruled the roost ever since, from the era of Scotland's Brian Clough and Argentina's Helenio Herrera to the days of Portugal's Jose Mourinho and the United States' Bruce Arena.

It may sound needlessly macho, but history bears it out — nearly all successful coaches are determined to do things their way. Few succeed at trying to keep everyone happy or worry about what people think of them.

Coach or Manager or Boss?

Historically in the United States, the person running the team has been known as the *coach*. In some places, such as England, the coach is instead known as a *manager* — and usually has additional responsibilities, such as a greater role in recruitment of players than a Major League Soccer (MLS) coach usually has.

Instead, in MLS, there's often a general manager or technical director who is ultimately in charge of the roster, although taking into account input from the coach who has to select from the players recruited.

What the role involves

A professional coach's role is to ensure a club puts out a team of 11 players — plus however many substitutes are allowed — for every game in the season. The coach must pick the most effective 11 players to take on the opposition, and *coach* (advise) them on how best to win the game. The coach's role has much more to it than that, however:

 ✔ **Dealing with the media:** At bigger clubs coaches must give interviews to television, radio, and newspapers in order to maintain a dialogue with the supporters. The more charismatic coaches are able to cultivate a relationship with the crowd that may insulate them from criticism when things go wrong.

✔ **Handling the roster:** The coach works with a general manager and other members of the club to build the club's roster, giving input on which players to sign and which to let go. The level of responsibility the coach has for this varies from country to country and even team to team.

✔ **Managing motivation and morale:** The coach is responsible for the man-management of the entire team roster. It's the coach's role to keep spirits and confidence high, encourage or criticize players when necessary, and ensure team members get along with each other and pull in the same direction.

✔ **Picking the team:** The coach selects the starters on the team from the available players on the roster. Team selection is a critical role, as the coach must balance factors such as the opposition, playing conditions, the physical condition of players, team morale, and current form in deciding which 11 players to send out every game.

✔ **Taking charge of games:** The coach reacts to events during games, coaching and supporting his team throughout the 90 minutes of play. He needs to make tactical changes and substitutions wherever he sees fit.

✔ **Taking the flak:** When things do go wrong, the coach is expected to shield his players from criticism and take it on the chin himself. He is seen as the figurehead of the club, and is ultimately responsible for everything that happens on the field.

In short, coaches are expected to keep 100 plates spinning at once — and if one smashes to the floor, the blame usually lands on the coach.

Chess — or all-out war?

There are as many different types of coaches as there are different human character traits, but in general two approaches to coaching exist:

✔ **The cerebral approach:** The coach concentrates on tactics, preparation in practice, and meticulous team planning. This type of coach treats soccer like chess, as intense tactical battles against the opposing coach, and sometimes moves his players around the field — and in and out of the team — like pawns on a chessboard. A modern coach who represents this approach is José Mourinho at Real Madrid.

✔ **The emotional, passionate approach:** The manager espouses pride in the team colors and tells his team to put everything into every challenge, a blood-and-thunder approach akin to waging war. The modern coach most famous for this is surely Sir Alex Ferguson at Manchester United.

Get your coaching licenses

If you want to become a qualified coach in the United States, you need to enroll in a US Soccer Federation coaching course. Contact your local state soccer association to find out the details of upcoming courses. To learn more about training to be a coach, see Chapter 9.

In practice, though, a truly great coach tries to balance both approaches. He may put more weight on one approach than the other, but he tries to get a mix that works. Ferguson wouldn't have won so many trophies at Manchester United without ensuring his teams were properly tactically briefed, while Mourinho creates a close-knit camaraderie with his teams that generates hard-fought wins.

Kicking It with Kids

If you're thinking of taking over as a coach of a youth soccer team, ask yourself a few questions before taking the plunge. If you're relatively new to soccer, are you willing to take the time to really learn the game so players can benefit from your knowledge? Does your work and family schedule allow you to take the time out to manage practices and games two or three times a week? Have you dealt with kids before, and if not, do you really have the patience to work with them?

As you prepare to get started coaching kids, you may like to keep one or two things in mind:

- **Kids get bored quicker than adults do.** Adults like to hang around at practice, chatting between drills, but children want to keep playing. If you keep children waiting, they get irritable and cross — and the session produces less beneficial results.

- **Positive feedback is essential.** It's no use shouting at a child who's trying his best to perform a skill in practice or to play well during a game. What gets a good response from an adult doesn't necessarily work with a child.

- **There's nothing wrong with winning and losing.** Kids love to compete, and think every game is the biggest since the last World Cup final — so if they've lost the game, don't tell them it's okay and that it doesn't matter. Just make sure they keep a sense of perspective and don't slip into a sulk or throw a tantrum. Explaining how they can use their feeling of frustration positively — to practice harder and play better next time — will stand them in good stead.

✔ **Tell the parents on the touchline to keep calm.** Some parents scream and shout throughout the game, transmitting an aggressive message to the young players. Such an attitude does nobody any favors. Honestly, sometimes the parents are worse than the kids.

Above all else, be prepared for each coaching session and game. Every practice should be planned to accomplish a particular goal, such as a focus on finishing skills or, with an older age group, to illustrate how to implement a particular tactical play.

On gameday, come ready with a starting lineup chosen and a plan for substitutes. Kids won't improve unless they play, so make sure that everyone gets some playing time regardless of ability levels.

Most of the coaching advice that follows below applies equally at youth level and adult level, but for the detailed lowdown on coaching kids, check out *Coaching Soccer For Dummies* by Greg Bach (Wiley).

Picking a Team

Selecting a best 11 to send out onto the field isn't just a matter of picking names from a hat. There is a lot to consider when picking your team from a roster of players that offers different options.

Assessing your roster

If you've just taken over as coach of a team or club, you've inherited a roster of players. Your first task is to take a look at each player in practice and figure out each player's strengths and weaknesses. This will help you know how to utilize them best and target areas where each player can improve with your guidance.

Doing the best you can to improve a player's performance and develop his or her skills is one of the crucial roles a coach plays. Is there a way you can improve a player's game, perhaps through practice drills, teaching him or her new techniques or with simple encouragement?

Perhaps a poorly performing player would benefit from playing in a different position. When Rafael Benitez took over as coach at Liverpool, Jamie Carragher was an under-performing right back. Benitez converted him into a central defender, a position he excelled at for seasons afterwards.

You need to evaluate each player's skills, strengths, and weaknesses, such as by asking the following:

- ✔ **Is the player mobile?** Soccer is an increasingly athletic game, and players who are unfit, lack flexibility, or are clumsy are likely to cause problems. An in-shape and mobile runner still needs the ability to play, but it's a crucial base upon which to build. Be sure to encourage good levels of fitness.

- ✔ **Does the player contribute defensively?** Teams can rarely afford to carry passengers when the other team is attacking. The very best strikers defend from the front by chasing down every ball and pressuring opposing defenders. Does the player stand around admiring his own shots and passes? Or does the player immediately harass opponents upon losing the ball in an attempt to win it back? Your team may need to battle to win games, so commitment is important.

- ✔ **How skillful is the player?** Not all players need to be involved with play for the whole 90 minutes. Creative playmakers, wingers, and strikers may only need a minute to change a game in your favor — and their talents make them worth their place, even if they're occasionally lax in the tackle.

- ✔ **What's the player's spirit like?** A player can have all the talent in the world, but if she lets her mood sour when the team is struggling it can have a detrimental effect on others. A sulking player may go missing, leaving the team effectively playing with 10 players — or may even get herself sent off in a fit of frustration, literally leaving the team a player down. Emphasize the importance of disciplined play.

- ✔ **Does the player capitalize on opportunities?** A striker can be hardworking and get himself into good positions, but if he repeatedly misses simple goalscoring opportunities, then that's just a waste of your team's good work. Perhaps such a player is better suited in a different position.

- ✔ **Does the player influence the team?** The best players take their team along with them, inspiring them to up their game. In an ideal world, a team would have 11 captains, all encouraging each other to reach more intense levels of play. Motivate individuals to take leadership roles.

- ✔ **What's the player's soccer intelligence like?** Can a player read the game well, spotting the killer pass or making the clever run? Or is she constantly caught offside or finding herself positioned miles away from the play?

Many other factors exist for a coach to consider, but simply by watching a player you will soon make up your mind about that player's strengths and weaknesses — that will help you identify how to improve the team and work to improve the player's skills.

Choosing a captain

A coach needs to select one or more members of his roster to be club captain. That player needs to have a good rapport with the coach, as well as be respected by the rest of the team. The captain needs to be a good communicator, a player who is likely to start most games — so she can fulfill her captain's duties on the field.

Being a captain is a big burden on an individual, so at youth level, teams often contain multiple captains all helping the team.

Selecting a first XI

Logic dictates that the coach wants to select the most talented players in each position, but you will need to consider three major factors:

- **Who's in form?** The manager wants to pick the players who are currently in good physical shape, on top of their game, and delivering the goods.

- **Does the player fit in?** There's no point picking a supremely talented player if he or she doesn't gel with the rest of the team or if his or her style of play doesn't work with the tactical system. Sometimes a lesser player may develop understandings with other team mates that are more beneficial to the overall system and that can't be replicated.

- **Should everyone play?** If the players are also children, the coach needs to give everyone the chance to play — otherwise, development of everyone's play on the roster won't be possible. For older players and especially at the adult level, you may instead need to focus on always starting the best XI to win games — and keep your job.

A coach won't necessarily be picking the best 11 players in his roster for every game, but rather the 11 who work best together as a unit. If a team plays a large number of games in a short amount of time, it may be necessary to rest better players to avoid injury and ensure they are fit for crunch games later in the season.

Deciding on tactics

A coach doesn't need to decide on one sole tactical approach — in fact, it's beneficial to the team if they learn several different ways of playing. However, chances are the coach in general prefers one particular method of playing and sets his team up accordingly.

Coaches may decide on a tactical approach reflecting the abilities of the players in their rosters; for example, if the team has several talented attackers, it would be pointless to play an overly defensive game. The coach may also opt for a certain approach as part of an overall philosophy — a coach may think the team will win a higher percentage of games by playing a long-ball game, and always stick with that approach.

Coaches also tweak, or sometimes completely change, their tactics and style of play depending on the opposition. This may even influence a change in starting selection. For example, if a dangerous winger like Cristiano Ronaldo is playing on the right wing, a coach may place an extra defender there to nullify the threat. Tactical changes may also take place during the game — if Cristiano Ronaldo is being double-teamed on defense on the right wing, his coach may switch him to the left wing instead.

Being Prepared

Unless you've already managed to land yourself a job at a professional league club, chances are you won't be able to appoint a large staff of assistant coach, fitness coach, goalkeeping coach, and talent scout. In fact, you may even have to perform the role of medic yourself, not to mention cutting the half-time oranges into segments. There's a lot of preparation to do.

If you're taking sole charge of a team, it's advisable to take a course in basic first aid in case you need to administer any during a game.

But being in sole charge doesn't mean you should isolate yourself. Take advice from trusted friends who come along to watch the games, and listen to the players, especially the senior ones, who may have practical and positive suggestions to make.

Practicing for success

When you have your roster of players together, it's time to prepare them for games. You will need to take them through fitness drills as well as honing their skills on the practice field. But you also have to make sure they're mentally prepared.

Setting goals

Adult players know the ultimate goal is to win games, but it pays to be realistic as well. At the start of the season do you expect your team to be challenging for a league title or a cup? If so, set out those parameters at the beginning; that way your players have a target in mind.

For younger players, remind them that playing the game well is just as important as wins and losses. Perhaps more importantly than telling the kids, remind the parents that your goal is to develop technique and skills that the players can benefit from in the future, rather than simply focusing on individual game results.

Being realistic in the short term does not necessarily breed pessimism or resignation!

Practicing

Putting your players through drills in practice will help hone their skills and prepare them for game situations. Here are a few popular drills:

- **Shooting drills** are a simple and popular option because everyone wants to score goals, and practicing to strike the ball accurately refines a player's technique. You can mix up shooting drills by having players focus on shooting low or high to the corners or by making them use their weaker foot to shoot.

- **Set pieces** show how to both defend and attack from free kicks and corner kicks. This can help identify who you should select to take set piece kicks, and encourage your players to attack the ball. Drills on defending at set pieces help players know how to lineup and guard attacking players.

- **Scrimmages** are a chance to put into practice all that you've been showing your team. Small-sided games are often a necessity — you probably won't have enough players at practice to do a full 11 versus 11 game — but this can be a benefit, as fewer players will mean each takes more touches. Don't be afraid to blow your whistle and stop a scrimmage to make a coaching point.

Explaining the tactics

Although you take players through drills in practice, you need to hammer home your tactical wishes in a briefing at the end of the last practice ahead of a game. You can use magnetic tactics boards or whiteboards to illustrate tactical situations, but remember to keep it short and sweet. Players get bored if your instructions last too long, and in any case they're likely to forget what you've told them.

Keep it simple. Your players need to recall this information when they're playing the game. Technical jargon will either confuse or be totally forgotten in the heat of battle.

Check out Chapter 5 for the lowdown on the various formations that may suit your team.

Players may find it easier to grasp certain concepts, and how they relate to them, if you show them videos of professional teams in action.

Motivating before the game

Find out how your players like to prepare for a game. Do they feel more relaxed listening to loud music in the locker room before the game, for example, or do they prefer silence?

Make sure all players are relaxed and happy. Some may need to be energized; others may prefer a calming arm around their shoulders.

Your players should already be well briefed tactically, so there's no need to go over any plans in detail. If you need to hammer home any reminders, keep them short and simple. All that's left is time for a rousing speech — or a brief *good luck* if you think that will suffice.

Making in-game decisions

Just because the referee has blown the whistle to start the game, it doesn't mean it's suddenly all down to the players. You need to keep working with your team as the game progresses — if they start to struggle, they'll be looking to you for help.

Touchline communication

Don't rant and rave on the touchline, even if a player is playing abysmally. If you lose your temper, players on your team are likely to get agitated or panicked, resulting in poor performance. Players specifically targeted by a touchline tirade from the coach are also likely to deliberately ignore him, looking away from the bench either in anger or embarrassment. You're unable to get any tactical changes or advice across to your players if you act this way. Pass messages and advice to your players calmly, through your captain if possible.

Tactical changes and substitutions

If a mismatch is occurring somewhere on the field to the detriment of your team, make efforts to switch things around. If a player for the opposition is running a defender ragged, either detail another player to switch with the defender or get him to double up on the attacker. Alternatively, you may think that your speedy winger may be happier against a slower defender on the opposite wing to the one he's currently playing on; if so, make the switch immediately, subtly if possible.

Successful coaches aren't afraid to make changes to the original battle plan. This isn't an admission that you got it wrong in the first place — just a mature reaction to events unfolding in front of you.

At some point in the game, unless things are going perfectly, you may want to make tactical changes to personnel. For example, a fast reserve striker may take advantage of a tiring defense during the latter stages of a game. But be careful not to use all your substitutions for tactical purposes too early: Your own players may tire, or pick up injuries, and you don't want to end the game with ten players or less.

Half-time

While the players rest at half-time you need to give them a pep talk. Players may need words of encouragement if they're working hard but getting no reward, praise if they're doing well, or some choice critical words if they're playing poorly. It may be time to instigate some tactical changes while you have everyone's ear, or make substitutions. It may also be time for a small rousing speech of encouragement to lift your team's spirits before they go out again for the second half.

Full-time

If your team has won, congratulate each member of your team. Making each player feel a crucial part of the victory emboldens them for the following game. Feel free to make any minor technical criticism — happy players are much more likely to take a small nugget of constructive advice on board after a win without taking offense.

If your team has lost, there's no point ranting and raving in the locker room after the game, unless several of your players have put in an abysmal performance (a lack of effort, perhaps, or needless red cards). It's always better to analyze the game at the next practice session, when tempers have cooled down.

Chapter 9

Getting the Game On

- -

In This Chapter

▶ Playing for fun

▶ Taking part and playing for a team

▶ Picking a team for kids

▶ Playing on in college

▶ Coaching from the bottom to the top of the game

▶ Becoming the man — or woman — in the middle

- -

Getting a game together takes a little bit of organizing skill; you can't just wander along to the local park and be confident of joining a pickup game. But don't fret: It doesn't take long to find somewhere to play and someone to play with. It's easy when you know where to look — and plenty of people are available to advise you along the way as well.

You may just want to have a semiregular pickup game somewhere, or perhaps you'd like to be a bit more serious and play for — or coach — a team in a local league. It may be your ambition to run a team of your own. Or perhaps you want to find the right place for your child to play. Whatever your aims, the following advice helps anyone to get onto on the field in time for kickoff, from the youth level to veteran play.

Playing Pickup Soccer

Pickup soccer is the easiest way to play the game. If you're looking to just kick a ball around and have some fun, it's worth asking if you can join in games played just for fun anywhere you can find them.

During the summer months taking a quick wander around the major parks in your town or city may pay dividends. Groups of players often arrange informal games, picking teams at random and getting on with the serious business of having some fun.

Solo players walking by — or even groups — often ask to join in. Unless the game's at a crucial stage, with plenty of players already taking part, the answer's often affirmative. It's a good way to meet other players — you may even end up agreeing to meet again for a regular game. And the players may put you in touch with a regular game with an organized team or club.

Word of mouth is often the best way to find out about possible vacancies in organized teams. It's worth keeping your ear to the ground. Check the Internet as well — many websites now help players find local pickup games in various sports, including soccer. The Meetup website (www.meetup.com) is a good place to start searching.

Finding Out about Teams and Leagues

Amateur teams and leagues range from absolute beginner levels up to semi-professional quality. Like professional soccer, at the amateur level leagues and teams are arranged by ability so you find ones for beginners as well as for experienced players. Some of the top amateur teams in the country even compete for national titles alongside professional teams in competitions such as the U.S. Open Cup.

Amateur soccer is guided nationally by the United States Adult Soccer Association (USASA), with their website (www.usasa.com) including all the details on affiliated competitions around the country.

Whether you're a beginner or a former college star player, the easiest way of getting a game of soccer anywhere is to join an existing team. Every state has its own association in charge of soccer in its area affiliated to the USASA. Do a quick Internet search to find the contact info for your local association and then give them a call. They can advise you of clubs to contact near you.

Don't be afraid to contact official soccer associations — that's exactly why they exist. Many young or inexperienced players assume soccer associations are busy dealing with professional matters, but someone is always prepared to help.

When you've got a list of local clubs and leagues, do a bit of research. Almost all organizations now have websites, so take a look around and see which look like they may be a good fit for you.

Consider carefully the details of the league and team you are interested in joining before signing up. Here are some key questions to ask:

✔ **Is the team men's, women's, or coed?** Choose whether you want to play with players of just one gender, or on a mixed team.

✔ **What standard is the league?** Have you played high-level college soccer and you're looking for a very competitive game, or have you never played before? Ask what the standard of play is.

✔ **What age group are you?** Are you finding a league for your child? Are you looking for adult-aged competition? Be sure to find a league that's the right age group for the player (see "Playing on past 30" later in this chapter for details on leagues for more mature players).

✔ **Where are the games?** Some leagues play on brand-new turf fields at city parks, whereas others hold their games on a muddy patch a long way outside of town. Check if the location is convenient for you, and ask if the field is in good condition.

✔ **How much does it cost to play?** Be sure to find out all the fees for your participation — do you have to pay extra for insurance? For team jerseys? Make sure to ask for the complete lowdown so you don't face unexpected costs later.

✔ **When are the games?** Most recreational leagues play on the weekends or on weekday evenings, so find one that suits your schedule.

As well as teams and leagues officially affiliated to their state associations, many cities also have recreational leagues run by commercial companies outside of the formal league structure. They often have teams made up of *independents* — individuals who are all new to the league — so you can join up with some fellow newcomers.

Be careful about signing up for a team in a league not affiliated with its state soccer association. There is less guarantee of good conditions, such as experienced referees, and you may not get the same insurance benefits in case of injury or an accident outside of an officially sanctioned league. Teams in unaffiliated leagues are also unable to compete in official regional and national competitions organized by the USASA.

Playing on past 30

Your aching bones may not thank you, but if you love playing soccer you won't want to stop just because you turn the wrong side of 30. Plenty of leagues exist to cater to players who don't want to spend their Sundays chasing around faster, younger players. These leagues are divided by age group for over-30s, over-40s, and even over-50s. The quality of play in these leagues can be high — though the players may be slower, they are usually experienced, and most know a trick or two to make up for a lack of speed.

Thousands of teams exist across the country, composed of beginners to professional-level players and everything in between. There's a competitive game — and hopefully a league — for you out there somewhere!

Running a Team

Maybe you've played for other teams in recreational leagues for a while, but now you want to start your own. It's not as daunting as it sounds if you take some simple steps.

Choosing a league

Like picking the right league to play in as a player, you need to pick an appropriate league for your team. Choose a league that matches your team's gender (men's, women's, or coed), age group, and skill level — if you have a team of beginners, don't pick a league advertised as "competitive."

Recreational leagues play on weekday evenings and at weekends. These leagues, which you can easily find on the Internet, are relatively hassle-free for teams to enter. For a flat fee paid by each team, the league organizes a field to play on, opposing teams to play, and referees.

Be sure to consider the cost of the league and where the games are played — will your players be able to make it to the games without too much inconvenience?

 Some recreational leagues aren't as strict about discipline as leagues with a long-established official disciplinary apparatus behind them. That's not to paint these leagues as lawless free-for-alls, but it's worth remembering this point.

Finding players

If you decide to start a team from scratch, you no doubt have the backbone of a team of players in mind — probably people you've played with before, or friends and acquaintances that you know play. But even if you think you have a full roster, it pays to get the word out through your social networks to see if you can unearth an extra talented player or two.

Paying dues

You need funds to get your team going. At the start of the season, you should work out the rough costs for the season. If your team is playing at a recreational level, your main costs include:

✔ League membership fees, which usually cover costs such as referee fees and field rental

✔ Purchase of jerseys

The total cost can be divided by the amount of players involved for the season.

Your team's finances can be supported by finding a sponsor willing to chip in a few hundred dollars towards your fees every season. Many bars sponsor sports' teams, so if there's one where you and your team mates would enjoy hanging out after every game, don't be afraid to ask.

Keeping to a schedule

The league administers the schedule of the competitions and lets you know when and where the games will be. They usually give you a complete list of games at the start of the season. When you have the schedule in hand, be sure to send it out to all your players so they can plan ahead. Every week ahead of a game, be sure to do a head count to make sure you have enough players available for the next game — this can be done through e-mails or phone calls.

Game officials

The league, or whatever other competition you enter, arranges referees for the game. This doesn't cost the club any money because the membership fee paid to the league covers the charge.

Getting serious

If you want to start a club that can compete in competitive regional and national tournaments, you have a lot of work to do. You need to consider the costs of traveling, obtaining all the jerseys and other equipment a team needs, disciplinary procedures when a player steps out of line, and keeping up social events to build club morale. Running a competitive club is time-consuming but can be very rewarding for you and your community if you can dedicate the resources to setting it all up. Make sure you have plenty of other committed people willing to help.

Taking the Game Indoors

Soccer isn't just about 11-a-side games. You also have small-sided games — predominantly with six or seven players on each team, as well as the relatively new sport of Futsal — that you play on indoor rather than outdoor fields. This can be a great way to keep playing during the colder months.

You usually play indoor soccer games on hard or artificial surfaces. A quicker game than 11-a-side, it's more end-to-end, with crisp passing and movement as greater features of the game. The smaller size of the field negates the need for long passing, and no sidelines exist: You can play passes off the walls around the field, which ensures a fast-paced game.

Futsal is a similar game with five players on each team, but with a smaller ball that gives less bounce. Ball skills are vital in Futsal; the game was created with developing dribbling in mind. Unlike other indoor soccer games, the ball can go out of play.

Commercially organized indoor leagues are common. As with commercial outdoor soccer, the league organizes everything for you: field, opposition, and officials. Games are often held on weekday evenings, a good alternative to weekend leagues.

Getting Your Kid Playing

Since the 1970s, youth soccer has grown to become one of the biggest participation sports in the country. Millions of children now play for teams in leagues run by the two biggest organizations in youth soccer, the U.S. Youth Soccer Association (USYSA) and the American Youth Soccer Organization (AYSO). Both offer well-organized, safe places to play across the country.

If you're planning to sign a younger child up to a team, consider whether he or she is ready for organized play — there is no need to rush a kid who just enjoys kicking a ball around for fun. Many children don't join teams until after the age of 10. Practices are usually twice a week, so it's a serious commitment for both the child and the parent.

Levels of play

Youth soccer clubs are made up of teams for different age groups and genders — make sure the club is playing at an appropriate skill level for your child's abilities. Club levels include:

- ✔ **Recreational:** Starting as young as four, kids can join teams that play small-sided games — with as few as three players on a team — to maximize touches and fun, with the score often not being kept at all.

- ✔ **Travel:** As a child gets older and more serious, more competitive levels of play can be found in travel soccer — so called because teams often travel frequently to play against other strong teams.

- ✔ **Academy:** The top youth teams for teenage players in the country are part of the United States Soccer Development Academy, which includes 80 teams from across the nation. Teams compete regularly in regional competitions, attempting to qualify for prestigious national finals.

Starting out with a team

When you think your child is ready for the challenge of playing in organized soccer, it's time to find a local team to join. Both the USYSA and the AYSO websites have online club directories that allow you to search for clubs near you by entering your zip code. You need to find out the fee any club charges to join — these vary widely. After you sign up your child, make sure they have the right equipment to bring to practice. The minimum needed is a ball, soccer shoes, shin guards, and bottled water. See Chapter 3 for more details on the gear needed to play.

Camping out

Taking a trip to a youth soccer camp can be a great way for kids to develop their skills. When choosing a camp, consider questions such as:

- ✔ How far do you want your child to travel?

- ✔ Does your child play recreationally, or do they need a competitive camp for a challenge?

- ✔ Does your child need to develop a special skill, such as in a goal-keepers' camp?

After you whittle down the choice, take a close look at who the camp director is — ideally an experienced coach — as well as at the camp facilities. Don't be afraid to ask plenty of questions before putting your money down on a camp.

High school soccer

In addition to playing for clubs, more than half a million boys and girls play for high school soccer teams. The high school soccer season is short, lasting for only around 15 to 20 games. The quality of coaching at high school level is variable, and some of the best players are encouraged or even forced by their club teams to forgo playing high school in order to focus on playing in elite club competition.

Making it in the academy

There are currently 80 teams in the United States Soccer Development Academy, a partnership between American soccer's governing body — the United States Soccer Federation — and the best youth clubs across the country. The aim of the Development Academy is to provide top-level training for players, with three mandatory training sessions for clubs in the program and a higher quality of play. Academy clubs compete against each other regularly in a 30-game season that lasts for ten months. Players on Academy rosters aren't allowed to play in high school soccer.

Academy clubs are divided into two age levels: under 15/16 and under 17/18. Most teams offer regular tryouts that are highly competitive. To find an Academy club near you, search the listing of clubs at the Development Academy website. Some Academy clubs charge expensive fees, whereas some teams — including some of those run by Major League Soccer clubs — are free to play for. As you'd expect, competition to get on those teams is intense.

Challenging the gifted player

Very gifted players quickly show it on the field and find opportunities to be challenged at stronger levels of play. This starts with select teams from each league picked to play against select teams from other leagues, and goes all the way up to youth national teams, theoretically the best players in the country in any given age group.

One route for a gifted youth player to progress is the U.S. Youth Soccer Olympic Development Program (ODP). Established in 1977 to train potential players for the nation's Olympic soccer teams, every state has its own ODP pool of players in each age group. The best players from each pool are selected for national training camps. Annual tryouts are held to identify players for the program, with players assessed on their technique, tactical awareness, athletic abilities, and attitude. Contact your state's youth soccer association to find out when these take place.

Playing in College

In the rest of the world, college soccer just isn't a big deal for serious players hoping for the chance to turn professional. But in the United States, it has long been a key springboard for hundreds of players who have gone on to play in Major League Soccer and professional leagues overseas. The National Collegiate Athletic Association (NCAA) runs college soccer with a prestigious national championship held every year.

Due to the establishment of Title IX in 1972 — a law that mandated equal provision of sports for men and women in federally funded colleges — women's soccer has grown enormously on campuses. There were still less than 100 varsity women's soccer programs by the end of the 1970s, but three decades on, there are now almost 1,000 of them.

There are three levels of play in college soccer.

The elite level

The best of the best, programs at the NCAA Division I level usually offer multiple soccer scholarships and the strongest coaching at the college level. The annual College Cup championship crowns the national champion. In the men's competition, founded in 1959, Saint Louis University has been the most successful program with 10 wins. The women's national championship began play in 1982, and University of North Carolina has been the dominant force, with 20 titles.

Lower-level NCAA play

Below the NCAA Division I level are a number of other levels with competitive programs, though the quality is more variable. Numerous professionals have come through programs at the NCAA Division II level, where athletic scholarships are also available. Athletic scholarships aren't allowed at the Division III level, but academic scholarships and financial aid are available so serious sports and academics can be combined.

Other competitive levels

Outside of programs affiliated to the NCAA, the National Association of Intercollegiate Athletics (NAIA) has hundreds of smaller colleges affiliated to it. The level of play here is similar to NCAA Division II. The men's championship dates back to 1959 and the women's to 1984. Many Christian colleges are affiliated to the National Christian College Athletic Association (NCCAA), with regional and national champions held annually. Two-year junior colleges can also provide a proving ground for players to transfer to NCAA schools.

Bruce Arena, who coached the United States men's national team between 1998 and 2006, began his collegiate soccer playing career at Nassau Community College in New York, becoming an All-American at the junior college before transferring to Cornell University in 1972. He became an assistant coach at Cornell in 1973, starting his storied coaching career.

Taking Up Coaching

If you have an eye for tactics and a strong ambition to lead a team, you can take charge of your own roster: Pick who plays, how they line up, and all the other duties and responsibilities that come with being the person in charge.

First steps

A good coach needs to be able to relate to his players. If you're already playing on a team, see if a leadership role suits you — be vocal on and off the field, and offer to assist your coach with any duties organizing practices. Talk tactics and strategy with other experienced members of the team. The more you think about the game and how teams are effectively organized, the readier you are to take up a coaching role yourself.

Getting qualified

Soccer's governing body in the United States, the U.S. Soccer Federation, offers coaching qualifications at five different levels, suitable for everything from learning the basics needed for coaching young kids to the complex business of running drills for a professional team.

The E certificate is the first rung on the ladder and prepares you to coach kids in the 9- to 12-year-old age bracket in an 18-hour course. You learn the rules of the game, how to run simple practice drills for small-sided games, and a few tactical nuances. You then are put through your paces in a couple of tests you need to pass to earn your license.

Next up is the D certificate, a 36-hour course for those who have their E qualification and want to dive in further after they have gained some coaching experience. This level introduces you to more fundamentals of teaching the technical parts of the game and ensures you understand age-appropriate drills.

Your local state association can inform of you of when and where E and D certificate courses are held. These classes are often held as 3- to 4-hour evening sessions so you don't need to take an 18-hour course all at once.

Moving up the ladder

After you've qualified from the E and D courses, consider whether you want to get really serious by moving up to the C level. Before you can do this, however, a year must pass from the date you received your D license, and it is highly recommended that you have extensive experience coaching in the 11-14 year age bracket.

The C course is a serious commitment, and you may need to travel some distance to a regional center in order to take it. The course lasts for nine days, including around 25 hours of classroom material and 45 hours out on the field. You study game video and run your own training sessions, receiving feedback from U.S. Soccer Federation instructors. As well as proving your abilities to run effective practice sessions, you also have to give a short oral presentation at the end of the course to show that you understand the material.

You need to be in good mental and physical shape for courses at the C level and higher. Make sure you're physically fit, and be ready to participate at all times: Being a coach is about being active, not passive.

The top level

If you want to coach at a serious level — for officially sanctioned teams over the age of 16, such as in college — you need to get your B coaching license. You must be at least 19 years old for this level, and you must have held your C license for at least one year. This is another nine-day course with almost 70 hours of lessons to take in, and at this level, you need to be able to think tactically about attacking and defending.

After you have passed your B course, all that's left is the A license. You must be at least 21 years old to take this course and have held your B license for at least a year. An A certification covers exploration of advanced technical, tactical, psychological, and physical elements of the game. After completing the 70-hour course, you're certified to teach adults at the professional level.

For more on the practical elements of coaching a team, see Chapter 8.

In addition to the A through E licenses, separate courses are also available if you want to focus on a single area of the game, such as goalkeeping, fitness, or youth coaching.

Becoming a Referee

If you don't fancy playing, but you want to take part in the game on the field you have only one other option: become one of the officials. If you want to become a referee you need to fulfill certain criteria:

- ✔ Have a workable level of fitness
- ✔ Possess good eyesight (including with the use of glasses or contact lenses)
- ✔ Demonstrate an ability for keeping your cool (because tempers can run high and you need to stay fair-minded at all times)

If you meet this criteria, you can register with your state soccer association for a basic refereeing course to get a national license from the U.S. Soccer Federation. This consists of several classroom sessions and practical examinations as you learn the fundamental rules of the game.

If you pass the exams, you're qualified to referee local amateur games — contact local leagues and let them know you are available. After you receive your license from U.S. Soccer, you need to get the right gear for a referee — a uniform, flags, cards, watch, cleats, and perhaps most importantly, a whistle. Make sure you keep an extra whistle on you at all games — there's nothing more useless than a referee with a broken whistle!

Game fees paid to referees vary from league to league and state to state. If you become an officially licensed referee, your local referee assignor can let you know the standard payment for your area.

Volunteer Roles

Perhaps you love soccer and want to get involved with a local amateur or professional team, but don't want to get involved as a player, coach, or administrator. You can choose among many volunteer roles with most teams, such as helping out at information booths at games or with recording statistics during a game. Ask a local team how you can help.

Sometimes those doing seemingly menial roles at the club are rewarded for their service. In 1986, when England's Oxford United won the League Cup in London, their head coach Maurice Evans generously gave his winning medal to the club's 72-year-old physiotherapist, Ken Fish. Evans even sent Fish up the famous Wembley stairs to receive the winner's medal.

Part III
Exploring the World of Soccer

In this part . . .

This part explores not only the major soccer club competitions that are played in North America, but those played at international level as well. We start the tour of planet soccer with an explanation of everything you need to know about the World Cup, including its history and format, as well as descriptions of some of the most memorable World Cup moments.

Next, we take you on a comprehensive guided tour of international soccer and the other major tournaments, such as the European Championships, the Copa America, and the CONCACAF Gold Cup. Away from the international arena, we talk about the major club and tournaments (both leagues and cups), introduce you to some of the great clubs who play in them, and explain, along the way, the whole business of what constitutes a club and the league it plays in.

To round off our voyage around the game, we provide you with everything you need to know about the burgeoning world of women's soccer.

Chapter 10

The World Cup

The International Olympic Committee and the NFL would argue otherwise, of course, but soccer's premier international trophy — officially called the FIFA World Cup, but known to everyone simply as the World Cup — is unquestionably the biggest sporting event on the planet.

The event people refer to as the *World Cup* is really the World Cup finals, a series of 64 games held in one country that serves as the finale of a worldwide qualifying process that takes nearly three years to complete. The World Cup finals are held every four years, a month-long festival of soccer featuring the best players and the greatest national teams, culminating in the biggest single one-off sporting occasion in the world of sport: the World Cup final.

This chapter describes everything you need to know about this amazing event: who takes part, how teams get to play in it, how the tournament is organized, and what happens during the finals. I also touch upon the most amazing moments in the history of the World Cup, from Diego Maradona's infamous "Hand of God" goal to Zinedine Zidane's headbutt.

The Biggest Show on Earth

The World Cup is organized by FIFA (the Fédération Internationale de Football Association or in English, the International Federation of Association Football), who govern soccer worldwide. Every single one of FIFA's 208 member countries — from giants like Brazil and Italy, to minnows such as Papua New Guinea and Montserrat — is allowed to enter the World Cup. But only 32 teams are able to participate in the finals tournament; considering that the host nation of the finals is automatically allowed entry, only 31 places are up for grabs. To determine who reaches the finals, the teams play in qualifying tournaments organized regionally.

The long and winding road begins

FIFA is split into the following six continental governing bodies, represented by a blizzard of acronyms:

- **AFC:** The Asian Football Confederation covers soccer throughout much of Asia. Russian soccer, however, comes entirely under the aegis of UEFA, even if a Russian club is, by any other measure, in Asia.

- **CAF:** The Confederation of African Football pretty much does what it says in Africa. Actually, the title is originally French — *Confédération Africaine de Football* — but it amounts to the same thing.

- **CONCACAF:** The home confederation for the United States, and an abbreviation that doesn't seem to do that much abbreviating. The *Confederation of North, Central American and Caribbean Association Football* is responsible for the game from Alaska down to the Panama Canal, including the islands of the Caribbean.

- **CONMEBOL:** The rather convoluted abbreviation for *Confederación Sudamericana de Fútbol* (if you're a Spanish speaker) or *Confederação Sul-Americana de Futebol* (if you speak Portuguese). Either way, CONMEBOL runs soccer in South America.

- **OFC:** The Oceania Football Confederation administers the game in the islands of the Pacific, in Polynesia, and in New Guinea. It also takes in New Zealand, though not, confusingly, Australia, which has been affiliated to the AFC since 2006.

- **UEFA:** The *Union des Associations Européennes de Football,* to give its full French title, is the governing body for soccer in Europe.

FIFA gives each of these continental governing bodies a certain number of World Cup finals berths to fill, and each runs their own qualifying campaign to determine who makes it to the finals.

The relative strength of the teams in each part of the world determines the number of places each continent receives. For example, in qualification for the 2014 World Cup, UEFA — which includes the reigning world champions Spain and four-times World Cup winners Italy — were given 13 berths to fill. By comparison, OFC — who've only ever sent four teams to the World Cup in the tournament's 80-year history — received just half a berth! (In practice, this *half berth* means the Oceania qualification group winners play off for a spot in the finals with the fourth-best team in the CONCACAF qualifiers.)

The shape of things to come

Due to an ever-fluctuating number of countries in the world, the qualification process has taken on many varied shapes since the first qualifiers were held for the 1934 tournament. (For the record, the first-ever World Cup in 1930 was invitation only.)

Each continent also prefers its own method to determine who wins through, but the process is always based on some sort of league format. So in South America all ten competing countries play each other, home and away, in one big league. The top four go through, and the fifth team goes into a playoff (in 2010, with the third-best team in Asia). But in Europe the 13 places on offer are decided by eight groups of six teams and one group of five. The winners of all nine groups go through, and the best eight group runners-up play off against each other for the remaining four qualification places.

It's a complicated process, but one that ensures every single nation has — theoretically, at least — a chance of making the finals.

The finals countdown

There would be no point putting all that effort into qualifying, only to lose your very first game at the finals and be sent packing straight back home. That's why FIFA has developed a structure that ensures all 32 finalists at the World Cup are guaranteed at least three games — therefore giving everyone at least a second chance of survival.

The structure of the World Cup finals is simple. In the first stage the 32 teams are drawn into eight groups of four. Each group is identified by a letter, A to H. FIFA seeds the draw — made roughly seven months before the start of the tournament — in terms of current ranking and historical performance to ensure all the best teams aren't drawn together in the early stages. Each group takes the form of a minileague, the teams all playing each other once. After all the teams have played all the games, the top two teams in the group qualify for the second round.

From the second round onwards, it's a single-elimination format. In the second round, each first-round group winner plays a runner-up from another group. After that is the quarter-finals, by which time things start getting really hot, then the semifinals and the final. The whole process takes, give or take a couple of days, a month. There are at least two games a day right up until after the quarters, whereupon in order to give the teams still standing a rest — and to make it totally fair — the two semis and the final are spread out over the last week.

The day before the final there's a third-place playoff. But players, coaches, and fans alike agree: Having gotten so close to the big one, nobody involved really wants to be there at all. Not least because, by now, everyone is anxious for the final. Now held on the last Sunday of the tournament, many millions of people worldwide watch the final. Over 500 million watched Spain beat the Netherlands in the 2010 final. Kickoff is invariably at a time that ensures European viewers (the biggest source of TV advertising revenue) watch the game in daylight hours.

From Montevideo to Johannesburg: Eighty Years of Top-Class Drama

With one exception (in 2002, when the finals were staged jointly by Japan and South Korea), one country has hosted each finals tournament. Uruguay was the first in 1930, and has been followed by Italy (1934 and 1990), France (1938 and 1998), Brazil (1950), Switzerland (1954), Sweden (1958), Chile (1962), England (1966), Mexico (1970, which was won by Brazil as shown in Figure 10-1, and 1986), West Germany (1974), Argentina (1978), Spain (1982), the United States (1994), South Korea and Japan (2002), Germany (2006), and South Africa (2010). In 2014, Brazil will host the tournament for the second time.

The 1930 tournament in Uruguay featured 13 teams from three continents (North and South America, and Europe), took a mere 18 days to complete, and was played in three stadiums in a single city, Montevideo. In 2014 the finals will feature 32 teams from across the world, take a month to complete, and take place in 12 stadiums in 12 cities. The tournament has come a long way since 1930 . . .

Uruguay and Italy set the template

Two teams dominated the early years of the World Cup. Uruguay won the inaugural event at home in 1930, before Italy repeated the trick four years later. The Italian success was forever tainted by rumors that the dictator Mussolini had paid a visit to the referee before the final against Czechoslovakia. But the Italian team was undoubtedly one of the greats, powered by the fearsome Luis Monti, and managed by the legendary Vittorio Pozzo, one of soccer's earliest tactical geniuses.

Italy retained the trophy in 1938, but understandably flopped when the World Cup resumed in 1950 after World War II. Most of the top Italian players were killed in the 1949 Superga air crash, laying to waste the famous Torino team, and the Italians insisted on traveling to the tournament in Brazil by boat. Exhausted, Italy bowed out without making an impression. Still, everyone expected the host nation Brazil to win — including the country's president, who congratulated his countrymen on their victory in a speech *before* the deciding game against Uruguay. Needing only a draw against Uruguay in the last game of a final-stage pool to win, Brazil conceded twice in the last 19 minutes to lose 2-1. There were suicides in Rio that night.

Figure 10-1: Brazil captain Carlos Alberto holds aloft the Jules Rimet trophy in 1970, Brazil's third World Cup triumph.

AFP/Getty Images

Brazilian brilliance

The years between 1954 and 1970 represent the World Cup's classic era, one dominated by Brazil, which soon recovered from the trauma of 1950. Reigning champion Uruguay lost its first ever World Cup game in 1954, in the semifinal against Hungary. It was hardly a shock, though: The Hungarians reinvented the sport playing smart soccer based around the revolutionary deep-lying playmaking of Nandor Hidegkuti and silky footwork of Ferenc Puskás. The Hungarians were reigning Olympic champions and hadn't lost for three years. Puskas' team was considered a shoo-in for the trophy, especially because the Hungarians faced West Germany in the final, who they'd beaten 8-3 in the group stage. But despite going 2-0 up in eight minutes, Hungary let West Germany back into the game, eventually losing 3-2.

The next Greatest Team in the World had no problem claiming the big prize: Brazil finally landed its first World Cup in 1958 thanks to the genius of the 17-year-old Pelé (see Figure 10-2) and tricky winger Garrincha. Brazil retained the trophy in 1962, but relinquished it in England four years later, Sir Alf Ramsey leading the home of soccer to its greatest achievement. People regarded Ramsey's team at the time as dour and defensive, failing to entertain throughout the tournament — until the final against West Germany, that is, when England suddenly burst into goalscoring life as Geoff Hurst became the first, and as yet only, man to score a hat trick in a World Cup final. (With a little help from an Azeri linesman — not Russian, despite the legend — who failed to spot his second goal hadn't crossed the line, admittedly, but not even the Germans argued that England had deserved to win on the day.)

Figure 10-2:
The incomparable Pelé, pictured in 1966 playing for Brazil against Sweden.

Popperfoto/Getty Images

There was no doubt about the entertainment in the 1970s finals in Mexico, considered the greatest in the history of soccer. England's Bobby Moore and Pelé embraced after a cat-and-mouse duel between England and Brazil under a psychedelic Guadalajara sun, and West Germany gained revenge for 1966 with a stunning comeback in León in the quarter-finals to put the champions out. England's exit mattered little though: Pelé's Brazil was destined to take the crown anyway, thrashing defensive hardmen Italy 4-1 in the final. Captain Carlos Alberto scored the most iconic goal in the history of the World Cup, ending a Brazilian multiplayer sashay down the entire length of the field with a blistering drive into the net. As shown in Figure 10-1, Brazil was awarded the Jules Rimet trophy permanently, having become the first nation to win the World Cup three times.

Germany and Argentina take center stage

The 1970 tournament was drenched in Mexican sun, but the 1974 version was soaked by German drizzle. Yet once again the World Cup was blessed by a burst of vibrant color: the brilliant orange of the Netherlands. The Dutch team was built around the elegant skill of Johan Cruyff, as shown in Figure 10-3. The Netherlands lit up the tournament with a new style known as Total Football, the idea being that any player on the field could play in any position — defense, midfield, attack — and often did so, interchanging with each other during the game. Like Hungary 20 years earlier, the Dutch team was considered to be miles ahead of all the other opposition, a hot favorite for the cup. And like Hungary 20 years earlier, the Dutch players were stymied in the final by a resolute West Germany, led by the brilliant Franz Beckenbauer, pictured lifting the World Cup in Figure 10-4. Along with the Hungarians, many agree that this Dutch team was the best never to have won the biggest prize in world soccer.

Figure 10-3:
The gifted Johan Cruyff at the 1974 World Cup playing for the Netherlands.

Figure 10-4:
Franz Beckenbauer, West Germany's winning captain in 1974.

The Netherlands felt more pain in 1978, once again losing in the final to the host nation, this time Argentina. The tournament is remembered for the goals of Argentinian striker Mario Kempes, the wonderful ticker-tape celebrations in the stadiums — and the murderous military junta running the country at the time, a sickening backdrop to the tournament.

Four years later in Spain, Italy became the second country to triumph for a third time. The Italians beat West Germany in the final, but the team is chiefly remembered for putting a rampant Brazil to the sword along the way, Paolo Rossi scoring three goals to deny the swashbuckling Zico, Socrates, and Falcão. West Germany was back in the finals in 1986 and again came up short, as Diego Maradona almost single-handedly dragged an otherwise average Argentina team to victory. Is the defining memory of that campaign the "Hand of God" goal palmed in by Maradona against England in the quarter-finals, or the perplexing 70-yard run he scored in the same game minutes later? Both will surely be remembered forever.

Argentina and West Germany both reached the final again in 1990. This Italian World Cup was a poor tournament, and bittersweet for the host nation and for England, who both lost in the semifinals on penalty kicks. There were tears, too, for Maradona, as in a drab final, West Germany took the honors over Argentina.

Brazil bounce back

On the way to the 1990 final, Argentina eliminated rivals Brazil in the second round. It was Brazil's most unsuccessful campaign since failing in the group stage in 1966. The team hadn't reached the final since 1970, so it decided from then on to play in a *European style* — in other words, eschewing the sometimes reckless *samba* soccer synonymous with Brazil since the 1950s in favor of a more pragmatic defensive approach. The decision paid immediate dividends. Brazil won the 1994 World Cup in the United States — though reaction to the win back home was muted in comparison to previous winning celebrations because many fans felt the team had jettisoned something unique in the pursuit of glory.

Brazil reached the final again in 1998, but the country's star striker Ronaldo suffered a seizure on the morning of the game and was rushed to hospital. In circumstances still unclear to this day, he wasn't even on the initial roster released before the game but with less than an hour to kickoff was back in the team. Ronaldo played as though in a daze, as did the other ten Brazilians. Host nation France, inspired by Zinedine Zidane, coasted to an easy 3-0 win.

Once again, though, Brazil bounced back. The 2002 Korea/Japan tournament was perhaps the poorest of all time in terms of overall quality, with only Brazil standing out. Ronaldo made up for his travails in 1998 by scoring both goals in the final, his team running out 2-0 winners over Germany. Brazil's run of reaching World Cup finals couldn't last forever, however, and in 2006 the Zidane-inspired French team beat Brazil in the quarter-final stage.

France could easily have won its second World Cup, proving to be marginally the better team in the final against Italy. But the French failed to press home their advantage after Zidane was sensationally sent off for headbutting Marco Materazzi in the chest, sending him flying (as shown in Figure 10-5). France then lost a tense penalty shootout. It was as dramatic a finish as any final in this grand old competition's history.

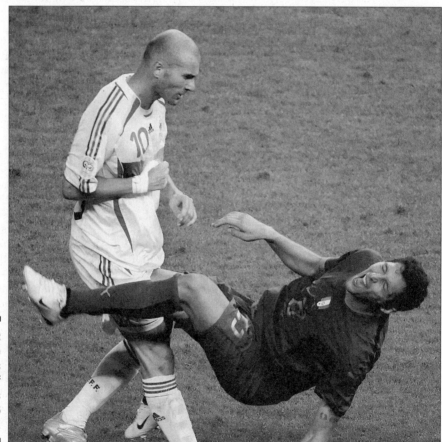

Figure 10-5: Zinedine Zidane's moment of madness in the 2006 final.

AFP/Getty Images

The 2010 finals themselves were notable for breaking new ground, because the World Cup was held on the African continent for the first time — in South Africa. Ground was also broken when Spain — long the biggest underachieving major national team — won the World Cup for the first time, defeating the Netherlands in the final. That meant heartbreak for the third time in a World Cup final for the Dutch, but there were few tears worldwide as the Netherlands' foul play proved second best to Spain's sublime technical passing and movement.

America on the World Stage

The United States men's national team has yet to win a World Cup, but it has had some shining moments and regularly competes on the biggest stage in soccer. Here's a quick recap of America's history in the World Cup:

- **1930 (Uruguay):** At the first ever World Cup, the United States achieved its best finish at the competition to date — finishing in third place out of the 13 competing nations. The U.S. lost at the semifinal stage to Argentina, 6-1.

- **1934 (Italy):** After qualifying by defeating Mexico 4-2, thanks to four goals by Buff Donelli, the United States lost to host nation Italy in the first-round knockout competition, 7-1.

- **1950 (Brazil):** At this World Cup, the United States earned its most famous single result, an amazing 1-0 upset of England in Belo Horizonte, the winning goal coming from Joe Gaetjens. The U.S. was eliminated in the first round group stage with losses to Spain and Chile, but the England game is still remembered with amazement today.

- **1990 (Italy):** Forty years passed before the Americans appeared at a World Cup again, with an inexperienced team losing to a veteran Czechoslovakian team in a 5-1 defeat as Eric Wynalda became the first U.S. player to receive a red card in World Cup play. Defeats to Austria and Italy consigned the Americans to elimination in the first round.

- **1994 (United States):** As the host nation, the United States felt the pressure but progressed to the second round thanks to a 1-1 tie with Switzerland and an impressive 2-1 win over Colombia. Eventual champions Brazil proved too strong for the Americans in the second round with a 1-0 win.

- **1998 (France):** The United States finished a disappointing last out of 32 teams, losing all three games — 2-0 to Germany, 2-1 to Iran, and 1-0 to Yugoslavia. The performances were not helped by controversy off the field, as head coach Steve Sampson dismissed team captain John Harkes just two months before the World Cup began.

✔ **2002 (Japan/South Korea):** Under head coach Bruce Arena, the U.S. team made it to the quarter-final stage, upsetting Portugal 3-2 in the group stage and beating Mexico 2-0 in the second round. Elimination came with a 1-0 defeat to Germany as the U.S. achieved its best finish in the World Cup in 72 years.

✔ **2006 (Germany):** With Bruce Arena still in charge, the U.S. team suffered a frustrating tournament. A 3-0 defeat to the Czech Republic was followed by a creditable 1-1 tie with Italy — though marred by red cards for the U.S.'s Eddie Pope and Paolo Mastroeni. A 2-1 defeat to Ghana in the Americans' final group game meant an early exit.

✔ **2010 (South Africa):** Bob Bradley took over as head coach for the first World Cup in Africa. The U.S. began the group stage by tying with both England and Slovenia. Qualification to the second round was secured in dramatic style, as Landon Donovan scored in the last minute for a 1-0 win over Algeria, the Americans' topping a World Cup group for the first time. In Johannesburg in the second round, Ghana defeated the U.S. after a rollercoaster game, winning 2-1 after extra time.

And so to 2014 . . .

You can be sure that the 2014 World Cup in Brazil will add a fantastic new chapter to this already-rich narrative. No event on earth offers as much drama; even the tournaments that in retrospect seem less than vintage — 1990 and 2002 spring to mind — were still roller-coaster rides of emotion when they were actually happening.

So which players will stamp their names all over the 2014 World Cup? And which teams have a realistic chance of making the final on July 13 at the Maracanã in Rio de Janeiro?

Teams to look out for

Brazil starts every World Cup as favorites, and this time will be no different: Twelve years will have passed since the South Americans' record fifth World Cup victory in 2002, but on home turf, no one will want to take on Brazil, especially armed with emerging star Neymar. Brazil's main competitor is likely to be Spain, the defending World Cup champions who have also won two consecutive European Championships, playing a hypnotic brand of possession soccer.

Some other usual suspects will likely line up, too. Argentina didn't have a particularly impressive 2010 World Cup under the auspices of the legendary Maradona, but the Argentinians usually come good. Italy made it to the final of the 2010 European Championship, and traditionally performs well at the World Cup. Germany, meanwhile, looks to have rebuilt its roster after a weak start to the 21st century, with plenty of young talent coming to fruition.

Among the wild cards, South American teams are likely to enjoy playing in Brazil; with Uruguay having reached the semifinals in 2010 in South Africa, it shouldn't be ruled out as a possible contender. Colombia has been picked as a dark horse at past World Cups, and could be one again this time. From Africa, Ivory Coast is packed with stars from Europe's top clubs, whereas North America's strongest contender is likely to be Mexico, the 2012 Olympic Games gold medalists.

As for the United States? Under German coach Jürgen Klinsmann, the Americans have been trying to install an attractive style of play and have two world class forwards in Landon Donovan and Clint Dempsey nearing the end of their careers. They will look to crown their international efforts in Brazil, but need a strong defense behind them against the very best the world can offer.

Players to watch

Lionel Messi isn't just the best player in the world at present — FIFA World Player of the Year in 2009, 2010, and 2011 — he's fast becoming mentioned in the same breath as Pelé and Diego Maradona, among the greatest ever. Unlike those two, Messi has yet to win a World Cup — in 2014, he will be determined to change that.

Brazil boasts the most exciting young forward in the world, Neymar (shown in Figure 10-6), along with an array of other glittering young talent. The Santos FC stud averaged over a goal a game so far in his brief international career, and if he keeps that up on home turf in 2014, his form could decide the tournament.

Spain's strength is in its team play, but that doesn't mean they lack individual talents. The Spanish team can boast David Villa as an option at striker, while its midfield is teeming with riches, including Barcelona's incisive passing trio of Xavi, Cesc Fàbregas, and the wonderful, bustling Andrés Iniesta. Portugal's Cristiano Ronaldo is still one of the most exciting players in the world to watch with his array of dribbling moves and free kicks, whereas England boasts a true star name in powerful striker Wayne Rooney. And when it's all over . . .

Figure 10-6: Brazil's talented Neymar — a star in 2014?

So a month of excitement awaits in 2014. And then?

Well, the World Cup heads to the giant landmass of Russia in 2018. In 2022, the Middle East will enjoy hosting the tournament for the first time, as the World Cup heads to Qatar — which is the smallest country to ever host the competition. The fun continues . . .

Chapter 11

Surveying the International Scene

The World Cup isn't soccer's only international tournament where nations face off head to head. Each continent holds its own international championship with rich and varied histories of its own.

Some championships are older than the World Cup itself — South America had its own as far back as 1917 — whereas others, like the FIFA (Fédération Internationale de Football Association, or the International Federation of Association Football) Confederations Cup, are still in their infancy. North America's own international competition is growing fast, but the European Championships are the most popular among both television viewers worldwide and for attendance in the stadium.

And then there are exhibition games between countries, where there's nothing at stake. Apart from your country's pride, that is . . .

Understanding the Point of Exhibition Games

An exhibition — sometimes called a *friendly* or a *scrimmage* — is a game where there is no competitive prize on offer whatsoever. Until soccer became organized in the early days into serious tournaments (see Chapter 2 for how the game developed), nearly all games had nothing formal at stake.

The very first international game ever played was an exhibition. It was contested between Scotland and England in Glasgow on November 30, 1872. The game ended 0-0 — the only time the two teams would play out a goal-less game until 1970.

After a while, countries started organizing meaningful tournaments. First the British nations — England, Scotland, Wales, and a pre-partition Ireland — set up the International Championship (known as the Home Internationals). Later, as we shall see, came the Copa America, the World Cup, the European Championship, the Confederation of North, Central American and Caribbean Association Football (CONCACAF, the governing body of soccer in the region) Championship, the Africa Cup of Nations, and others — but even so, countries still play exhibitions to this day.

These days, exhibitions are staged mainly to help countries prepare for their official tournament games. With much less pride at stake against different opposition, coaches are able to experiment with new and previously untested players, formations, and tactics. Coaches can make up to six substitutions in these games, three more than in official tournament conditions.

But countries still arrange the odd prestige exhibition game, at which pride is at a premium. Even if there's no cup at stake, the United States doesn't want to lose to Mexico, or vice versa.

Playing for North American Pride

North America's Continental Championship for Nations is known as the CONCACAF Gold Cup. It was founded in 1991 and replaced its predecessor, the CONCACAF Championship, which ran from 1963 to 1989, as the region's premier competition.

The CONCACAF Championship years

The very first CONCACAF Championship in 1963 was hosted by El Salvador, featuring nine teams with games played in two cities. A final pool of round-robin games determined the winner, with Costa Rica finishing ahead of hosts El Salvador in second place. The competition was then held every two years until 1973, when it switched to taking place every four years — and also doubled as the qualification tournament for CONCACAFs World Cup entrants.

By the time of the final competition in 1989, six different nations had won at least one CONCACAF Championship title. The United States was not one of them, during a long, lean period for the American team — it was won three times each by Costa Rica and Mexico, and once each by Guatemala, Haiti, Honduras, and Canada.

Onto the Gold Cup

Doubling the CONCACAF Championship up as a World Cup qualifying tournament had made some sense in earlier years, but in the late 1980s, CONCACAF decided there would be more prestige — and more money — in hosting a showpiece competition operating as a regional championship every two years. So in 1991, the CONCACAF Gold Cup was born.

The timing coincided with an upswing in the fortunes of the United States' men's national team, who had just qualified for the World Cup in 1990 (the first time in 40 years), and the country was also set to host the World Cup in 1991. With a wide array of large stadiums available across the country — although designed for other sports than soccer such as football and baseball — the United States was chosen as host for the inaugural Gold Cup. The competition was a success, with a crowd of over 40,000 attending the first Gold Cup final held at the Memorial Coliseum in Los Angeles on July 7, 1991, and the host nation took its first ever regional title with a win over Honduras after a penalty shootout.

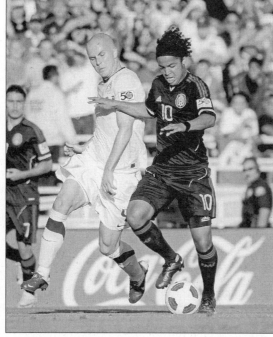

Figure 11-1: Mexico's Giovanni Dos Santos battles with the United States' Michael Bradley for the ball during the 2011 CONCACAF Gold Cup.

Getty Images

The Gold Cup has been held every two years since and has always been hosted or co-hosted by the United States; in 1993 and 2003, it shared that duty with Mexico. Those two countries have jostled to become the most successful in the competition. Mexico can boast six Gold Cup titles to the United States' four, including most recently thanks to a 4-2 win for the Mexicans in the 2011 final over the United States (two of the teams' stars are pictured jostling for supremacy in Figure 11-1). Canada is the only nation to have broken this duopoly, with a victory in 2000.

Winning European Prestige

The UEFA European Football Championship — formerly known as the European Nations Cup — is the international championship of Europe, held every four years. It's one of the most-watched sporting events in the world: Over 100 million fans worldwide tuned in on television for England versus Italy at the 2012 European Championships. Across the Atlantic in the United States, that year's tournament averaged over one million viewers per game.

Since 1984, the European Championships have been known colloquially as The Euros, with the year appended. So the 1984 event was called Euro 84, the 1988 staging Euro 88, and so on. Since the turn of the millennium, the full year has been used: Euro 2000, Euro 2004, Euro 2008, Euro 2012, and, coming soon, Euro 2016 . . .

The early years

The Union of European Football Associations (UEFA) held the first European Championship finals in France in 1960. Only four teams competed — the final tournament was effectively the two semifinals and final of an elimination tournament. Host France was the favorite, but despite being 4-2 up in its semifinal against Yugoslavia with 15 minutes to go, lost 5-4. The final would be won by the Soviet Union, whose star player was goalkeeper Lev Yashin, still said by those who saw him play to be the greatest of all time.

The 1964 tournament was held in Spain, which had defaulted from the 1960 event after its right-wing dictator General Franco had refused to allow the communist Soviets into his country for the quarter-final qualifier. This time, with UEFA threatening to take the tournament away from the Spanish, he allowed the defending champions in. Franco would be pleased at the way things panned out, Spain beating the Soviet Union in the final.

The host nation won for the second successive tournament in 1968, with Italy defeating Yugoslavia, which had now been runner-up twice in three stagings.

The famous West German team of Franz Beckenbauer, Gerd Muller, and Gunther Netzer won the 1972 finals, held in Belgium, but was powerless to retain its trophy in Yugoslavia four years later. In that 1976 final, it was beaten by Czechoslovakia in a penalty shootout; Antonin Panenka scored the decisive penalty with one of the cheekiest kicks of all time, a deft chip straight down the middle.

Ever since the 1976 final, a cheeky penalty chipped into the center of goal, sending the keeper helplessly diving either to the left or right, has been known as a "Panenka."

The Euros go large . . . and even larger

The 1976 finals had been extremely popular, so for Euro 80, UEFA decided to allow eight teams to compete in the finals. Two minileagues of four teams would compete, with the group winners facing each other in the final. West Germany regained the trophy it had lost four years earlier, beating Belgium in the final, but it was a poor tournament that didn't stay long in the memory.

The format was slightly reconfigured for the 1984 version in France, with a semifinal stage coming after the opening group phase. If the 1980 tournament was totally forgettable, this one was perhaps the greatest ever: Midfielder Michel Platini scored nine times in five games as host nation France claimed its first trophy, spectacularly beating Portugal 3-2 in a dramatic semifinal, before beating Spain in the final.

Euro 88, held in West Germany, was another memorable classic. After losing two World Cup finals in the 1970s, the Netherlands finally got its hands on some silverware, beating the Soviet Union 2-0 in the final. The game, and the tournament, will always be remembered for Marco van Basten's sumptuous volley in the final, a dipping cross crashed in from an almost impossible angle to the right side of the Russian goal.

Euro 92 in Sweden was less memorable, although the tournament did offer up perhaps the biggest fairy tale in the history of the European Championship. Denmark failed to qualify, but was handed a reprieve when Yugoslavia, which had topped its qualification group, descended into civil war and could not compete. Denmark surprisingly made it all the way to the final, where the Danes beat reigning world champions Germany 2-0.

By now the Euros were becoming almost as popular as the World Cup, so UEFA decreed that Euro 96, held in England, would be competed by 16 teams. The host nation looked as good a bet as anyone, especially after England trounced much-fancied Netherlands 4-1. But the English met Germany in the semifinal, losing on penalties. Germany beat the Czech Republic in the final, thanks to Oliver Bierhoff, who scored the first golden goal to decide a major tournament.

Golden goals were introduced in the mid-1990s by FIFA to decide tied games in big tournaments which went to extra time. If a goal was scored at any point during extra time, the scoring team would automatically win the game. Golden goals were not popular because they gave the losing team no opportunity to come back. They were first replaced by *silver goals,* which allowed the game to continue to the end of a half in extra time, before the concept was abandoned altogether after Euro 2004.

The Euros in the new millennium

Euro 2000, held jointly by the Netherlands and Belgium, was a huge success, with many high-scoring and dramatic games. The Netherlands was beaten in the semifinals by Italy, missing two penalties during normal time. The Italians so nearly won the trophy, leading France 1-0 in the final with seconds to go, but Sylvan Wiltord whipped in a dramatic equalizer, before David Trezeguet scored a spectacular golden goal in extra time.

Euro 2004 was a quieter affair. Otto Rehhagel's Greece team was considered dour, not that anyone on the team cared: The Greeks amazingly won the tournament against all the odds, smothering reigning champions France, the much-fancied Czech Republic, and host nation Portugal (twice — in the opening game of the tournament, then in the final).

Euro 2008 was held in Austria and Switzerland, with Germany reaching the final after defeating surprise package Turkey at the semifinal stage. The Germans, however, had no answer for Spain, who had been by far the best team in the tournament. Spain won the final thanks to Fernando Torres's single goal, adding a second European Championship to the one it won way back in 1964.

The 2012 tournament was held jointly by Poland and Ukraine. It was won by Spain, who not only successfully defended its title from 2008, but became the first country to hold the World Cup while winning consecutive continental championships — in 2010, the Spaniards had won the World Cup for the first time. Spain sealed victory with an impressive performance in the final against Italy, who had surprised many by defeating Germany at the semifinal stage (see Figure 11-2). Spain crushed Italy 4-0 in Kiev to claim the title again.

2012 was the last ever staging of the European Championship to feature just 16 teams — UEFA has decided that in 2016, the tournament will be contested by 24 countries. From its origins back in France 56 years previously, when four teams battled it out for the title, the Euros will have come a long way when they return to French soil in 2016.

Getty Images

Figure 11-2:
Action from
the Euro
2012 game
between
Germany
and Italy.

Ruling the Roost in South America

Although it took the Europeans until the swinging sixties to start up their own international tournament, the South Americans had already been up and running for half a century. The South American Championship — known since 1975 as the Copa America — is the oldest international soccer tournament outside of the Olympic Games.

It was first held on an unofficial basis in 1910, then officially in 1916, when it really got going. The championship has been held ever since, though at irregular intervals. Sometimes, as in the 1920s, there was one held every year; other times, there have been breaks of up to eight years (1967 to 1975).

How it's organized

The Copa America is organized by the ten member countries of the South American governing body CONMEBOL (Confederación Sudamericana de Fútbol, or Confederação Sul-Americana de Futebol): Argentina, Bolivia, Brazil, Chile, Colombia, Ecuador, Paraguay, Peru, Uruguay, and Venezuela.

All teams automatically qualify — and are usually joined by two invitees to make the numbers up to a more draw-friendly 12. In 2007, for example, Mexico and the United States were invited. In 2011, the guests were Mexico and Costa Rica. Once again, the Mexican team has been invited to take part in the 2015 tournament, along with Japan.

The teams will be split into three groups of four, with the top two in each group advancing to the quarter-final knockout stage. The best two third-placed teams will also go through.

The oldest — and the best?

The South American Championship has only recently been decided in the latter stages by elimination ties culminating in a final. Traditionally, the tournament was organized in a group, with the top team in the league winning the trophy.

Argentina won the very first tournament, which they organized in 1910 and featured only themselves, Uruguay, and Chile. The real thing started six years later when Brazil joined the party. Uruguay won that one as well as the following championship a year later in 1917.

The championship would be held every year between 1919 and 1927, with Uruguay and Argentina the dominant forces. But soon its staging would become extremely erratic, with several CONMEBOL members showing little interest in the trophy at all, either sending second-string teams or simply not bothering to enter whatsoever.

An erratic history

Whereas all CONMEBOL members enter the competition nowadays, that hasn't always been the case. In fact, it was only in 1975 when every single one of CONMEBOL's ten countries deigned to enter the same tournament.

The *big three* of Argentina, Brazil, and Uruguay entered more often than not. Between the mid-1930s and late 1950s, the championship was held — usually — every two years. But despite emerging as kingpins on the world stage, Brazil struggled to win its continental championship: Uruguay has become the most successful country in the competition, winning the Copa America for a record 15th time in 2011, as shown in Figure 11-3.

Figure 11-3:
Uruguayan players hold the Copa America aloft after victory in the 2011 final against Paraguay.

LatinContent/Getty Images

The championship nearly ground to a halt in the 1960s and 1970s. Most of the continent's big-name players now plied their trade in Europe, and getting them back to play out a month-long tournament became a major hassle. Only four championships were staged between 1963 and 1983, with the two in the 1970s won by minnows Peru (1975) and Paraguay (1979). It seemed the big three could no longer be bothered, sending teams of players who would get nowhere near a World Cup roster.

The Copa's revival

But the status of the tournament slowly grew again. CONMEBOL had rebranded it as the Copa America in 1975, then introduced a World Cup and Euro-style finals tournament in 1993. A group stage followed by elimination games and a final game would generate television revenue and raise the tournament's profile. There would also be guest spots for other countries, such as Mexico and the United States. Suddenly all the CONMEBOL countries were interested again.

Argentina won the first staging of this new format in 1993 — still its last success on the international stage — beating guest entrant Mexico in the final thanks to a late goal from Gabriel Batistuta. Uruguay beat Brazil on penalties in the 1995 final, before Brazil won what was at the time only its fifth title in 1997, triumphing over host Bolivia. (By comparison, both Argentina and Uruguay had 14 titles to their names.)

Since then, Brazil has finally become dominant in the Copa America, winning in 1999, 2004, and 2007. The Brazilians' victory streak was broken in 2011, when Uruguay claimed its 15th title, defeating Paraguay in the final.

The Copa America is now held on a regular four-year cycle. The next tournament will be held in Chile in 2015.

Taking the African Title

The Africa Cup of Nations was launched in 1957 by African soccer's governing body, the Confederation of African Football (CAF). Initially a three-team invitational event, it has grown into the largest competition in Africa — and one whose influence and popularity is growing rapidly, as world-class African players are now common at the world's top club teams.

The tournament is often referred to as the African Cup of Nations — but drop the adjectival "n" because the proper name is the Africa Cup of Nations. Even to this day, many newspapers and websites get this wrong!

The ACN: A slow burner

The first tournament, held in Sudan in 1957, wasn't much of an event. South Africa was initially scheduled to play, but refused to field a multiracial team, citing its apartheid policy, and was forced to withdraw. This meant Ethiopia made the final by default — it refused to countenance a three-team round-robin — but were stuffed 4-0 in the final by Egypt.

Many countries in Africa were too poor to compete — or were still colonized — so it took a while for the competition to grow. The same three teams competed in 1959 — and this time Ethiopia was forced to accept a three-team minileague — with Egypt again prevailing.

Ghana and Tunisia were the star teams of the 1960s. Ghana's team — known as the Black Stars, or the Brazil of Africa — won in 1963 and 1965, and carried political significance, too. Ghana's head of state, Kwame Nkrumah, thought that a successful soccer team would show the world an independent African nation could prosper on the big stage. "It showed we could do things for ourselves and achieve positive results," said Ghana's star striker Joseph Agyeman-Gyau, looking back decades later.

The tournament caught on, and by 1968, 15 teams wanted in. By now, too many entrants meant qualification was required for the first time. The CAF decided to hold the ANC every two years, a symbol of its success.

The cup catches fire

After the number of participants increased, so too did the number of winners. Between 1968 and 1980, the Democratic Republic of Congo, Sudan, Republic of Congo, Morocco, and Nigeria all won the title for the first time.

Cameroon would be the team of the 1980s, reaching three finals in a row between 1982 and 1986, winning twice. Nigeria was also a big player, reaching five finals between 1980 and 1994; it bookended that period with two victories, losing three finals in between.

South Africa came out of the sporting wilderness in the early 1990s. It failed to qualify in 1994, its first tournament back since the abolition of apartheid, but hosted the event in 1996 — and won its first-ever title.

Since then, Egypt (champions in 1998, 2006, 2008, and 2010) and Cameroon (champions in 2000 and 2002) have dominated, though the most recent edition in 2012 was won by Zambia, defeating Côte d'Ivoire in a penalty shootout.

The cup will be held again in 2013 in South Africa, because the competition is now held in odd-numbered years so that the tournament no longer clashes with the World Cup.

Winning Elsewhere

The two other confederations — the Asian Football Confederation and the Oceania Football Confederation — stage their own tournaments as well. FIFA also recently launched the Confederations Cup, contested by the champions of each confederation. And, of course, there's the Olympic Games.

Asian Cup

The Asian Cup is the continental soccer tournament in Asia, contested between members of the Asian Football Confederation. The trophy was held every four years from 1956 until 2004, at which point the four-year cycle jumped back a year in order to avoid clashes with other major tournaments such as the European Championships. The last Asian Cup was held in 2011, with the next one to be held in 2015.

Japan is the most successful Asian Cup participant with four wins, followed by Saudi Arabia and Iran with three wins apiece. South Korea has won the trophy twice, while Israel, Kuwait, and Iraq have each won it once.

Not all the former or current member nations of the AFC are from Asia: 1964 winner Israel, for example, left the confederation in 1974, and Australia, formerly of Oceania, joined in 2006.

OFC Nations Cup

The Oceania Football Confederation runs the OFC Nations Cup. It has been staged eight times and won four times apiece by New Zealand and Australia, with Tahiti the only other team to win the trophy — the most recent edition in 2012. New Zealand — a minnow on the world stage — is nevertheless the only sizeable nation left in the competition since Australia defected to the Asian Football Confederation in 2006.

Olympic Games

An official soccer tournament was first held at the 1904 Olympic Games held in St. Louis. It was won by Canada (represented by a club team called Galt F.C.); the United States took silver. The tournament was held again in 1908 and won by Great Britain. The Brits also won gold in 1912, and after a hiatus for World War I, were expected to win again in 1920 — but Norway eliminated Britain in the first round, Belgium winning instead.

The 1920 Olympic final is the only international final ever to be abandoned. Belgium was 2-0 up when Czechoslovakia walked off the field after having a man sent off. The Czechs later complained about the referee — who was in his 70s — but to no avail, Belgium being awarded the gold medals.

Uruguay won in 1924 and 1928, a precursor to its 1930 World Cup win. At this point, with FIFA having launched the World Cup, the Olympic tournament declined in importance.

During the Cold War era, the Olympics status as a wholly amateur tournament allowed Communist countries to circumvent regulations using technicalities over employment: All sportsmen were considered amateurs by communist states, though in practice they were full-time athletes, usually employed by the army. As a result, between 1952 and 1980, every single title was won by a nation in the Eastern Bloc.

The tournament was revamped in the early 1990s as a competition for players under 23 years old, with each team able to field three over age players. Since then the Olympics have been notable for the first African successes at a major tournament — Nigeria in 1996 and Cameroon in 2000 — followed by Argentinian wins in 2004 and 2008, and a first-time triumph by Mexico in 2012.

All countries affiliated to FIFA and the International Olympic Committee can enter, with qualification usually won through under-21 continental tournaments held by the various FIFA confederations.

One team that has never won the Olympic gold is . . . Brazil! The nation is obsessed with picking up the one major trophy it has never won, but has been unable to do so, despite sending along World Cup winners like Ronaldo, Ronaldinho, Rivaldo, and Roberto Carlos. It came closest in 2012, but lost in the final to Mexico.

Confederations Cup

The FIFA Confederations Cup is held a year before every World Cup, in that World Cup's host nation. It is contested by the winners of the European Championship, Copa America, Africa Cup of Nations, Gold Cup, Oceania Nations Cup, and Asian Cup, plus the reigning World Cup holders and the host nation.

The Confederations Cup started life as an invitational tournament held in Saudi Arabia: the King Fahd Cup. Argentina won the inaugural tournament in 1992, followed by Denmark in 1995, before FIFA took over the running of it and renamed it the Confederations Cup.

Since the relaunch in 1997, Brazil has won the trophy three times, France twice, and Mexico once. The United States' best finish came with second place in the 2009 tournament, a run that included a famous victory over European champions Spain in the semifinal.

Looking at the Game All Over the World

From Brazil, Argentina, and Spain at the top, all the way down to Brunei Darussalam, Anguilla, and St. Lucia at the bottom, there are over 200 countries affiliated with FIFA. Some have a richer history than others, of course: The following sections cover some nations you are sure to hear about.

United States

The United States men's national team has a longer history than most people realize — in November 1885, the first (unofficial) international game played outside of Great Britain took place when a team of Americans took on Canada in Newark, New Jersey. The United States also appeared at the first World Cup in 1930, achieving its highest finish to date — third place. The Americans lost at the semifinal stage to Argentina.

The United States appeared again at the next World Cup in 1934, losing its only game. In 1950, the Americans created one of the great upsets in World Cup history — with a 1-0 win over England in Belo Horizonte, Brazil. But the American team lost both of its other games in the competition, and the United States did not appear again at the World Cup until 1990, a long, barren spell that reflected the struggles of professional soccer in the country.

The United States team returned to the World Cup in 1990, and hosted the next edition in 1994, reaching the second round (losing there to eventual champions Brazil). Helped by the launch of Major League Soccer (MLS) in 1996, the United States has qualified for every tournament since — its best finish in this streak coming in 2002, when Bruce Arena's team reached the quarter-final stage (losing to Germany). It has also become a powerful force in regional competition, with four CONCACAF Gold Cup titles claimed.

The United States' team colors are red, white, and blue, and its international games are hosted in stadiums from coast to coast. The most famous American players, past and present, include Alexi Lalas, Eric Wynalda, Claudio Reyna, Landon Donovan, Clint Dempsey, and Tim Howard.

Canada

Canada's sporting interest was focused on hockey rather than soccer in the 20th century and didn't appear in the World Cup finals until 1986. Canada lost all three games in that World Cup and, to date, that remains its only World Cup finals participation. Canada has fared better in regional play, winning the CONCACAF Championship in 1985 and the CONCACAF Gold Cup in 2000.

Canada plays in red and white colors with home games played in various cities, though most frequently in recent years at Toronto FC's BMO Field.

Mexico

Mexico's love of soccer far exceeds that of its fellow North American nations, though it has yet to go past the quarter-final stage of the World Cup — reached in both 1970 and 1986, years in which the country hosted the competition itself. Mexico has won the Confederations Cup once (1999) and the CONCACAF Gold Cup six times, a record.

Mexico's uniform colors are green and white, and the team is nicknamed *El Tri.* The most famous Mexican players include Hugo Sanchez and Cuauhtémoc Blanco from days gone by, and Javier "Chicherito" Hernandez today.

Brazil

Brazil is the most successful international soccer team in the world. It's the only nation to have competed in every single World Cup finals tournament and has lifted the trophy five times (1958, 1962, 1970, 1994, and 2002). The 1970 team, built around Pelé, is recognized by many as the best in the history of the game. Brazil has also won eight Copa America titles (1919, 1922, 1949, 1969, 1997, 1999, 2004, and 2007) and three Confederations Cups (1997, 2005, and 2009).

Brazil's home jersey is yellow with green trim. The team plays the majority of its home games at the Maracana stadium in Rio de Janeiro. Brazil's best-known past and present players include Pelé, Zico, Rivaldo, Ronaldo, and Neymar.

England

England played in the first-ever international game, against Scotland in November 1872. England and Scotland were the best teams in the world for the next 20 or 30 years — though that's only because many nations had yet to take up the game or to arrange international games. England refused to compete in the World Cup until 1950 — and when the English did deign to join in, they lost 1-0 to the United States. But England got back up to speed quickly and won the World Cup in 1966. England has not reached another major final since, coming closest with semifinal appearances at the 1990 World Cup and Euro 96.

England's home jersey is white. The team plays home games at Wembley Stadium in London. Famous players (of the past and present) include Stanley Matthews, Tom Finney, Bobby Moore, Kevin Keegan, Paul Gascoigne, David Beckham, and Wayne Rooney.

Italy

Italy is the only European country to have won the World Cup four times (1934 as the host nation, 1938, 1982, and 2006). It has also won one European Championship (as host in 1968) and reached the final again in 2012, losing to Spain.

Italy's home jersey is blue. The team plays its home games at stadia all around the country. Italy's best-known former and current players include Dino Zoff, Gianni Rivera, Franco Baresi, Paolo Maldini, and Mario Balotelli.

Germany

Germany is the most successful European soccer nation, having won three World Cups (1954, 1974, and 1990, all as West Germany), and three European Championships (1972 and 1980 as West Germany, 1996 as Germany). An independent East Germany team existed between 1952 and 1989, but won zero trophies — although it did win the only meeting between the two teams, 1-0, during the 1974 World Cup finals.

Germany's home jersey is white, with black trim. The team plays its home games at stadia all around the country. Germany's famous past and present players include Franz Beckenbauer, Gerd Müller, Lothar Matthäus, Jürgen Klinsmann, and Thomas Müller.

France

Pioneers in French soccer take the credit for creating the World Cup, the European Championship, and the European Cup. It was a while, though, before the French national team gained some reward for the country's contribution to world soccer. In 1984 France won its first title, the European Championship. France would add a second in 2000, but not before winning the nation's first World Cup in 1998 as the tournament host.

France play in blue, occasionally with red trim. The team plays its home games at the Stade de France, Paris. The best-known past and present French players include Raymond Kopa, Michel Platini, Zinedine Zidane, and Frank Ribery.

Spain

Spain won the 1964 European Championship, but for so long were the bridesmaids of the game in Europe. Although Spanish clubs were dominant on the continent, the national team struggled. But the Spanish finally won another international title in 2008 with the European Championship, and has followed up with a remarkably dominant run since, winning a first World Cup title in 2010 and then repeating as European champion in 2012.

Spain plays in red with yellow trim. The team plays its home games all over the country. The most famous Spanish players past and present include Emilio Butragueño, Raul, Andres Iniesta, and Xavi Hernandez.

Argentina

Argentina contested the first-ever World Cup final in 1930, but did not win the prize until beating the Netherlands at home in the 1978 final. Thanks to the genius of Diego Maradona, Argentina added a second World Cup crown in Mexico in 1986. The South Americans have won the Copa America 14 times and one Confederations Cup (1993).

Argentina's home jersey has vertical sky-blue-and-white stripes. The team plays the majority of its home games at El Monumental stadium in Buenos Aires. Argentina's most famous past and present players include Daniel Passerella, Diego Maradona, Gabriel Batistuta, and Lionel Messi.

Uruguay

Uruguay won the first World Cup, in 1930, and the second World Cup it entered, in 1950. It wasn't until extra time in the semifinals of the 1954 tournament that it tasted defeat in the competition. The South American team has also won 15 Copa America titles, the last in 2011.

Uruguay's home jersey is sky blue. The team plays its home games at the Estadio Centenario, Montevideo. Uruguay's best-known players from past and present include Juan Alberto Schiaffino, Héctor Scarone, Enzo Francescoli, and Diego Forlan.

Chapter 12

Playing Together: Clubs and Leagues Around The World

Club soccer is the bread and butter of the game: As the old saying goes, you can change your religion, leave your wife or husband, but you can't get rid of your favorite team when you've picked one as yours.

There are thousands of major soccer clubs in the world. In this chapter, I explain how clubs started springing up in England during the 1860s and then all across the world, up to today's teams in Major League Soccer (MLS), North America's premier club competition.

Clubbing Together

From multinational concerns like Manchester United and Real Madrid, all the way down to weekend recreational teams run for fun, a soccer club is, in the final analysis, a group of people who have *clubbed together* to play the game. The members of that club can then practice with each other in preparation for playing competitive games with representative teams from other clubs.

The very first clubs

Some form of soccer has been played in England for centuries, but up until the mid-1800s, games were always played by a disorganized rabble. Then university teams, elite private school teams, factory teams, and pub teams began to spring up — educational establishments, workplaces, and bars were natural social places for people to get together and arrange official games.

But something more concrete needed to be established. Nobody knows exactly when the first made-to-order soccer-only club was set up — universities in London, Edinburgh, and Dublin all stake claims to having done so between the 1820s and 1840s — but we do know that in 1857, the first non-university club was set up: Sheffield FC.

And that's when the club scene really began to kick off.

Within three years, Sheffield FC had a local rival — Hallam FC — and regular games between the two were established. Clubs began to spring up all over England, and within a decade the FA Cup had been set up.

As competitive soccer became popular, so did the clubs, and vast numbers of spectators would turn up to games in order to cheer on one team or the other. Soccer was suddenly big business.

The rise of the super clubs

Economic and social factors mean that some clubs are always going to be bigger than others. Clubs from major cities, for example, can draw on wider support than ones from smaller cities and towns.

For example, Celtic and Rangers, coming from Glasgow, the third most populous city in the United Kingdom, were always going to be bigger clubs than Caledonian and Clachnacuddin from the small Highland city of Inverness.

But many of the biggest names in soccer today also benefitted from being successful at precisely the right times in the sport's development: the 1950s and 1960s, when televised soccer and the European Cup caught the public's imagination.

This meant teams such as Manchester United, Real Madrid, and AC Milan became huge deals in their countries. Other clubs such as Liverpool and Bayern Munich also benefitted in the 1970s, as TV turned soccer into a glamour sport.

Alongside already established European behemoths like Arsenal, Rangers, Celtic, Juventus, and Barcelona, these new clubs slowly began to dominate domestic and international club soccer — though the balance would not tip totally in their favor until the 1990s.

The name game

What's in a name? Some clubs have the simplest of monikers — Liverpool FC, São Paulo FC, and Toronto FC are called what they are for obvious reasons: They're Football Clubs (FCs) from the city named. But other names offer more than geographical clues.

Some explain how a club was founded back in the midst of time. In England, Sheffield Wednesday was, up until 1929, simply called The Wednesday — after the cricket club from which it sprang in the 1860s. Wednesday was the day of the week the cricketers played their games.

Arsenal in London, meanwhile, was formed as a works team — of the Royal Arsenal munitions factory in Woolwich.

Common components offer other clues. Teams with *United* in the title were, more often than not, formed as a result of a merger between two smaller local clubs. In Spain, the prefix *Real* — meaning Royal — denotes royal patronage and suggests the club has been favored, historically at least, by the Establishment. (Real Madrid, the team supported by the dictator General Franco, is an example of this.)

In the United States, some MLS teams are named with a nod to the history of a club's location — the San Jose Earthquakes and Chicago Fire both refer to a city's rebirth after disaster — whereas others follow European name styles mentioned above (DC United and Real Salt Lake), or are even named after the team's sponsor (Red Bull New York).

The smaller clubs

Between 1960 and 1990, smaller, provincial clubs still won titles across Europe: Burnley and Derby County won the English league, Kilmarnock and Dundee United became champions of Scotland, and Hellas Verona landed the Italian title. But as the balance of power tilted, it became increasingly harder for teams outside of the major clubs to win league titles.

After a while, even major cup competitions were rarely won by smaller clubs. In England, for example, since 1991, only Portsmouth (2008), Everton (1995), and Manchester City (2011) have taken the FA Cup from the grasp of the self-styled Big Four of Arsenal, Chelsea, Liverpool, and Manchester United.

It's a shame, and a state of affairs that has caused quite a bit of disillusionment in fans of clubs outside the select few in the biggest European leagues, as trophies are almost impossible to land. However, fans are nothing if not resourceful, and most have rationalized why they still follow the sport despite the chances of seeing their team lift a cup being slim: It's not only about winning anyway; it's about the fun of belonging. That passion is shown by the way fans support their teams through thick and thin, joining together to sing songs, travel to road games, and create giant banners as shows of support (like the one shown in Figure 12-1).

Figure 12-1:
Chicago Fire
fans show
their sup-
port with a
huge
banner.

Organizing Clubs Today

These days, many clubs are major multinational organizations, with hundreds of front office employees, even at some of the so-called "smaller" clubs
in the lower divisions. But how are they set up, and who works for them?

The players

A soccer club would be a fairly pointless enterprise without a roster of players.
So it goes without saying that all clubs employ them. Not all clubs maintain
a full-time playing staff, though. A club in the Scottish Third Division, pulling
crowds of 300 spectators per week, is unable to maintain a full-time roster. So
they field part-time players, paying them a flat fee for each appearance.

Move up the leagues, however, and clubs become full time, employing a
sizable roster of players on increasingly large salaries. As a very rough-and-
ready rule, an average full-time club will employ around 30 players. The really
big clubs, however, sometimes contain upwards of 50 full-time players on
their rosters, plus assorted reserve and promising youth players on full-time
contracts.

The roster of a top-flight team usually contains at least three players for each
position.

Buying, selling, and nurturing

Clubs have two methods of finding new players. They either nurture them from a young age, training them in their youth academies and developmental teams and eventually starting them in the first XI, or acquire them from another club.

In most of the world, if a team acquires a player from another club, they usually have to pay a transfer fee. This is to effectively buy out the player's contract with another club. After a fee has been settled upon, club and player agree to a new contract between them.

In North America, a trade is much more common than a transfer involving a fee — team A will give up player X to team B in exchange for player Y, for example. Sometimes, draft picks and money are also included to sweeten the pot.

Occasionally, players are waived by their clubs, receiving nothing for them. This is usually when they are no longer required by the club, and it will be cheaper to write off their contract than to pay them any further salary.

Clubs can also sign players who are out of contract. They do not have to pay the player's former club a fee to do this.

The head coach

The most important person at any club is the head coach. More often than not, he has the final say in who plays in each game, the tactics for each game, and any substitutions and tactical changes during a game. (To learn more about coaches, check out Chapter 8.)

Different coaches take different approaches to the job. Some are highly tactical, insisting their players work within a rigidly defined predetermined system. Others manage by the force of their personality, either charismatically or through fear and discipline.

Brian Clough, for example, led Nottingham Forest to the 1979 and 1980 European Cups, yet paid no heed to tactical systems whatsoever. Managing on gut instinct, he either shouted and bawled at his players, or put a comforting arm around them, depending on his mood. Occasionally, he would even get them drunk before a game. Idiosyncratic, maybe, but it worked.

Suffice to say, the personality of a team — and sometimes an entire club — rests on the personality of its coach. This goes some way to explaining why, if the team embarks on a losing streak, the head coach is usually the first person to be fired, ushering in a new era.

Outside North America, the head coach often goes by the name of "manager" and is also responsible for the buying and selling of players, giving the boss much greater control over the roster.

Technical staff

A head coach surrounds himself with a team of assistants that form his *technical staff*. The most important role is of assistant coach. Also known as the "number two," the assistant coach gives the boss advice and support.

Often an assistant is an expert in a particular field — a defensive coach, for example, or a goalkeeping guru working solely with the goalkeepers on the roster.

The coach is assisted by fitness coaches, customized tactical coaches for defenders, attackers, and goalkeepers, and medical staff such as physiotherapists, sports therapists, and masseurs.

The club also appoints scouts, whose job it is to watch other teams in order to find potential new players, as well as assess how upcoming opponents play tactically.

Ownership

Methods of club ownership vary from country to country and even within countries. In the United States, at the highest level of Major League Soccer (MLS), clubs are centrally owned by the league, with owners of each club also league shareholders. In the lower leagues, clubs are usually individually privately owned.

Overseas, many clubs are actually owned by their supporters as membership-based clubs — Barcelona, for example, is controlled by their fans. Hundreds of thousands of *socios* pay a membership fee to join the club, and vote to elect the club president, empowering that person to spend their budgets as they see fit. And in Germany's Bundesliga, it's a rule that clubs must be majority owned by supporters, even at the biggest such as Bayern Munich.

In England, clubs in the Premier League are usually privately owned with few restrictions on who can purchase any team, though at the lower levels, increasing numbers of teams are now owned by fans through democratic groupings of fans known as *supporter trusts*.

Transfer windows

Up until comparatively recently — 2003, to be precise — soccer clubs could transfer (meaning trade) players whenever they wanted. This means they could buy players from, and sell them to, other clubs at will.

However, FIFA now decrees that there are only two transfer windows per year allowing transactions between clubs. A long transfer window — lasting a maximum of 12 weeks — can be opened roughly between two separate domestic seasons.

A shorter one — lasting a maximum of one calendar month — can be opened at a predetermined point roughly in the middle of a domestic season.

Clubs cannot buy players when their domestic windows are shut, although they can in principle agree to deals in advance for players to move during a future window.

In addition, a player from a club whose domestic window is shut can still be sold to a club whose domestic window is open.

The final day of an open window is known as Transfer Deadline Day. These are always big media events, with much expectation of a flurry of last-minute deals, but can often be a complete anti-climax should no big-name moves occur!

However ownership is organized, the owners employ a front office charged with the everyday running of the club, though they retain overall control and ultimate power.

A chief executive is usually employed to oversee the front office and day-to-day running of the club, looking after budgets, and liaising between ownership and the head coach.

When it comes to the big decisions — namely whether to fire the head coach or not — club ownership has the final say.

Owners can often be controversial. In the 2000s, major English clubs such as Manchester United and Liverpool were taken over by American investors not trusted by the clubs' fan bases, and were seen to be putting profit over investment in the teams' success.

However, other recent buyouts have been welcomed more by fans. Elsewhere in England, the Russian billionaire Roman Abramovich's purchase of Chelsea saw major investment in the team, followed by unprecedented levels of success for the club. Manchester City, too, has recently benefitted from similar money-is-no-object investment.

Clubs also benefit from cash injections by major corporate sponsors — in 2012, General Motors agreed to a deal to sponsor Manchester United for $559 million over seven years, with the English club adorning their jerseys with General Motors' Chevrolet brand in return.

Many European teams are actually part of larger sporting clubs that also run teams for sports such as volleyball, basketball, or ice hockey. Istanbul-based Galatasaray, for example, fields teams in 14 other sports besides its most famous endeavor, a soccer team that has won the Turkish league 18 times.

Competing in Club Competitions

There are two types of club competition: leagues and cups. All countries run a league over the course of a single season, and most hold at least one cup competition at some point during the same season.

Seasons

This is a fixed period of time during which all domestic club competitions are held. At the opening of a season, no competitions have been started. By the end of it, all the winners of every competition will have been determined.

There is usually only one season every 12 months, though they do not necessarily cover the year January through December. For example, the MLS season traditionally starts in March and ends the following November. In some countries, such as Mexico, the season is split into two periods with a break in between — known as the *Apertura* and the *Clausura*.

Seasons run at different times across the world, at dates often dictated by local weather systems. To illustrate, whereas most North American leagues run roughly along the aforementioned MLS time frame, southern European leagues run during the winter months as the milder weather makes playing conditions feasible for play long into the season.

Each season is preceded by a *pre-season,* which sees clubs play exhibition games in order to attain optimum levels of fitness and assimilate new signings into the team.

Every season has at least one *transfer window,* allowing clubs to sign new players and sell existing ones.

There are also the designated International Weeks during the season, when the best players appear for their national teams. Leagues do not have to break for these, but as clubs are obliged to release players for international games such as World Cup qualifiers, a *rest week* is sometimes scheduled.

The first-ever league

The Football League — and the concept of league soccer — was the brainchild of William McGregor, a Scottish director of Aston Villa in the 1880s.

At the time, the only competition Villa could enter — because it was the only one that existed — was the FA Cup. It was held every year, but if a team was knocked out in the first round, they would have only one competitive game per season. It wasn't much of a money spinner.

McGregor decided to act. Villa was one of the biggest clubs of the day, so he wrote to the chairmen of several other big teams — including Blackburn Rovers, Preston North End, West Bromwich Albion, and Bolton Wanderers — proposing a groundbreaking idea.

"Every year it is becoming more and more difficult for football clubs of any standing to meet their friendly engagements and even arrange friendly matches," he wrote. "I beg to tender the following suggestion as a means of getting over the difficulty. It is that 10 or 12 of the most prominent clubs combine to arrange home and away fixtures each season."

Having penned the letter in March 1888, McGregor saw his idea implemented quickly. That September, it was up and running. The world would soon follow.

Leagues

The concept of league soccer was born in England in 1888, when the Football League was formed. It was the first in the world. Now almost every country which plays organized soccer operates its own league system.

How leagues work

In most countries, a league is a round-robin tournament. All entrants play each other — usually twice, each team home once — and gain points depending on results. Usually a team is awarded three points for a win, one for a tie, and none for a defeat.

According to results and points awarded, teams are then arranged into a table, placing them in order of points won, top to bottom. After all the games have been played, the top team is declared the champion.

In the United States and some other countries, a twist is added to this idea with an additional postseason playoff competition to decide the champions. In MLS, the league is divided into two conferences, and the top teams from each take part in a postseason playoff contest to determine the overall winner.

As a general rule, if teams are level on points, they are separated on goal difference (the difference between goals scored and conceded). The team with the highest positive goal difference wins. Should goal difference be level, the team with the higher number of goals scored wins. And if the teams are still level after that, the champion may be decided in a playoff game, or even by the toss of a coin!

Goal difference doesn't always decide the order of teams level on points, though. In Major League Soccer, the 2012 season saw teams separated first on goals scored — the team with more goals rewarded — with goal difference only used to settle the tie if the number of goals scored happened to be the same for each team. At other times, head-to-head results between teams are used as the first tiebreaker instead.

Divisions, promotion, relegation, and pyramids

Of course, because most countries have many teams, they cannot realistically all play each other, home and away, in one huge league. So leagues are comprised of a hierarchy of several divisions. In some countries such as England, clubs can move up or down each season depending on results — this is called promotion and relegation. But in North America, the top tier of soccer — Major League Soccer — is a closed system of franchises, with a new one granted only to expand the league when the owners decide to do so. The league is instead divided into two conferences (East and West), with the top teams in each meeting in the playoffs.

The overall structure of soccer in each country is often called a Pyramid, because of the general shape of the hierarchy: After the top few divisions, there are usually very many more local divisions towards the bottom.

To illustrate, the top of the American soccer pyramid looks like this:

✔ **Level 1:** Major League Soccer (19 teams)

- **Eastern Conference:** Chicago Fire, Columbus Crew, DC United, Houston Dynamo, Montreal Impact, New England Revolution, Philadelphia Union, Red Bull New York, Sporting Kansas City, Toronto FC

- **Western Conference:** Chivas USA, Colorado Rapids, FC Dallas, Los Angeles Galaxy, Portland Timbers, Real Salt Lake, San Jose Earthquakes, Seattle Sounders, Vancouver Whitecaps

✔ **Level 2:** North American Soccer League (11 teams)

Atlanta Silverbacks, Carolina RailHawks, FC Edmonton, Fort Lauderdale Strikers, Minnesota Stars, New York Cosmos, Ottawa, Puerto Rico Islanders, San Antonio Scorpions, Tampa Bay Rowdies, Virginia

✔ **Level 3:** United Soccer Leagues (11 teams)

Antigua Barracuda, Charleston Battery, Charlotte Eagles, Dayton Dutch Lions, Harrisburg City Islanders, Los Angeles Blues, Orlando City, Pittsburgh Riverhounds, Richmond Kickers, Rochester Rhinos, Wilmington Hammerheads

Between 1985 and 1995, there was no top-level outdoor professional league in the United States. Instead, indoor soccer was briefly seen as the sport of the future as the Major Indoor Soccer League (MISL) attracted large crowds. Indoor soccer proved to be a fad, but there's still a successor Major Indoor Soccer League playing in several American cities during the winter months.

Apertura and Clausura

In most countries, there is usually only one league championship held per season. However, in many Latin American countries — such as Argentina, Uruguay, and Mexico — the season is split into two separate halves, *Apertura* and *Clausura* (Opening and Closing).

Both sections — Apertura and Clausura — have their own champions, with no results carrying over to decide the winner. Some countries then stage a final game between both champions to decide an overall season champion.

Cups

Nearly all countries hold at least one domestic cup competition, based on elimination games. The basic principle is simple: The tournament is divided into rounds, with all team names going into a hat and being drawn — usually randomly, but sometimes on a seeded basis — to face one other entrant.

The teams typically play each other in a one-off game, the name of the winner of each game going back into the hat for the next round — which now has half the number of clubs as it did before — and the losers having been eliminated.

The process continues until there are only two teams left standing. They then play off in a final game to decide the tournament winner.

Round 1: 32 teams

Round 2: 16 teams

Round 3: 8 teams (this round is known as the *quarter-final*)

Round 4: 4 teams (this round is known as the *semifinal*)

Round 5: 2 teams (this round is known as the *final*)

Some cups are organized so teams play each other once at home each, the winners on aggregate score going onto the next round.

Compared to leagues, the winners of cups are less likely to be the *best* team in the competition, as draws are usually random and teams have no margin for error in a one-off game. This means the overall quality of cup competitions are often lower, but with the likelihood of shock results and *giant-killing* — when a small team beats a bigger one — greater, they are often more dramatic and exciting.

Playing in the Big Leagues

Some leagues are bigger than others. The teams taking part in them have more fans and more money, and consequently get the best players and the greatest amount of media attention. This section focuses on the leagues you're most likely to hear about from around the world.

USA and Canada: Major League Soccer

Professional soccer in the United States had two huge false starts. The American Soccer League, created in 1921, lasted only a decade. Then the North American Soccer League, launched in 1967, sputtered out 17 years later, despite at one point coaxing Pelé from retirement to play for the New York Cosmos. However, as a condition of landing the 1994 World Cup, FIFA (Fédération Internationale de Football Association, or the International Federation of Association Football) and the governing body of soccer in the United States, the U.S. Soccer Federation, agreed that a new professional outdoor league would be formed. And it has been third-time lucky, with the 1996-launched Major League Soccer currently going from strength to strength.

The league consists of 19 teams, divided into two conferences, Eastern and Western. Each team plays 34 games, with an unbalanced schedule meaning every team plays more often against teams in their own conference than those in the opposing conference.

At the end of the regular season, the team with the most points wins the Supporters' Shield trophy. But more important is that the top five teams in each conference proceed to the MLS Cup playoffs to decide the overall champion.

In the playoffs, each conference features a play-in game between the teams who finished fourth and fifth in the conference. The winner advances to the Conference Semifinal, home-and-away games with the winner of each series determined by aggregate score over the two games. The winners of each of those series move on to the Conference Championship. Home-and-away matchups then determine the overall Conference champion.

The Conference Champions then meet in the MLS Cup final, a one-off game that is hosted by the team in the final who boasted the best regular season record. The winner is the MLS champion.

Among the most successful MLS teams are DC United, the Los Angeles Galaxy (shown in Figure 12-2 winning the MLS Cup for the third time), the Houston Dynamo, the San Jose Earthquakes, the Chicago Fire, Sporting Kansas City, the Colorado Rapids, Real Salt Lake, and the Columbus Crew.

The winners of the Supporters' Shield and the MLS Cup are rewarded with berths in the following season's continental championship, the CONCACAF Champions League (Confederation of North, Central American and Caribbean Association Football), with a chance to be crowned as the best club in the region (see the section "Competing on the International Stage," later in this chapter).

Figure 12-2: LA Galaxy team members celebrate winning the 2011 MLS Cup.

Getty Images

Since the 1980s, many of the top American players have made their livings playing in professional leagues overseas, following trailblazers like John Harkes, Eric Wynalda, and Kasey Keller. U.S. goalkeeper Brad Friedel currently holds the record in the English Premier League for most consecutive games played, with 310 at the time of writing.

Mexico: Liga MX

Mexico's top tier has been playing nationally since 1943, with 18 teams taking part in a season each year that is divided into two chronological championships: the *Apertura* (opening summer session) and *Clausura* (closing winter session).

Each session features a league tournament with every team playing each other once at home. When those games have been completed, the top eight teams in the standings then qualify for a playoff competition, with home-and-away games in an elimination format seeing the winner of each series decided by aggregate score.

Among the most successful teams in Mexico are Chivas de Guadalajara, Club América, Toluca, and Cruz Azul.

England: The FA Premier League

The Football League was established in 1888, featured 12 teams, and quickly expanded. A second division was added four years later, a third in 1920, and a fourth in 1921, whereupon the two lower divisions became regional leagues, the Third Divisions North and South. In 1950, they became national Third and Fourth divisions.

That four-division setup — with a top flight of 22 teams — was maintained until 1992, when the country's top 22 clubs broke away from the Football League to form an elite division: the FA Premier League. The old Second, Third, and Fourth Divisions initially became the First, Second, and Third Divisions of a revamped Football League; the divisions are now the Championship, League One, and League Two.

Nowadays, the FA Premier League is contested by 20 teams. The winners are crowned champions of England (just as the winners of the Football League were in the years before the formation of the Premier League). Three teams are relegated from the league each year, to be replaced by three from the Championship (the top two teams and the winners of a playoff competition among the teams finishing in the third through sixth places).

Teams in the FA Premier League include: Arsenal, Chelsea, Everton, Liverpool, Manchester City, Manchester United, and Tottenham Hotspur.

As of 2012, Manchester United has won the most English championships, with 19 total, one ahead of Liverpool with 18. All of Liverpool's titles were won before the advent of the Premier League, whereas United has won 12 Premier League titles.

From 1994 to 2007, the FA Premier League was known as the FA Premiership. In North America, it's typically known as the English Premier League, or EPL for short.

Italy: Serie A

Italy was one of the first European countries to launch a national championship — the first title was awarded in 1898, in a tournament that involved four teams and lasted the grand total of *one* day — but after it got going on a larger scale, the champions would be decided in a playoff final between regional champions. It wasn't until 1929 that a national league was established, forming the divisions Serie A and Serie B. The setup remains the same to this day.

Serie A is contested by 18 teams. The winners are crowned champions of Italy, and are awarded the right to wear the *scudetto,* a tricolor shield, on its jerseys the following season.

Major teams in Serie A include Milan, Internazionale, Juventus, Roma, Lazio, and Fiorentina.

Juventus is the most successful team in Serie A history, with 28 title wins. Internazionale and Milan jointly hold the second-most successful records, with 18 victories apiece.

Teams are allowed to wear a golden star for every ten title wins. Juventus therefore has two on their jersey, Internazionale and Milan one.

Spain: La Liga

The Spanish operated several regional leagues until 1929, when the national *La Liga* was formed, comprising two divisions: the *Primera* (first) and *Segunda* (second). Initially the top division only contained ten teams, but the competition swiftly grew: Today the Primera has 20 teams, whereas the Segunda has 22.

The winner of La Liga is crowned the champion of Spain. The bottom three teams in the division are relegated to Segunda Division, while the top three teams in Segunda win promotion.

Real Madrid and Barcelona are the big players in La Liga; Real has won the title 32 times, Barca 21 — including three straight from 2009 to 2011, fired by Argentina's Lionel Messi (see Figure 12-3). Atletico Madrid, Athletic Bilbao, and Valencia have nine, eight, and six titles between them, while Real Sociedad can boast two. Deportivo la Coruna, Sevilla, and Real Betis all have one title apiece — meaning that there have only been eight champion clubs in Spain, the lowest number in any of the major soccer nations.

Figure 12-3: Lionel Messi tries to add to his prolific goalscoring tally for Barcelona.

GettyImages

Germany: Bundesliga

Soccer has been played in Germany since the 1870s, but it took nearly 100 years for a nationwide professional league to be set up. For much of the 20th century, Germany's national champions were determined by a playoff between winners of regional tournaments. But in 1963 the German Football Association (DFB) launched the country's first national league: the Fussball-Bundesliga (more commonly referred to simply as the Bundesliga).

It's contested by 18 teams, the winner becoming the champion of Germany. The bottom two teams are relegated to a secondary league known as *2.Bundesliga.*

Teams in the Bundesliga include Bayer Leverkusen, Bayern Munich, Borussia Dortmund, Hamburg, Schalke 04, Werder Bremen, and Wolfsburg.

The league was won by seven teams in its first seven seasons, but since has been totally dominated by Bayern Munich, which has won 22 Bundesliga titles. The next most successful Bundesliga team is Borussia Monchengladbach, which has won only five times — the last of which in 1977.

Brazil: Campeonato Brasileiro Serie A

As mentioned earlier, most Latin American countries split their seasons into two halves — Apertura and Clausura (Opening and Closing) — and have a champion for each. Brazil is the only South American country to operate a more traditional single league along European lines. Twenty clubs compete in the league, the winners are crowned champions, and the bottom four clubs are relegated to Serie B.

Whereas teams compete in a national league, they also compete in local state leagues. These are historically important — Brazil is such a big country, a national league was only considered viable in 1971 — and the champions of the state leagues are treated with the same reverence as the national title winners.

Knocking Out a Winner

Most domestic soccer associations organize one or more cups, organized on an elimination or *knockout* basis. Although these are usually won by the big clubs that also dominate the league system, there's always the chance of a shock result — if not in the final, then in one of the preceding rounds. This gives cup competitions their drama, not unlike March Madness in college basketball.

FA Cup

The Football Association Challenge Cup is a knockout cup competition open to all teams in the top ten levels of English league soccer and is the oldest in the world, founded in 1871. Over 700 teams regularly enter the competition.

The draws are totally random — and unseeded. There are six qualifying rounds for the competition proper. In the first round, the 48 teams from the Football League's Leagues One and Two are entered into the draw, along with 32 qualifiers. Teams from the FA Premier League and Football League Championship enter at the third round, which signals the point at which there are 64 teams left in the competition. The sixth round is the quarter-final stage.

The third round is one of the most glamorous days in the soccer calendar, as small clubs have a chance to be paired with the Manchester Uniteds and Arsenals of this world. Very occasionally, a small team upsets the odds to cause a giant-killing shock. The last amateur nonleague team to beat a top-flight team was Sutton United, who knocked out Coventry City in 1989.

All ties up to this point are played as one game, the first team being drawn from the hat playing at home. Should the game be drawn, there is a replay at the home of the second team drawn from the hat. Should that game be drawn, 30 minutes extra time is played — and if there is still no result, a penalty shootout decides who goes through.

Manchester United is the most successful club in FA Cup history, with 11 wins as of 2011–2012. Arsenal is right on United's heels, with ten victories. Tottenham has won the Cup eight times, Liverpool, Chelsea, and Aston Villa seven apiece.

The U.S. Open Cup

The United States has its own long-running national cup competition, one modeled after England's FA Cup. The U.S. Open Cup has been contested since 1913, making it one of the oldest such competitions in the world. For many decades it was dominated by amateur teams from the enclaves of ethnic urban areas. These players brought a love of soccer with them from the old world, such as New York's Greek Americans, who won the competition three successive times in the late 1960s.

Nowadays, the tournament is dominated by MLS teams: They began entering the competition in 1996 when MLS kicked-off, and since then all but one U.S. Open Cup competition has been won by an MLS team (the Rochester Rhinos of the A-League proved the exception in 1999). The leading MLS teams in the cup are the Chicago Fire with four wins, Seattle Sounders with three titles, and the LA Galaxy and DC United with two apiece. But none have yet matched the most successful teams in U.S. Open Cup history, Bethlehem Steel and Maccabi Los Angeles, who dominated in the 1920s and 1970s, respectively.

The tournament is still open to all amateur and professional teams affiliated to the U.S. Soccer Federation, with 64 teams qualifying for the competition in the 2012 edition, won by Sporting Kansas City of MLS.

Other famous cups

Nearly every country runs its own national knockout cup competition. Notable cup competitions include:

- ✔ Spain: Copa del Rey (won most times by Barcelona — 26)
- ✔ Germany: DFB-Pokal (Bayern Munich — 15)
- ✔ Italy: Coppa Italia (Roma and Juventus — 9)
- ✔ France: Coupe de France (Marseille — 10)
- ✔ Brazil: Copa do Brasil (Gremio and Cruzeiro — 4)

The European Cup: Born in Paris (and Wolverhampton)

In 1954, the Wolverhampton Wanderers, the reigning champions of England, hosted a series of prestigious midweek exhibition games against top teams from mainland Europe under fancy new floodlights. Some of the biggest clubs in world soccer — such as Racing Club, Moscow Dynamo, and Spartak Moscow — came to Wolves' Molineux stadium. All were defeated.

But nobody expected Wolves to beat Honved, whose team contained six members of the legendary Hungary team that had humiliated England 6-3 and 7-1 during the previous year. Wolves won 3-2, though, prompting London's *Daily Mail* newspaper to trumpet "WOLVES: CHAMPIONS OF THE WORLD!" the day after.

Noting this with some disdain, Gabriel Hanot, the editor of the French newspaper *L'Equipe*, took the *Mail* to task. "Before we declare Wolverhampton is invincible, let them go to Moscow and Budapest," wrote Hanot. "And there are other internationally renowned clubs: AC Milan and Real Madrid to name but two. A club world championship, or at least a European one."

Within the year, UEFA had taken Hanot's idea and ran with it, inaugurating the first European Cup in the 1955–1956 season. Wolves eventually qualified for the new tournament in 1959 — only to be eliminated in the first round by the German team Schalke.

Competing on the International Stage

Clubs don't just play soccer within their own borders, though. They also compete with clubs from other countries, in competitions which are often more prestigious than the domestic leagues and cups.

European Cup/UEFA Champions League

The European Cup was launched in 1955, an unseeded knockout cup tournament between the reigning champions of all European leagues. The first five trophies were won by Spain's Real Madrid, before Portugal and Italy shared the spoils in the early 1960s, and Benfica, AC Milan, and Internazionale added their names to the roll of honor.

Glasgow Celtic would become the first club from Britain — and indeed northern Europe — to win the European Cup in 1967. Manchester United followed in their wake the year after. By the end of the 1970s, Ajax Amsterdam and Bayern Munich had both won three times, with Liverpool and Nottingham Forest landing the trophy twice each. The 1980s saw Liverpool win two more trophies before they were embroiled in the Heysel disaster at the 1985 final, which saw English clubs banned from Europe for six seasons. The late 1980s and early 1990s were dominated by Milan, though Eastern Bloc teams finally made their mark, too, with Romania's Steaua Bucharest (1986) and Red Star Belgrade (1991) winning the trophy.

In 1992–1993, the tournament was rebranded the UEFA Champions League, the format changing from unseeded knockout to seeded round-robin groups, guaranteeing competitors a certain number of money-spinning games. In 1998, entrants other than the national champions were allowed to take part.

The new format — up to four teams per country enter — means there is now an established elite, many of the same giant clubs participating year in, year out. Paradoxically, however, no team has retained the trophy in the Champions League era.

The most successful European Cup and Champions League team is Real Madrid, who has won the trophy nine times. Milan has seven wins to its name.

Format

All countries choose league position as its qualification criteria to award its allotted places in the Champions League for the following season's competition.

England, for example, has four places. The FA Premier League champions and second and third placed teams qualify for the group stage of the Champions League automatically. The fourth-placed teams must go through the preliminary rounds.

The group stages involve eight groups of four teams. The draw is seeded, with seedings based on past performances in Europe. After playing each other home and away, the top two teams in each group go through to the knockout stages. (The third placed teams go into the knockout stage of the Europa League.)

The competition is then a straight cup knockout. All rounds are unseeded, and matches randomly paired, apart from the first knockout round: Group winners must play group runners-up, and no two teams from the same country can be paired.

The decision to play the 2010 Champions League final, and all subsequent finals, on a Saturday evening — in order to maximize TV audiences across the world — broke with tradition. The game had always previously been played on a Wednesday evening.

Although the tournament is now officially called the UEFA Champions League, it's still also referred to as the European Cup. The two terms are interchangeable (although the use of the latter may point usefully to someone's age).

CONCACAF Champions League

Self-consciously named after its European equivalent, the premier international club competition in North America, Central America, and the Caribbean isn't the money-spinner that its namesake in Europe is, but there is still plenty of prestige at stake as the top teams from across the region take part.

The CONCACAF Champions League is organized by the governing body of soccer in the region, the CONCACAF. The tournament was known from 1962 to 2008 as the Champions Cup until its rebranding as the Champions League starting in 2009.

As well as getting a new name, the competition was reorganized to guarantee teams from the bigger countries more games in the group stage — much like the changes made in Europe.

But whatever it's called, one nation has utterly dominated the competition: Since 1962, Mexican teams have taken the title a remarkable 28 times. Costa Rica sits second in total titles with six, whereas the United States is rather lowly in the region, having only had two champions crowned — DC United in 1998 and the Los Angeles Galaxy in 2000. Not surprisingly, the top three clubs in the competition have all been Mexican: Cruz Azul and Club América each have five titles to their name, whereas Pachuca has won four. The top non-Mexican team is Costa Rican club Saprissa, with three titles.

Copa Libertadores

South America staged its first international club championship in 1948, with Brazilian club Vasco da Gama winning a tournament staged by the Chilean club Colo Colo. But the event lost thousands of dollars, and the idea was put on the back burner. It was revived in 1960 in the wake of the successful launch of the European Cup, with UEFA offering to stage a world championship game — the Intercontinental Cup — between the European champions and any South American equivalent.

Penarol of Uruguay was the winner of the first two stagings of the newly minted Copa Libertadores, with Pelé's Santos winning in 1962 and 1963. Independiente of Argentina then matched the feat in 1964 and 1965 — and would become the most successful team in the tournament's history, with seven wins notched up by 1984.

Boca Juniors of Argentina has dominated the tournament since the turn of the millennium, winning the trophy four times between 2000 and 2007.

Format

The format is similar to the UEFA Champions League. After a preliminary round, eight groups of four teams are drawn, the two top teams after a round-robin tournament progressing to the knockout stages.

Other continental tournaments

Africa, Asia, and Oceania also hold their own Champions League tournaments. Along with the winners of the European Cup and the Copa Libertadores, all victorious teams qualify for the FIFA Club World Cup.

Intercontinental Cup/FIFA Club World Cup

The Intercontinental Cup had a checkered history. Founded as an annual playoff between the champions of Europe and South America in 1960, in order to name a semiofficial "world club champion," the games often descended into needless violence. Matchups between Celtic and Racing Club, Manchester United and Estudiantes, Milan and Estudiantes, and Feyenoord and (are you noticing a pattern?) Estudiantes all ended in mass brawls.

During the 1970s, many European champions decided not to take part — Ajax, Bayern Munich, Liverpool, and Nottingham Forest all turned down invitations — and the competition suffered as a result.

In 1980, the tournament — previously played over a two-game series with each team hosting one game — moved to Tokyo for a one-off final, where it was regularly contested up until 2004, by which time it had been superseded by the FIFA Club World Cup.

FIFA's new baby was launched in 2005 and is contested annually by the champions of all six continental confederations. The format is a straight elimination tournament, but seeded so the champions of Europe and South America qualify automatically for a semifinal spot on either side of the draw.

As of season 2012–2013, all seven competitions have been won by a team from the two powerhouse confederations of Europe and South America. Three Brazilian teams have won the trophy — São Paulo, Corinthians, and Internacional — while four European teams have triumphed — Barcelona, Internazionale, AC Milan, and Manchester United.

Chapter 13

Focusing on Famous Clubs

*H*undreds of thousands of soccer clubs exist on Planet Soccer, so picking the top few and pleasing everyone is always going to be an impossible task.

I narrowed it down by picking the biggest and most successful clubs overseas — and as you see in this chapter, *biggest* and *most successful* are nearly always the same thing — along with some of the best known on this continent.

This chapter gives you some very selective histories of the top clubs in North America and around the world. (For more about the international competitions in which these clubs play, see Chapter 12.)

Shooting Stars in North America

Soccer in the United States and Canada has had an up-and-down history, but the launch of Major League Soccer (MLS) in 1996 means some teams are now settled as permanent additions to the landscape. South of the border in Mexico, though, teams have much longer and more storied histories behind them.

Chivas de Guadalajara

Mexican soccer's most dominant club has been Club Deportivo Guadalajara — better known as *Chivas,* the Mexican word for *goats,* the Guadalajara-based club's longtime nickname. Founded back in 1906, the team is a national institution and arguably the best-supported in the country. Chivas has won 11 national championships in the professional era, along with a Confederation of North, Central American and Caribbean Association Football (CONCACAF) Champions Cup win in 1962. In 2011, Chivas reached the final of the Copa Libertadores, as a special guest in South America's prestigious continental championship.

The club has an unusual policy of only allowing players of Mexican heritage to play for the team. Many of Mexico's top players have been stars at Chivas, including most recently Manchester United's Javier "Chicherito" Hernandez.

Chivas opened a new home stadium, Estadio Omnlife, in 2010. The club's home jersey has vertical red-and-white stripes.

Club América

Along with Chivas, Club América from Mexico City claims to be the best-supported team in the country. They play in the gigantic Estadio Azteca — which can cram in over 100,000 fans — and are known as *Las Águilas,* or *Eagles* in English.

Founded in 1916, América has won ten national titles and five CONCACAF Champions Cup/League trophies — in 1977, 1987, 1990, 1992, and 1996, an era of great success for the club.

América can lay claim to having some of the greatest Mexican players of all time appear for them, including Hugo Sánchez and Cuauhtémoc Blanco, along with an array of international stars.

DC United

DC United, based in Washington, D.C., was founded in 1996, but quickly earned a reputation as the powerhouse of Major League Soccer — also launched that year. DC won both the MLS and U.S. Open Cup titles in that year, and now have a total of 12 trophies in the cabinet. However, the last of DC's MLS Cup titles was back in 2004, and the club continues to look to move to a new home venue to replace the aging RFK Stadium.

DC is also one of only two American teams to win continental honors, with the CONCACAF Champions Cup title in 1998. DC's primary colors are red and black.

LA Galaxy

The Los Angeles Galaxy is one of the founder members of MLS, and since the league's first season in 1996 has enjoyed great success, becoming regular-season champions four times and winning the MLS Cup end-of-season play-offs three times. Galaxy made world headlines in 2007 with the signing of England and Real Madrid midfielder David Beckham, who led the team to LA's fourth MLS Cup title win in 2011.

The Galaxy isn't the first soccer team in Los Angeles. Others have included the LA Kickers, the hilariously titled LA Salsa — the team was owned by a restaurateur — and most famously the LA Aztecs, who played in the North American Soccer League (NASL) during the 1970s, signed Johan Cruyff and George Best, and had Elton John as a co-owner. Another MLS team, Chivas USA, also plays at the Galaxy's own stadium, the Home Depot Center.

New York Cosmos

The original Cosmos went out of business in 1985, along with the original North American Soccer League (NASL), but the team's exploits in the 1970s mean the Cosmos name remains well-known today, and a new Cosmos team joined the new North American Soccer League (now the second tier of American soccer) in 2012.

The New York club was a prime mover and shaker in the first NASL, which briefly popularized soccer in the United States during the 1970s and astonished the world by goading Pelé out of retirement in 1975. In 1977, Pelé's final season, the Cosmos boasted a team also starring Brazil's 1970 World Cup winning captain Carlos Alberto and West Germany's 1974 World Cup winning captain Franz Beckenbauer. The original Cosmos won Soccer Bowl titles in 1972, 1977, 1978, 1980, and 1982.

The largest crowd the original Cosmos ever attracted is still the record attendance for a playoff soccer game in the United States — 77,691 for a game at Giants Stadium, with the Fort Lauderdale Strikers the visiting team. The Cosmos won 8-3.

Seattle Sounders

Some teams are measured by the size of their trophy cabinet, but though they have won some silverware, the Seattle Sounder's biggest impact since they began play in MLS only back in 2009 has been the size of the club's crowds. The Sounders set MLS attendance records in each of its first three seasons, filling what's now known as CenturyLink field with crowds often over double the size of the MLS average attendance league-wide. In 2012, Seattle's average home crowd in the MLS regular season was 43,143.

Seattle also won the U.S. Open Cup each time in its first three years of MLS play (2009, 2010, and 2011) and then lost in the final in 2012. The club succeeded a lower division team of the same name, while the North American Soccer League saw a team called the Seattle Sounders play from 1974 to 1993. The Sounders play in blue and bright green.

Banding Together In Europe

Europe — or to be more precise, England — was the home of the first-ever soccer clubs. The oldest, Sheffield FC, formed in 1857, is still going today in the local northern leagues. Sheffield has long been usurped in importance by some other big names, though. Although England was first out of the blocks, forming soccer teams from the mid-1800s onwards, the rest of Europe wasn't far behind. It wasn't long before the continent boasted some of the most evocative institutions in sports. If you want to know more about the trophies European clubs compete for, see Chapter 12. (Note here that Europe's premier competition, the Champions League, was known as the European Cup until 1992, and is referred to by both names.)

AC Milan

AC Milan (or simply Milan) has been the most successful club in Europe over the past two decades, winning five Champions League titles between 1989 and 2007. The club was a founding member of the Italian league, but didn't enjoy any sustained success until after World War II. In the 1950s, Milan — built around Swedish trio Gunnar Gren, Gunnar Nordahl, and Nils Liedholm, and Uruguay's 1950 World Cup hero Juan Schiaffino — won several titles and reached the 1958 European Cup final, losing to dominant Real Madrid. Five years later Milan became the first Italian team to win the European Cup, beating reigning champions Benfica.

Come on, you red-blacks!

Wherever you go around the world, soccer teams are nicknamed according to the color of their jerseys: In England, Manchester United, Liverpool, and Arsenal are known as *the reds,* while Everton, Chelsea, and Portsmouth are *the blues.*

It's not very original — and not particularly romantic in plain old English. However it's all much more lyrical in Italian — and the nicknames are worth learning because people often use them to describe both teams and their fans in English-speaking Serie A reports.

Here are the most frequently used nicknames:

- ✔ *Viola* **(purple):** Fiorentina (from Florence)
- ✔ *Nerazzurri* **(black-blues):** Internazionale
- ✔ *Bianconeri* **(white-blacks):** Juventus
- ✔ *Biancocelesti* **(white and sky-blues):** Lazio (of Rome)
- ✔ *Rossoneri* **(red-blacks):** Milan
- ✔ *Giallorossi* **(yellow-reds):** Roma
- ✔ *Azzurri* **(blues):** The Italian national team

Milan won another European Cup in 1969, but went into a decline and was relegated for the first time in its history in 1980 as punishment for its part in a betting scandal. It won immediate promotion, but was relegated again, this time simply for not being very good. In 1986 media magnate (and future Italian prime minister) Silvio Berlusconi bought the club and injected large sums of money. Within three years a Milan team starring Dutch trio Ruud Gullit, Marco van Basten, and Frank Rijkaard was the champion of Europe. The team has been a regular fixture in Champions League finals ever since, the high point being a 4-0 win over Barcelona in 1994; the low an inexplicable loss against Liverpool in 2005 after being 3-0 up at half time.

Milan plays in red and black jerseys at the San Siro. The team has won the European Cup 7 times and the Italian championship 18 times.

Milan was founded by English expats, which is why the name doesn't take the Italian form *Milano.*

Ajax Amsterdam

Ajax is the largest and most famous of Dutch soccer's biggest three teams — most of the major prizes in the Netherlands have been historically shared out among Ajax, PSV Eindhoven, and Feyenoord of Rotterdam.

Ajax's golden period came in the early 1970s with a team starring Johan Cruyff, Ruud Krol, and Johan Neeskens. They pioneered *Total Football* — where every player could interchange positions as the game developed — and won three European Cups in a row between 1971 and 1974. The club discovered the great striker Marco van Basten in the early 1980s, before a youthful team added another Champions League title in 1995.

Ajax is from Amsterdam, Netherlands. Its home stadium is the Amsterdam Arena. The team plays in white jerseys with a thick red stripe down the center, and Ajax has won the Champions League 4 times, the UEFA Cup once, and the Dutch championship 31 times.

Arsenal

Arsenal hails from North London, though the team was formed south of the River Thames in 1886, at an ammunition factory works team in Woolwich. Arsenal moved north to the Highbury neighborhood in 1913 and within two decades became one of the most successful clubs in the country: In the 1930s, inspired by influential coach Herbert Chapman, Arsenal won five league titles — the first club from the south of England to become champions — and two FA Cups.

Apart from a league and cup double in 1971, Arsenal didn't enjoy sustained success again until relatively recently. The London team won the league twice under George Graham in 1989 and 1991, then two more league and cup doubles after the arrival of Arsene Wenger in the mid-1990s (1998 and 2002). Once infamous for workmanlike soccer — the opposing fans' chants of "1-0 to the Arsenal" and "Boring, boring Arsenal" say it all — they've since become a much more attractive team to watch.

Arsenal plays in red jerseys with white sleeves at the Emirates Stadium in London. The club's arch rivals are Tottenham Hotspur, though Arsenal also enjoys rivalries with other major London clubs such as Chelsea and West Ham United. In addition, Arsenal often clashes with Manchester United, a result of numerous title battles in the late 1990s and early 2000s.

Arsenal won perhaps the most dramatic league title of all. In 1989, Arsenal needed to win by two clear goals at Liverpool to snatch the championship from the Merseyside club — and did so, with Michael Thomas famously making it 2-0 deep into injury time.

Herbert Chapman: The visionary who changed soccer

Herbert Chapman, Arsenal's coach between 1925 and 1934, was always on the lookout for innovative ideas. Among other things, in the early 1930s he:

✔ Advocated that one man should pick the England team (it was chosen by committee until 1963)

✔ Installed floodlights at the club's stadium, Highbury (though Arsenal wasn't allowed to use them until the 1950s)

✔ Introduced a stadium clock to inform the crowd how much time was left in the game

✔ Got the London Underground to change the name of nearby Gillespie Road stop to Arsenal

✔ Introduced numbers on the back of jerseys

Chapman died suddenly of pneumonia while still in office in 1934. The club erected a bust of the great man, which stands in Arsenal's Emirates Stadium to this day.

Barcelona

Barcelona is one of the two dominant clubs in Spain, the other being Real Madrid. Based in the country's capital, Madrid is seen as the establishment club and a symbol of a unified Spain; Barcelona represents the region of Catalonia and symbolizes that nation's autonomy.

Barca has long been one of the most glamorous teams in world soccer, attracting the biggest names from around the world — the famous Hungarians Sándor Kocsis and Zoltán Czibor in the 1950s, Johan Cruyff in the 1970s, Diego Maradona in the 1980s, and Lionel Messi today. The team had to wait until 1992, however, to win its first Champions League. Since then they've added two more Champions League titles, in 2006 and 2009.

Barcelona plays in blue-and-red stripes. The club's stadium, Camp Nou, is the largest in Europe, seating nearly 100,000 fans. Barcelona has won three Champions Leagues, four Cup Winners' Cups, and three UEFA Cups.

Bayern Munich

Bayern Munich is Germany's biggest and most successful club, though they didn't become a dominant force nationally until the late 1960s. Since then, Bayern has won more titles than any other German club, becoming the most loved — and paradoxically the most hated — club in the country.

Bayern's heyday came in the 1970s, when a team starring defender Franz Beckenbauer, striker Gerd Müller, and goalkeeper Sepp Maier — the backbone of West Germany's 1974 World Cup winning team — won three European Cups in a row between 1974 and 1976. Bayern became champions of Europe again in 2001, just two years after a painful 2-1 defeat to Manchester United in the 1999 Champions League final, after going into injury time a goal to the good.

Bayern historically plays in mostly red colors, with a dash of blue as well. The club calls the Allianz Arena home, a stadium they share with city rivals 1860 Munich. Bayern has won four Champions League titles.

Bayern is such a dominant force in Germany that it only takes a couple of defeats to spark talk of a crisis at the club. It's for this reason that people often refer to them as FC Hollywood.

Benfica

Benfica is Portugal's most successful and internationally renowned club, even though in recent years the team has been forced to play second fiddle to Porto. Benfica's golden era came at the start of the 1960s, when a team built around striker Eusebio won the European Cup in 1961 and 1962. Success abroad has since eluded Benfica, though the Portuguese club did at least reach the European Cup final in 1988 and 1990.

Benfica is from Lisbon, Portugal, and plays in red jerseys. The name of Benfica's home stadium, Estádio da Luz, translates as Stadium of Light, but Luz is in fact a district of Lisbon.

Benfica's nickname is *The Eagles*. Before each game, a trained eagle called Vitoria is released to fly once around the stadium.

Celtic

Celtic is, along with fellow Glasgow giant Rangers, one half of arguably the biggest rivalry in world soccer. The club is most famous for the trophies won in the 1960s and 1970s under legendary coach Jock Stein. Celtic won nine league titles in a row, including the 1967 European Cup with a team whose farthest-flung member had been born 30 miles away from Celtic's home stadium. Celtic remains the only Scottish team to have won Europe's premier club competition.

Today, Celtic regularly wins Scottish soccer's biggest prizes, and occasion-ally enjoys good runs in Europe. Under wily coach Martin O'Neill, and with the skillful striker Henrik Larsson up front, Celtic reached the 2003 UEFA Cup final, but lost 3-2 to José Mourinho's Porto team.

Celtic team members play in green and white hoops. The Glasgow club's home stadium is Celtic Park, though it's more commonly referred to as Parkhead.

Celtic is pronounced *sell*-tik and not, as you may assume, *kell*-tik.

Celtic is the best-supported team in Ireland, reflecting the team's genesis as a sporting club for Irish Catholic expats in the late 1800s.

Chelsea

For years Chelsea was the Nearly Club of London: always capable of putting on a good show but never quite winning the prize. Up until the 1990s Chelsea had only one league title (1955), League Cup (1965), FA Cup (1970), and Cup Winners' Cup (1971) to show for the club's efforts since forming in West London in 1905. The club was more noted for style than substance — Chelsea's players were better known for being spotted out on the 1960s "swinging London" scene than for anything they achieved on the field.

But that began to change from the mid-1990s when the club attracted big-name coaches such as Glenn Hoddle, Ruud Gullit, and Gianluca Vialli. The London club won two more FA Cups around the turn of the millennium (in 1997 and 2000) and another Cup Winners' Cup and the League Cup in 1998. Then Russian billionaire Roman Abramovich took over the team, and Chelsea became one of the most successful teams in Europe. Chelsea bought big-name stars with Abramovich's cash, and in 2004 appointed coach José Mourinho, who won back-to-back titles for the club. In 2012, Chelsea finally landed the biggest prize of all for the first time, winning the Champions League.

Chelsea's uniform is all blue, and the team plays at Stamford Bridge. Chelsea's historical rival is Fulham, but it also has cross-city rivalries with Tottenham, West Ham United, and Arsenal.

Up until the 1950s Chelsea's logo consisted of a local icon — a Chelsea Pensioner. (*Chelsea Pensioners* are members of a retirement home for former army soldiers.) The club was at the time considered something of a quaint joke, having won nothing, so in 1952 coach Ted Drake ordered the badge to be changed to a rampant lion. Within three years Chelsea had won its first league title!

Internazionale

Internazionale has always been one of Italian soccer's powerhouses — it's the only club never to have been relegated from Serie A — though its name will always be associated first and foremost with the mid-1960s. That's when coach Helenio Herrera unleashed a defensive style of play called *catenaccio* — Italian for *padlock* — and led the team to European domination, winning the 1964 and 1965 European Cups.

For many years the club struggled to match those achievements of the 1960s, despite spending more money than any other team in Europe during the 1980s, 1990s, and the first part of the 2000s. Inter's big spending has finally paid off in recent years, with several Serie A titles won along with the Champions League claimed in 2010.

Internazionale is from Milan, Italy. The team's uniform consists of blue-and-black vertical stripes. Internazionale play at the San Siro, a stadium shared with AC Milan.

People often refer to Internazionale as Inter Milan, but this is technically incorrect: It's like saying Arsenal London or Everton Liverpool. If Internazionale seems too much of a mouthful, a simple *Inter* will suffice.

Internazionale was forced to change its name during Mussolini's fascist era because foreign associations were frowned upon. Temporarily known as Ambrosiana, the name was changed back the minute Mussolini was usurped during World War II.

Juventus

Juventus is a strange beast: The club is not the best-supported team in its own home town of Turin (that honor goes to Torino), but Juventus is the bisest-supported in all of Italy. That's partly because the big Fiat car factory in Turin historically attracted workers from all over the country, but mainly because Juve (pronounced *yoo-vay*) is domestically the most successful club in Italian soccer.

The club — nicknamed The Old Lady — has won a record 27 Serie A titles, though success on the continent has been limited, with only two Champions League wins. The team's first win came in 1985, in the wake of the Heysel tragedy (see the sidebar "Liverpool in the 1980s: Triumph and tragedy"); the second in 1996 came with a team led by strike duo Gianluca Vialli and Fabrizio Ravanelli. Until 2006 Juve had always played top-flight soccer, but was then demoted for its role in a match-fixing scandal.

Liverpool in the 1980s: Triumph and tragedy

Liverpool was undoubtedly the team of the decade in the 1980s. In that time they won the league title six times, the FA Cup once, four League Cups, and three European Cups.

But amid the triumphs came two defining tragedies that shaped the future of English soccer. In 1985, before Liverpool's European Cup final against Juventus, fans of the two teams clashed at Heysel Stadium in Brussels, Belgium. After throwing missiles at each other, a section of Liverpool's support chased after

Juventus fans, forcing them to flee. A wall collapsed and 39 people were killed. English clubs were banned from European competition until 1991, Liverpool for a further 12 months.

Then, at Liverpool's 1989 FA Cup semifinal against Nottingham Forest at Hillsborough, home of Sheffield Wednesday, 96 fans were crushed to death when mistakes made by police and stadium organizers forced too many supporters into a small fenced pen.

Juve plays in Turin, Italy, and team members wear black-and-white striped jerseys. Juve's home stadium is the brand new Juventus Stadium, which replaced longtime home Stadio delle Alpi in 2011. Juve has won two Champions League titles, three UEFA Cups, and a Cup Winners' Cup.

Juventus has English club Notts County to thank for its jersey colors: A traveling Juve committee member was on vacation in England in 1903 and liked County's black-and-white striped jerseys so much that he took a set home for his team to wear.

Liverpool

Liverpool owes its existence to city rivals Everton, who used to play at Liverpool's current home stadium Anfield, but in 1892 left following a dispute with the stadium's owner, John Houlding, over rent. Houlding, left with an empty stadium on his hands, decided to form another club — and Liverpool FC was born. The team quickly became one of the most successful clubs in the country, winning the league in 1901.

The pivotal moment in Liverpool's fortunes came in 1959 when the club appointed maverick coach Bill Shankly, who led the English team to three titles and a first-ever FA Cup triumph in 1965. Even more trophies came in the 1970s and 1980s under his successor Bob Paisley, who won three European Cups. Joe Fagan (another European Cup) and Kenny Dalglish continued Liverpool's dominance of the decade on the field. Off it, however, Liverpool suffered the twin disasters of Heysel and Hillsborough (see the sidebar

"Liverpool in the 1980s: Triumph and tragedy"), and in 1991 Dalglish resigned due to the pressures of the job. Since then Liverpool has yet to win the league again, though in 2005 the club won the Champions League in amazing fashion under Rafael Benítez, coming from 3-0 down to beat Milan in the final.

Liverpool team members play in all red at Anfield. The club's city rivalry is with Everton, but even greater bitterness exists between Liverpool and Manchester United.

Liverpool was the first English club to win a treble of major titles: In 1984, Joe Fagan's first season in charge as coach, the team landed the League, League Cup, and European Cup. Liverpool also became the first English club to win three cups in one season: In 2001, under Gerard Houllier, the club won the FA Cup, League Cup, and UEFA cup.

Manchester City

Until recently, and despite enjoying levels of success most teams in the country would give their back teeth for — two league titles, four FA Cups, and a Cup Winners' Cup won during the 20th century — Manchester City earned itself a reputation for hapless failure. That's partially down to the ill-fortune of being city rivals with Manchester United, one of world soccer's biggest powers, and coming a poor second by comparison.

But that's all changed recently. New ownership in the form of Sheikh Mansour took over in 2009 and has since invested well over a billion dollars in the club to buy City the best players money can bring, helping the club win the FA Cup in 2011 and a first league title in 44 years with Premier League honors claimed in 2012. No longer does City play second fiddle to United in the trophy-hunting stakes in Manchester.

City team members play in sky blue and white at the City of Manchester Stadium, the club's home since 2003.

The club's fans will tell you that theirs is the only team in the city of Manchester. Rivals United are technically situated in the neighboring borough of Salford.

Manchester United

Manchester United is one of the biggest clubs in soccer, often topping the lists as the world's best supported and most valuable team. Manchester United was always a big club in England, ever since its formation as Newton

Heath in 1878, but after World War II, and the appointment of the legendary Matt Busby as coach, the institution grew and grew.

Busby created three great teams. The first won the FA Cup in 1948 and United's first league title in 41 years in 1952. His second — a youthful team known affectionately as The Busby Babes — won back-to-back leagues in the mid-1950s, but the Babes were tragically cut down in their prime in an air crash at Munich Airport in 1958. See the nearby sidebar "The Babes perish at Munich" for more information.

The third, starring the triumvirate of Bobby Charlton, George Best, and Denis Law, won more titles in the 1960s and the 1968 European Cup. A barren period followed in the 1970s and 1980s, but the appointment of Alex Ferguson as coach saw the club enjoy outstanding success in the Premier League era, the pinnacle of which was the 1999 treble of league, FA Cup, and Champions League, a feat unprecedented in English soccer.

United has won the most English championship titles with 19, including 12 in the past two decades alone. The club plays in red, black, and white at Old Trafford. United's city rival is Manchester City, although it also regularly locks horns with (by increasing levels of bile) Arsenal, Leeds United, and Liverpool.

United owes its existence to a runaway dog. Club forerunners, Newton Heath, held a fundraising fete in 1901 from which the captain's dog fled. The daughter of a wealthy local businessman found the dog and wanted to keep it. On tracing the dog, the captain struck a deal with the businessman: His daughter could keep it in exchange for investment — and a deal was done.

The Babes perish at Munich

On February 8, 1958, Matt Busby's young Manchester United team entered the history books in the most tragic way possible. United had hoped to do so in happier circumstances, by winning the European Cup, and had just reached the semifinals by winning at Red Star Belgrade.

But on the way back, after a refueling stop at Munich airport, the team's plane crashed while taking off in a blizzard. Seven members of the team were killed on impact; an eighth, the star man Duncan Edwards, died 15 days later in hospital. Red Star asked UEFA to name United as honorary champions of Europe that season, but UEFA insisted the show had to go on. Milan beat a hastily cobbled-together team in the semifinals. United had to wait until 1968 to lift the European Cup; Busby finally reached his holy grail.

It was the second major plane crash to hit soccer in a decade: In 1949 Torino's all-conquering Il Grande Torino team was wiped out in a crash at Superga, a hill overlooking Turin.

Marseille

Although the French national team has won World Cups and European Championships, and French bureaucrats were responsible for founding FIFA, the World Cup, and the European Cup, French club teams have failed to enjoy much success on the big stage. Reims and St Etienne both reached European Cup finals, but it was only in 1993 that a club from France became champions of Europe.

Olympique de Marseille — known as l'OM in France — had been expected to win the 1991 European Cup final, but froze on the day, allowing Red Star Belgrade to take the title. But two years later, l'OM surprised Milan 1-0 in the first-ever Champions League final. Defender Basile Boli scored the only goal, and midfielder Didier Deschamps lifted the trophy. It was the greatest achievement by any French club — though it was later tainted when Marseille was found to have bribed opponents en route to winning the French league the previous season. Marseille has yet to win a major trophy since the scandal, but remains the biggest club in France.

Marseille team members play in all white with light-blue trim, and the team's home games are at the Stade Vélodrome.

It's often erroneously reported that Marseille was stripped of its 1993 Champions League win as a result of the infamous match-fixing exploits. But the team was simply relegated from the French top flight and banned from European soccer.

Porto

Porto — from Portugal's second city — was for years considered to be the third club in the country, behind the Lisbon giants Benfica and Sporting Lisbon. But in 1987 the team won the European Cup, beating Bayern Munich in the final with the aid of a cheeky back-heeled goal from the Egyptian genius Rabah Madjer. And ever since Porto has been the dominant club in the country.

Porto enjoyed its grandest years in 2003 and 2004, after little-known coach José Mourinho took over the club and led the team — which contained future Chelsea stars Ricardo Carvalho and Deco — to victory in the UEFA Cup, then the Champions League the following season. Further success in Europe has since eluded Porto, but domestic domination continues apace.

Porto members play in blue-and-white stripes at the Estádio do Dragão.

Old Firm, old problems

The rivalry between Celtic and Rangers — collectively known as The Old Firm — is one of the most intense in world soccer.

The two Glasgow clubs are far and away the largest, best supported and most successful in Scotland, totally dominating all other clubs in terms of trophies won. (No other team, for example, has won the league since Aberdeen in 1985.)

The clubs are infamous for their sometimes sectarian rivalry. Celtic was formed by a Catholic priest and has strong links with the Irish republican community; Rangers is staunchly Protestant, very much the club of the UK establishment.

Up until the late 1980s Rangers had an unwritten rule not to sign Catholic players. Celtic has always been more open-minded in this regard. These days, though, neither club operates such a restrictive policy.

Fans, too, are encouraged not to sing sectarian songs. In the past, Celtic fans would chant pro-IRA songs and Rangers supporters would sing about the Irish famine. This is less a problem than it was, though incidents do still occasionally occur.

The Portuguese league is one of the more predictable in world soccer. Since it was launched in 1935, Porto, Benfica, or Sporting Lisbon have won it on all but two occasions: Belenenses of Lisbon (1946) and Boavista of Porto (2001).

Rangers

Rangers is the best-supported team in Scotland, gaining support from all over the country as well as in the club's Glasgow base. Rangers hold the world record for domestic title wins — currently the only team to have won its country's league title over 50 times — but the Glaswegians have never been able to translate that success internationally, although Rangers did win the 1972 Cup Winners' Cup.

Rangers matched Celtic's record of nine-in-a-row league titles in the mid-1990s under the leadership of Walter Smith, who soon left the club to manage Everton and then Scotland. But Smith returned in 2007 to enjoy more glory, leading the club to the 2008 UEFA Cup final, which Rangers lost to Zenit St Petersburg, and then another Scottish league title. A financial crisis engulfed the club during the 2011–2012 season, and Scotland's soccer authorities enforced a relegation of Rangers to the fourth division as the club restarted itself as a new business entity.

Rangers team members play in blue jerseys, white shorts, and black socks. The club's home stadium is Ibrox, Glasgow. Rangers enjoy a fierce rivalry with fellow Glaswegian club, Celtic.

Rangers are often referred to as *Glasgow Rangers,* but the official name of the club has no reference to the club's home city: The name is simply Rangers Football Club.

Ibrox has been the scene of two of soccer's worst stadium disasters. A stand collapsed in 1902, killing 25 fans. Then, in 1971, 66 supporters died in a crush on an exit stairwell. As a result of the 1971 disaster, Ibrox became all-seater, and one of the grandest (and safest) stadiums in the land.

Real Madrid

Despite the constant claims of others, Real Madrid is without question the biggest club in the world. The Spanish club has won the Champions League a record nine times, and has over the years fielded many of the game's truly great players. Real is also the most successful club domestically in Spain — though detractors will tell you the team earned many of its titles thanks to the influence of Spanish dictator (and Real fan) General Franco.

Real's legendary status was sealed in the 1950s, when a team starring Alfredo di Stéfano, Francesco Gento, Raymond Kopa, and Ferenc Puskás won the first five European Cups ever held, a run culminating in a famous 7-3 victory over Eintracht Frankfurt in the 1960 final. Although Real added a sixth European Cup victory in 1966, the European trail went cold for 32 years, though a high point in between was five consecutive Spanish titles in the 1980s, with strikers Emilio Butragueño and Hugo Sánchez dominating the goalscoring charts.

Then the club won three more Champions League in 1998, 2000, and (spectacularly, thanks to a wonderful volley by Zinedine Zidane) in 2002. Real has since pursued a policy of buying some of the biggest names in world soccer, such as David Beckham, Cristiano Ronaldo, Kaká, and Karim Benzema.

Real Madrid team members play in all white at the Santiago Bernabéu stadium in central Madrid.

Real Madrid is the only club to have fired its coach after winning the Champions League. It got rid of Jupp Heynckes in 1998 because he hadn't won the Spanish league. Real also sacked two-time Champions League winning coach Vicente del Bosque in 2003, just after winning the league.

Rivalries and derbies

There's not a club on the planet that doesn't have a rivalry with another. Ever since Hallam FC was formed in 1860, in order to give Sheffield FC a game, animosities have developed between different clubs. (By way of example, it only took two games before Sheffield and Hallam started throwing haymakers at each other.)

Rivalries are usually local (though there are exceptions to this rule). More often than not, warring clubs come from the same or neighboring towns and cities. In Britain, a game between two rivals is known as a *derby*.

Famous local rivalry games around the world include Celtic and Rangers (Scotland); Arsenal and Tottenham Hotspur (England); Roma and Lazio (Italy); Spartak Moscow and CSKA Moscow (Russia); and Corinthians and São Paulo (Brazil).

But rivalries aren't always local: In Spain, Barcelona and Real Madrid lock horns in fiercely contested games known as El Clásico, and in Mexico, América from Mexico City and Chivas from Guadalajara play in El Súper Clásico, feverishly anticipated clashes. Similarly, most Major League Soccer teams are considerable distances from each other, but some games are still definitely rivalry material. On the West Coast, clashes among the Portland Timbers, Seattle Sounders, and Vancouver Whitecaps make up the Cascadia Cup, the unofficial name of the Pacific Northwest region.

Tottenham Hotspur

Tottenham Hotspur — known to many simply as Spurs — is one of the biggest clubs in England, though Spurs' roll of honor doesn't particularly reflect this. The club's only won two league titles, yet far less famous teams such as Portsmouth, Burnley, and Preston North End have won the same amount, and outfits such as Huddersfield Town and Blackburn Rovers have won more. But Tottenham's fame is guaranteed because they produced one of the most attractive sides of all time in the early 1960s. The team, managed by Bill Nicholson and starring Dave Mackay, John White, and (later) Jimmy Greaves became the first team to win the league and FA Cup double in the 20th century — in 1961! — and then landed England's first European trophy (the 1963 Cup Winners' Cup).

That Spurs team was committed to playing attractive soccer, a philosophy summed up by the team's outspoken captain Danny Blanchflower's famous comment, "Football is about glory, about doing things in style and with a flourish, not waiting for the other lot to die of boredom." The club has struggled to live up to these lofty ideals since, though Spurs has won the FA Cup eight times, a record bettered only by Manchester United and Arsenal.

Tottenham Hotspur team members play in white with dark-blue trim at White Hart Lane, London. Spurs enjoys a fierce rivalry with fellow North London club Arsenal.

Spurs was not the first English club to sign players from overseas, but did lead the way in signing truly top-class stars from abroad. In the summer of 1978, in a deal still remembered fondly today, Spurs signed midfielders Osvaldo Ardiles and Ricardo Villa, both of whom had just won the World Cup with Argentina.

Making It in South America

While clubs were springing up all over mainland Europe in the late 1800s and early 1900s, the same thing was happening in South America, thanks to British expats taking the game across the seas. As a result, the continent boasts many of the oldest and most famous clubs in the world.

Boca Juniors

Along with River Plate, Boca is one of the two biggest clubs in Argentina. The team plays in Buenos Aires and is historically the team of the working class. Even though he didn't play for the club for a particularly long time, Diego Maradona is Boca's most famous player. Boca hadn't won an international trophy until triumphing in the Copa Libertadores (the south American club championship) in 1977, but now the club holds the world record of most international titles (18) won along with AC Milan.

Boca team members play in blue jerseys with a yellow stripe across the chest. The club's home stadium is La Bombonera, Buenos Aires.

Club representatives decided on Boca's color scheme as part of a wager, the club agreeing to adopt the flag colors of the next ship to dock at La Boca port. A Swedish vessel sailed in, with the country's blue and yellow flag flapping in the breeze, and so Boca's famous color choice was decided.

Flamengo

Flamengo is the biggest club in Brazil and the representative team of the working classes in Rio de Janeiro. The team shares a rivalry with its more middle-class rival Fluminense, from which Flamengo was formed in 1911 by a splinter group. It wasn't until the 1980s that Flamengo made its mark on the world stage, thrashing Liverpool 3-0 in the Intercontinental Cup in 1981 with a team starring Brazilian midfield legend Zico.

Fla, as the team's known, plays in black and red at both the Maracanã and Gávea stadiums in Rio and has won the Copa Libertadores once.

Fluminense

Moneyed British expats founded Fluminense in 1902, and to this day they're seen as the team of Rio's upper classes. Flu, as it's called, is one of the most successful teams in Brazil, though it's had no success on the international scene, a dreadful record for such a big club. Flu was relegated twice during a barren 1990s, but such is its status that political maneuvering quickly saw the team reinstated to the top flight.

Flu team members play in red-and-green stripes at both the Maracanã and Laranjeiras stadiums in Rio.

Rivalry games between Fluminense and Flamengo — known as the Fla-Flu — historically draw huge crowds. In December 1963 a game between the two teams at the Maracanã drew 194,603 spectators. Even the official paying attendance of only 177,656 made it the best-attended club game in world history, a record that stands today. Sure enough, it ended 0-0.

Independiente

Independiente may be the "third club" in Buenos Aires, losing out in the glamour stakes to city rivals Boca Juniors and River Plate, but the team has won more Copa Libertadores than any other club on the continent. However, its achievements are very much in the past — Independiente won its last Copa Libertadores in 1984. The club has struggled to match its illustrious achievements since, yet remain one of Argentinian soccer's big names.

Independiente's uniform is red. The team's home stadium is the Estadio Libertadores de América and has won a record seven Copa Libertadores titles.

Independiente's modern malaise can be illustrated by the fact that its most famous player, to this day, remains Raimundo Orsi, who played for Argentina in the 1930 World Cup final and then scored for Italy as it won the 1934 version.

Millonarios

Millonarios of Bogota, Colombia, hasn't won the Colombian championship since 1988 and has never even reached the final of the Copa Libertadores. But it remains without question the most famous name in Colombian soccer for the team's money-splashing exploits in the 1950s. That was when the Bogota club signed world soccer's biggest names, contravening all FIFA transfer protocol when Colombia ran an illegal breakaway league. Alfredo di Stéfano took his first steps to greatness there, eventually leaving the club for Real Madrid. The glory days are now long gone, but the luster of Millonarios remains.

Millonarios team members play in all blue at El Campín.

A local journalist gave Millonarios its name. In the 1930s the club — then called Deportivo Municipal — pushed for a professional league in soccer, so the journalist wrote "the Municipalistas have become the Millonarios." The name stuck, and a new identity was born.

Nacional

Nacional of Montevideo is one of the two historically dominant teams in Uruguay. The club supplied most of the players to Uruguay's 1924 and 1928 Olympic champion teams, and the country's 1930 World Cup winning roster. In 1941 Nacional enjoyed a perfect league season, winning all 20 games in the Uruguayan Primera Division, one of which was a 6-0 win over arch-rivals Peñarol. This win came in the middle of what is now called Nacional's *Quinquenio de Oro*: the Golden Five Years. Nacional has won three Copa Libertadores.

Nacional team members play in white jerseys at both Parque Central and Estadio Centenario.

Nacional claims to be the oldest team in Uruguay, formed in 1899. However, rival Peñarol insists its team is older because the club was initially formed by English expats as the Central Uruguay Railway Cricket Club in 1891, before becoming totally Uruguayan in 1913. The controversy rages to this day.

Peñarol

Peñarol of Montevideo is Nacional's rival for the title of biggest club in Uruguay. The club is the most decorated in Uruguay, having won the most domestic titles in the professional era and five Copa Libertadores, two more than

Nacional. Along with Nacional, Peñarol has dominated the Uruguayan game over the decades, with 37 league title wins in the professional era. The club famously provided the bulk of Uruguay's victorious 1950 World Cup team, including the two players who scored in the final against Brazil, Juan Schiaffino and Alcide Ghiggia.

Peñarol team members play in yellow-and-black stripes at both Estadio Las Acacias and Estadio Centenario and have won the Copa Libertadores five times.

Since the Uruguayan league turned professional in 1931, Peñarol and Nacional have shared the title for all but ten seasons. All the five other teams to have won titles — Defensor Sporting (4), Danubio (3), Bella Vista (1), Central Español (1), and Progreso (1) — also come from the capital city Montevideo. No other country's league has been totally dominated by a single city like this.

River Plate

River Plate is the *other* great team in Buenos Aires, Argentina, rivaling the working-class outfit Boca Juniors. River is traditionally seen as the club of the rich in the city, though despite winning many domestic titles, the team took until 1986 to win its first Copa Libertadores, with Uruguayan midfielder Enzo Francescoli the star of that team. Although rivals Boca can boast Diego Maradona as a star ex-player, River has arguably a more stellar roll call, featuring the likes of future Real Madrid midfielder Alfredo di Stéfano, 1978 World Cup winning striker Mario Kempes, and Milan and Chelsea striker Hernán Crespo.

River team members play in white jerseys with a red diagonal sash. River plays at El Monumental, and has won two Copa Libertadores.

The rivalry between River Plate and Boca Juniors — known as the Superclasico — is perhaps the most intense in world of soccer. Nearly 75 percent of Argentinians are said to either support or strongly express a preference for one team or the other.

Santos

Brazilian club teams have been nowhere near as successful as their international team. There's no better example of this than Santos — which despite winning two Copa Libertadores all the way back in 1962 and 1963 is still by far the most famous Brazilian club in the world. Why is this? Because it was the club team of Pelé, the most famous star ever to have played the game. Pelé was the beating heart of a team that also won the Intercontinental Cup twice, beating two different European champions in Benfica and AC Milan. The club — based in São Paulo — has never enjoyed such success since, but its fame refuses to diminish.

Santos is based in Santos, São Paulo. The team wears black-and-white striped jerseys, plays at Vila Belmiro, and has won two Copa Libertadores.

Although Santos remains the most famous Brazilian club, the club's neighbor, São Paulo, is the most successful. São Paulo has won three Copa Libertadores, more than any other Brazilian team, and more domestic league titles than anyone else.

Looking at Some of the Best of the Rest

Soccer took a serious hold in Europe and South America before anywhere else in the world, so it's only natural the majority of famous clubs are from those continents. But that doesn't mean the rest of the world are lacking major institutions of their own.

Of course, there are simply far too many to list, but I've chosen a select few. (Ask me next year and I'll no doubt pick a completely different group of teams.)

Al-Ahly and Zamalek

Egypt is the most successful African soccer nation, so it's not surprising the country boasts the fiercest (and most long-lasting) club rivalry. The two Cairo teams, Al-Ahly and Zamalek, have been at it for a century now — the former began life in 1907, the latter four years later.

Al-Ahly is the dominant partner in the rivalry, having won 36 Egyptian titles and seven African Champions League crowns, both records. The feats meant Al-Ahly was titled African Club of the 20th Century by CAF, African soccer's governing federation. But although Zamalek has won a mere 11 domestic titles by comparison, it's only two African Champions League wins behind Al-Ahly, with five wins.

Ten teams in flight

Some soccer clubs are more famous for their wonderful names than anything else. Here are ten of my favorites, some of which are sure to appeal to the inner child:

- **Prima Ham FC (Japan):** Prima Ham was founded by workers at a food company. It has since changed its name to Mito Hollyhock.

- **Deportivo Moron (Argentina):** Moron is a district in Buenos Aires.

- **Club Destroyers (Bolivia):** Having never won a Bolivian title, this second-tier club struggles to live up to its name.

- **The Strongest (Bolivia):** The oldest club in Bolivia. A battle in a 1930s war between Bolivia and Paraguay was named after this club, after several players and staff members took up arms.

- **Eleven Men in Flight (Swaziland):** This Swazi soccer club is surely the most romantically named in the world . . .

- **Queen of the South (Scotland):** . . . although these chaps from Dumfries, southern Scotland, run them close.

- **Botswana Meat Commission (Botswana):** This Lobatse-based team must be one of the better-fed teams in the world.

- **Big Bullets (Malawi):** As you'd expect, the most successful club members in the country are sharpshooters.

- **Mysterious Dwarfs (Ghana):** This first-division club is more commonly known as Ebusua Dwarfs, which isn't as catchy.

- **Corinthian Casuals (England):** Formed following the merger of two famous English amateur teams, Corinthians and Casuals. Corinthians were famous in the 1880s and 1890s for holding exceptional sporting values, which went as far as a refusal to attempt to save penalties awarded against them. (The feeling was, a foul in the box should be punished by a goal.)

Asante Kotoko and Hearts of Oak

Asante Kotoko and Hearts of Oak are the two largest clubs in Ghana, one of the most historically successful countries in African soccer. Asante Kotoko, from Kumasi has won the African Champions League twice, whereas Hearts of Oak from Accra has won it once. Between them the two teams have won over 40 domestic titles.

Asante's heyday came in the 1970s and 1980s, and Hearts became dominant in the late 1990s. Tragically, Hearts' Champions League winning season, in 2000, was overshadowed first by a riot at the Champions League final and then by a crush at its stadium in May 2001, which killed 126 fans. The club has bounced back from tragedy to win five Ghanaian championships since then.

Raja Casablanca

Wydad of Casablanca (WAC) is historically the biggest club in Moroccan soccer history, but in the last two decades it's been astonishingly superseded by city rivals Raja Casablanca. Raja only won its first domestic title in 1988, but by the end of the century — having won consecutive league championships from 1996 to 2000 and adding three African Champions Leagues in 1989, 1997, and 1999 — it was ranked third in the CAF's African Club of the 20th Century poll.

Chapter 14

Women's Soccer

You can't ignore the elephant in the room: There'll always be sports fans, usually male and set in their ways, who argue that women's sports such as soccer aren't worth watching.

Until the 1970s, soccer in the United States and much of the rest of the world was mostly played by men. But in recent decades, women's soccer has taken great strides, becoming a hugely popular participation sport. Professional women's soccer is more exciting and more competitive by the day — in 2011, the Women's World Cup held in Germany broke viewing records for the sport around the globe.

As this chapter explains, women's soccer has overcome big obstacles to become the successful sport it is today — and the United States has a particularly rich history in helping to develop the sport, with Americans among some of the best women's soccer players of all time.

From Beijing to London: How It All Began

Women's soccer has a history as long as the men's game, with Chinese women from the Han Dynasty (roughly 200BC to AD200) featured in pictures juggling with a ball. Sadly, due to a mixture of apathy and oppression, the female game was overtaken by the men's when soccer as you know it today really kicked off during the late 1800s and early 1900s.

While the men were getting their acts together in Britain with the formation of the Football Association in 1863, the prevailing mood of Victorian Britain deemed soccer to be anything but a feminine pastime. Many doctors were also wheeled out to advise that it was medically harmful to the female form, some even suggesting that kicking a ball would render a woman unable to have children.

But in March 1895 the first competitive "ladies" game was held in Crouch End, North London. In truth, it was more a political event than a sporting one: Suffragette Nettie Honeyball founded her British Ladies Football Club "with the fixed resolve of proving to the world that women are not the ornamental and useless creatures men have pictured. I look forward to the time when ladies may sit in Parliament and have a voice in the direction of affairs." (Women were yet to be given the vote at this point in history.)

The game was considered a success, though, a North London representative XI beating its South London counterparts 7-1. More than 10,000 supporters watched, and newspapers reported that the unreconstructed crowd spent the first ten minutes highly amused at the sight of women playing soccer but were soon won round by the excitement of the game. "I imagine that women players may, after some further practice, develop a style of play which may be both vigorous and graceful," reported the *Manchester Guardian*'s Lady Correspondent.

A month later Honeyball took the two teams around the country on an exhibition tour. The game they played at the home of Reading FC broke the club's attendance record previously held by a men's game between Reading and Luton Town. Opportunities for the women's game to thrive and prosper definitely existed, and during World War I its popularity went through the roof in Britain. It's worth noting, though, that while men's soccer leagues were forming at the same time across the Atlantic, in the United States no such comparable organization was made then in American women's soccer.

Dick, Kerr Ladies get popular . . .

In October 1917, Alfred Frankland, a clerk at the Dick, Kerr & Co. munitions factory in Preston, England, encouraged women working there to set up a soccer team (shown in Figure 14-1). Frankland had watched the workers attempting to kick a ball through an open window during their lunch hour and decided that the women were more accurate and skillful than the men.

Frankland organized a charity event at Deepdale, the home of local club Preston North End, and on Christmas Day that year 10,000 fans — starved of soccer with many of the men away at war and the Football League suspended — turned up to watch the event. It was a great success: Dick, Kerr beat a women's team from a nearby foundry 4-0, and the game raised a large sum of money for a local hospital.

Figure 14-1:
The Dick,
Kerr Ladies'
team.

Popperfoto/Getty Images

The men's league restarted in 1919, but the popularity of the women's game — a more skillful, less physical spectacle — continued to grow. A game on Boxing Day in 1920 between Dick, Kerr and St Helens drew 53,000 spectators to Everton's Goodison Park, and an unofficial England–France international (effectively Dick, Kerr versus a French team) attracted 25,000 fans.

In 1922, Dick, Kerr Ladies sailed to North America for a tour of Canada, but on arrival they were forbidden from playing by Canada's Football Association. Instead, they traveled to the United States and played eight games against top American professional men's teams (there were no known women's teams for them to play). Dick, Kerr Ladies won three games out of the eight, much impressing a curious American audience.

. . . and the Establishment gets sexist

Women's soccer had also become popular in other countries, including the Netherlands and Germany. But with popularity came jealousy, resistance, and finally oppression. In 1896 the Dutch Football Association (KNVB) banned a game between Sparta Rotterdam and an England XI. And worse was to come in England.

In 1919 a women's game at Newcastle United's St James's Park drew 35,000 fans and raised — in today's terms — nearly $500,000 for charity. Two years later the same club banned women from using the stadium, because club directors were worried that the sport would eclipse the men's in terms of popularity.

Political concerns also existed. Dick, Kerr had played a series of charity games to raise money for miners who had been laid off — rubbing up the wrong way the stuffy establishment figures at English soccer's governing body, the Football Association (FA) — and the very fact that these games raised so much money for charity highlighted to the general public the amount of money soccer games actually raised (and how much was being pocketed by the owners).

The FA launched an attack on the women's game. They orchestrated a smear campaign, accusing Dick, Kerr and other teams of fiddling their expenses and effectively stealing money from the charities. And they wheeled out the doctors again to provide spurious medical evidence that "violent leg strain" would leave women unable to have children.

In December 1921 the FA used those "health concerns" and accusations of financial impropriety to ban women from using men's fields. "The game is unsuitable for females and ought not to be encouraged," they wrote.

The FA didn't apologize for these slights until 2008, 37 years after they lifted their ban on women's soccer.

The women fight back

The women responded staunchly: Five days after their FA ban in 1921 they formed an English Ladies FA, which kept the flame lit during several dark decades for the sport. Dick, Kerr Ladies continued to play across the country until the 1960s, and a team called Manchester Corinthians prospered in the 1940s and 1950s. Women also attempted to stage meaningful tournaments, such as the English Ladies FA Challenge Cup in 1922 (won by Stoke Ladies FC) and a Championship of Great Britain and the World (Dick, Kerr beat Edinburgh 5-1 in 1937, with the exact score reversed the following year).

But unable to use the country's existing soccer infrastructure, women's teams were effectively banished to the sidelines, able to play only the very occasional exhibition game.

However, women's soccer was gaining popularity across the globe, with thousands of young women taking up soccer in the United States, China, Germany, the Netherlands, and all across Scandinavia. In 1957 women formed a body called the International Ladies Football Association, followed by the Fédération Internationale et Européenne de Football Féminin in 1969. Manchester Corinthians won an unofficial women's European championship. Then in 1970 and 1971 Denmark won unofficial World Cups. The games didn't generate much media interest, but soccer associations around the world sat up and took notice.

The FA lifts the ban — and FIFA gets serious

In 1970 and 1971 several national associations, notably those of France, West Germany, and England, lifted their bans on women's soccer. The move wasn't totally altruistic — the FAs were concerned they didn't have control of the women's game now it was becoming popular — but nevertheless it was a positive step.

The game began to take off worldwide. In 1975 the first Asian championship was held. In 1984 Europe followed suit, holding their first championships. And during the 1980s more unofficial world tournaments were held — five stagings of the Mundialito in Italy and Japan between 1982 and 1988, a world invitational in Taiwan in 1987, and a FIFA-sponsored jamboree in China in 1988. It was enough to persuade FIFA (Fédération Internationale de Football Association, or International Federation of Association Football) to launch an official Women's World Cup, and the first was held in China in 1991.

The women's game had finally booked its place at the top table.

The Game Today

Several major women's leagues exist across the world, from dominant nations such as the United States, Germany, and China, to smaller countries playing catch-up — like England.

The United States

The modern women's game in the United States really began to take off in the 1970s following legislation known as Title IX that mandated equal access to equally funded athletic programs without any differential treatment based on sex at federally funded educational institutions such as colleges.

This led to a massive increase in funding for women's sports, and one of the biggest beneficiaries was college soccer. From just a handful of varsity women's soccer programs in the late 1960s, over 200 were established by 1985. Participation by girls in youth soccer simultaneously exploded, feeding colleges with girls experienced in the sport by the mid-1980s — at the end of that decade, over two million American girls were regularly playing organized soccer.

Teams such as Anson Dorrance's powerhouse University of North Carolina's women's team developed enormously talented players, providing half the roster for the United States team as it headed to the inaugural FIFA Women's World Cup held in China in 1991 — a competition the Americans won.

This helped raise the profile of women's soccer in the United States, though things really took off when the American team won the World Cup for the second time in 1999. On this occasion, the victory came on home soil, and record numbers of fans — an average of 38,000 per game, including 91,000 at the Rose Bowl in Pasadena for the final — watched Mia Hamm's and Brandi Chastain's achievements.

The 1999 national team's success — with millions tuning in on television — led to the first of two major efforts to launch a professional league in the United States, neither of which lasted more than a few seasons. The Women's United Soccer Association (WUSA) was the first to try. It lasted three seasons between 2001 and 2003, but overspending doomed a league that couldn't attract enough fans to cover its expenses. Despite smaller budgets, the same proved true of Women's Professional Soccer (WPS), launched in 2009 but only lasting until 2011.

In late 2012, it was announced that a new professional women's league would begin play in 2013, featuring national team players from the United States, Canada, and Mexico. Maybe third time will be a charm for professional women's soccer in North America.

Rest of the world

Other leagues across the world are more established, with thriving and successful leagues in Germany, Italy, China, Sweden, and Norway established since the 1970s. In England, a new professional league — the FA Super League — was launched in 2011.

Probably the strongest of the bunch is the German league, as shown by the dominance of German teams in pan-European competition (see the following sidebar "The Women's Champions League"). In South America, club soccer is not as advanced as in Europe, though a continental competition — the Copa Libertadores de América de Fútbol Femenino — was formed in 2009.

The Women's World Cup

The first — unofficial — women's world championship was held in Italy in 1970. Denmark won, beating the hosts in a Turin final. The Danes held onto the trophy the year after, again beating the host country — this time Mexico — in the final.

The Women's Champions League

In Europe, the UEFA Women's Cup was launched in 2001, a competition for the best teams in the continent. Teams qualified by winning their national league, or winning their cup if no league competition existed.

German teams have dominated the cup, with teams from Germany winning six of the titles between 2002 and 2012. The first winner, in 2001–2002, was FFC Frankfurt, which went on to land another two stagings of the competition.

France's Olympique Lyon has recently been dominant, winning in both 2011 and 2012, and the trophy has also headed back to Sweden twice, with Umea winning both times. England can only boast one victory, when Arsenal won the cup in 2007.

As of 2009–2010, the tournament was renamed the Women's Champions League. Similar to the men's version, nonchampions are now also permitted into the competition.

Five more unofficial tournaments, the Mundialito, were held between 1982 and 1988 in Italy and Japan — the Italians winning three and England two — but in 1986 FIFA established a women's committee, and the ball was set rolling for a proper World Cup.

Two trial runs took place. In 1987 Chinese Taipei hosted and won the Women's World Invitation Tournament. Then in 1988 Norway won the Women's FIFA Invitational Tournament in China. The stage was set for the first FIFA Women's World Cup, to be held a mere 61 years after the men's inaugural World Cup.

1991: The First World Cup

The first Women's World Cup was held in China. Twelve nations competed, and the tournament was considered a huge success. It was dominated and won by the United States, the country winning its first major trophy of any kind.

The winning team boasted a forward line known as the Triple Edged Sword: Michelle Akers, Carin Jennings, and April Heinrichs scored 20 of the 25 goals tallied by the United States during the tournament. Akers scored twice in the final as the Americans beat Norway 2-1 in Guangzhou.

The tournament comes of age

The United States looked to defend its title four years later in Sweden, but lost star striker Akers within 10 minutes of the team's very first game of the tournament. The Americans still made the semifinals but were dispatched by Norway, which went on to win the trophy, beating Germany 2-0 in the final.

The 1999 tournament in the United States was the most successful yet. China looked like the most powerful team, with striker Sun Wen scoring seven goals en route to the final and the Chinese crushing defending champions Norway 5-0 in the semis. But China found the host nation to be an immovable object in the final, and the United States won 5-4 on penalties after a goalless draw.

The attendance of 90,185 for the 1999 final — held at the Rose Bowl, Pasadena — was the largest ever for a women's sporting event. The game is also remembered for Brandi Chastain's celebration upon converting the winning penalty: She removed her jersey to reveal her sports bra.

In 1999 the number of teams involved in the finals increased to 16, a number that's stayed the same since then but will rise to 24 for the 2015 edition. The 2003 and 2007 competitions, held in the United States and China respectively, were both won by Germany, which had by now become the powerhouse nation in women's soccer, thanks in no small part to the goalscoring exploits of Birgit Prinz. Held in Germany, the 2011 edition of the tournament was a great success on and off the field, though the host nation was knocked out surprisingly early — Japan scooped the crown for the first time, defeating the United States in the final.

Other Major Tournaments

Whereas the men's tournament at the Summer Olympics has been running for over a century, the women's event was only launched at the 1996 Games in Atlanta. The United States has dominated the Games, winning four of the five gold medals on offer in 1996, 2004, 2008, and 2012. Only Norway has managed to shove the United States off the top podium, beating them in the 2000 final to claim gold.

The other medals have been divvied up between the usual suspects in the women's game. Brazil has two silvers, China one silver, Japan one silver, and Germany three bronzes.

Third in the pecking order behind the World Cup and the Olympics is an invitational tournament that nevertheless carries great prestige. The Algarve Cup is held annually in Portugal, with 12 teams invited. The United States has won eight Algarve Cups, the best record of any nation.

Like the World Cup, Germany and Scandinavia have dominated the European Championship. Germany has won six out of seven European titles (1991, 1995, 1997, 2001, 2005, and 2009) with only Norway breaking its run in 1993. German superiority doesn't look like it's slipping any time soon: The team's 6-2 win over the best-ever England team in the 2009 final was a stunning display of the country's domination in European women's soccer.

The oldest surviving women's international tournament is the Asian Cup, which was first held in 1975. Over the years China has dominated the competition, winning the title eight times. North Korea and Taiwan are next on the roll of honor with three wins apiece.

The determination of the Asian Cup's organizers in the 1970s and early 1980s in the face of political pressure from the stuffy suits at FIFA was an important factor in the world governing body eventually agreeing to stage a women's world championship.

Major International Teams

The women's international game only really took off in the late 1980s, so few teams have been able to claim a place in the pantheon of soccer as of yet. As the sport develops and creates a longer history, that's bound to change. Meanwhile all I can do is note the achievements of some of the sport's major nations.

United States

The United States women's team is the most successful in the world, more often than not found at number one in the FIFA world rankings. The United States has won two Women's World Cups (1991 and 1999) and four Olympic golds (in 1996, 2004, 2008, and 2012). The team also won eight Algarve Cups.

The team played its first game in 1985. Notable players past and present include Kristine Lilly, Mia Hamm, Michelle Akers, Hope Solo, and Abby Wambach.

Germany

Germany's team has won the World Cup twice (in 2003 and 2007), making it the only nation to have won both men's and women's stagings of the tournament. By also finishing runners-up once, the Germans boast the best record of any nation in the World Cup. Germany has also been the dominant force in European soccer, winning the UEFA continental championship six times — an outstanding record when you consider only seven tournaments have taken place.

Germany played its first game in 1982. Notable players past and present include Birgit Prinz, Inka Grings, Silvia Neid, Doris Fitschen, and Martina Voss.

Japan

Japan became the first Asian nation to win either the men's or women's World Cup with its victory at the 2011 edition held in Germany. Led by Homare Sawa, named World Player of the Year that same year, Japan defeated the United States in a penalty shootout in the final after a 2-2 tie. Japan then reached the final of the Olympic Games competition the next year, but the Americans had their revenge in the final, winning 2-1.

Japan has played in every Women's World Cup since 1991. Japan's best known players include Homare Sawa, Aya Miyama, and Shinobu Ohno.

Brazil

The Brazilian women's team has yet to match the success of its male equivalent — it has yet to win a global title such as the World Cup or Olympic Games — but it has produced some of the best individual players in the world, such as five-time FIFA Player of the Year Marta. Brazil has come very close to a world title — the South Americans finished in third place at the 1999 World Cup and was the runner-up at the 2007 World Cup. There was further heartbreak to come for Brazil, the loser in both the 2004 and 2008 Olympic Games finals. Without a strong domestic league, Brazil remains dependent on brilliant talent coming through and usually moving on to leagues overseas.

The team played its first international in 1985. Notable players past and present include Marta, Cristiane, Formiga, and Sissi.

Great Players

The women's game may not get the same media exposure as the men's, but that doesn't mean it's short of stars. In the following sections I look at just a few.

Lily Parr (England)

Alfred Franklin, the coach of the famous Dick, Kerr's Ladies team, discovered Lilian Parr in 1920. Fourteen-year-old Parr was playing for local rivals St. Helens as a dynamic forward. Parr was an instant success, scoring 43 goals in her first season with Dick, Kerr's Ladies. One newspaper of the time reported that there was "probably no greater football prodigy in the country" than Parr.

In a lengthy career spanning 31 years she scored over 900 goals for Dick, Kerr's Ladies and Preston Ladies. Despite smoking vast quantities of Woodbine cigarettes, she was hard-running and powerful, her shot the stuff of legend. Before an exhibition game in the early 1920s a male professional goalkeeper challenged Parr to take some penalties against him. Minutes later he was found rolling around on the floor, having got in the way of one particularly strong wallop. "Get me to the hospital as soon as you can," the keeper wailed. "She's broken my arm!"

Parr was women's soccer's first star name, arguably the sport's only one until the game really took off in the late 1980s and 1990s. Parr died in 1978, but she was posthumously rewarded for her achievements by becoming the first woman to be inducted into the Hall of Fame at the National Football Museum in England.

Kristine Lilly (United States)

Kristine Lilly holds the world record for the number of international appearances in both women's and men's soccer. She played in 352 games for the United States, scoring over 130 goals. Lilly made her debut as a 16-year-old midfielder in 1987, and within four years was part of the United States team that lifted the first-ever Women's World Cup.

She also played in the United States' 1999 World Cup winning team, and was one of the heroes in the final against China, making a goal line clearance in extra time to avoid almost certain defeat. Lilly also featured in the United States' Olympic gold-winning teams of 1996 and 2004. She retired in 2007.

Mia Hamm (United States)

The bandy-legged Brazilian legend Garrincha isn't the only World Cup winning soccer player to have overcome childhood disability. As a toddler Mia Hamm (shown in Figure 14-2) had to wear corrective shoes in order to treat a club foot. The condition was rectified, and Hamm went on to become a trailblazer in women's soccer.

Over a 17-year career with the United States national team she won two World Cups (1991 and 1999) and two Olympic gold medals (1996 and 2004), and was named the first-ever FIFA Women's World Player of the Year in 2001, an award she held onto the following year. Hamm retired in 2004 having scored a frankly preposterous 158 goals in 275 games, more than any player — male or female — in the history of the game to that point.

Hamm was one of only two women to be named in Pelé's FIFA 100 selection, a list collated for FIFA's centenary in 2004 of the 125 greatest-living players in the game.

Time & Life Pictures/Getty Images

Michelle Akers (United States)

Along with her former United States team mate Mia Hamm, Michelle Akers is one of only two women to be named in the FIFA 100, a greatest-living-players' list that celebrated the world governing body's centenary in 2004. It was no surprise she was selected: In 153 appearances for her national team between 1985 and 2000, Akers scored a remarkable 105 goals.

Her high point was the 1991 World Cup, when she topped the tournament scoring charts with ten goals. Five of them came in one incredible quarter-final game against Taiwan, and she also scored both goals in the United States' 2-1 victory over Norway in the final. Akers was also a member of the 1999 World Championship winning team.

Sun Wen (China)

A powerful striker, Sun Wen (shown in Figure 14-3) was the top scorer at the 1999 World Cup but was denied a world title when China lost to the United States on penalties in the final. She did, however, gain some personal reward: She became the first-ever woman to be nominated for the Asian Football

Confederation player of the year award and was the first player to be picked in the inaugural draft for the first professional women's league in the United States.

Sun Wen was voted FIFA Women's Player of the Century in 2002, an award she shared with the United States forward Michelle Akers.

Figure 14-3:
Chinese striker Sun Wen.

Getty Images

Birgit Prinz (Germany)

Birgit Prinz was a star of the Germany team that triumphed in the 2003 and 2007 World Cups. A prolific goalscorer, she holds the record for the most goals scored in World Cup history with 14. Prinz scored a remarkable total of 128 goals in 214 games for her country. Prinz also achieved amazing success at club level, leading her Frankfurt team to a league, cup, and European treble in 2008.

In 2003, Italian men's team Perugia offered Prinz a contract, which would have made her the first female player in Serie A. She politely declined the offer.

Gearing Up

According to FIFA's Laws of the Game (check out Chapter 4 for more on these), women soccer players must play in the same uniform as men: jerseys, shorts, socks, and cleats. Predictably, however, women have occasionally attempted to tinker with this basic setup.

In September 2008, a Dutch women's team called FC de Rakt attracted worldwide publicity when the team's players replaced their shorts with skirts. This was initially thought to be against the rules, but as the players also wore pants underneath their skirts FIFA decided they were technically in compliance. The move didn't do much for the advancement of women's soccer as a sport — they were also wearing tighter jerseys — though it did benefit their website, with hits going through the roof.

Staggeringly, the man in charge of world soccer, FIFA president Sepp Blatter, has also mooted such ideas. In 2004 Blatter announced that women should "play in more feminine clothes" to increase the popularity of the game. "They could, for example, have tighter shorts," Blatter wondered aloud.

Blatter's unreconstructed views drew widespread criticism. "As footballers we have to think practically," responded Norway's Lise Klaveness. "If the crowd only wants to come and watch models then they should go and buy a copy of *Playboy*."

Kelly Smith (England)

Kelly Smith is widely considered to be the greatest player England has ever had — since the FA ban was lifted in 1971 and the sport entered the modern era, anyway. A skillful, ball-playing striker, Smith has been the star woman in the all-conquering Arsenal team, with a record of more than one goal per game for the club. Smith really came to national prominence during England's run to the quarter-finals of the 2007 World Cup, during which she scored four goals. She's widely remembered for celebrating one goal by taking off her shoe and kissing it. Her feats earned her a lucrative transfer to the now-defunct Women's Professional Soccer league, playing there for the Boston Breakers between 2009 and 2011. This was Smith's second stint in the United States because she was previously the first English player to feature in the first American pro women's league, the also-now-defunct Women's Soccer Association.

Marta (Brazil)

Many consider Marta Vieira da Silva (just Marta for short) to be the most skillful player in the world at present, one of the main reasons the Brazilian team — previously unheralded in the women's game — has become a major force in recent years. She was the top scorer at the 2007 World Cup, leading her team to the final, though Brazil lost to Germany. Marta nevertheless picked up the award for player of the tournament. She has also been honored by having her footprint pressed in cement at the Maracanã stadium in Rio de Janeiro, the first woman to make the hall of fame at the great stadium.

In her Brazilian hometown of Dois Riachos, Marta wasn't allowed to play soccer as a small child because she was a girl. She kept practicing anyway, and moved to Sweden when she was 17 to pursue her dream of becoming a professional soccer player.

Part IV
The Fans' Enclosure: Following the Game

"No, nothing's wrong. They just like us to be here when the Chicago Fire is playing the Dallas Burn."

In this part . . .

This part is where to come if you want to get seriously into becoming a soccer fan. Here I tell you everything you need to know in order to get yourself to a game and make the most of the experience. I also cover the media outlets which can improve your knowledge of the game, and how to get the most enjoyment out of watching it being played on television.

I also tell you about the best sources of soccer information across a range of media such as radio, newspapers, magazines, books, and websites, and I delve into the many different soccer-related pastimes you can take part in, from joining a supporter group to playing video games.

Chapter 15

Going to the Game

The sights, the sounds, the smell . . . there's nothing quite like going to a big soccer game. Although it's exciting to watch soccer on television — and watching on TV is how the vast majority of fans are first exposed to the beautiful game — attending a game in the flesh makes you feel truly involved in a way you can never be while sitting in front of a screen.

Preparing for the Game

If you're lucky, you live near a team that plays in the highest tier of American soccer — Major League Soccer (MLS) — where you find the best level of professional league play in the country. But even if there isn't an MLS team near you, there may be clubs nearby that play in lower level professional leagues such as the North American Soccer League (NASL) or the United Soccer Leagues (USL). There may also be occasional exhibition games held between clubs and countries from overseas. No matter which game you want to attend, the first thing you need to get is a ticket if you want to see a game.

Season tickets

The best way to make sure you can attend every game is to purchase a season ticket. These guarantee you the same seat in the stadium for every home league game in a season, and often come with additional benefits such as a ticket to an exhibition game against a big team visiting from overseas.

You also save money if you intend to go to games regularly — season tickets usually work out to a considerable discount on the price of admission compared to buying tickets for single games. The difference is you have to outlay more money up front, though payment plans are sometimes offered — ask your local team.

Season ticket holders often have extra rights, such as first option on purchasing tickets for postseason playoff games or major exhibition games — which are in limited supply — and the ability to purchase additional tickets for home games.

Keep an eye out for the dates that tickets are released for sale exclusively to season ticket holders. If there are still any tickets remaining, they go on general sale. Dates are announced on club websites and social media outlets like Twitter and Facebook, and can also be found by calling the ticket office.

Choosing where to sit

Whether you're buying a season ticket or a single ticket, you may be given several options for where to sit. As a general rule, the nearer you are to the center circle in one of the stands running the length of the field, the more expensive the seat will be. This is because those positions give you the best view of the field.

However, other factors may influence your decision. Supporter groups often gather behind a goal and create a unique atmosphere — with drums banging and songs going all game — that some fans want to be nearby, or even in the middle of.

Buying a single ticket in advance

If you're not a season ticket holder, you can still buy a single ticket in advance or at the box office on the day of the game — though you only have a choice of seats from the remaining available seats in the stadium (if there are any left).

For the club's biggest games of the year, it's often unlikely that any tickets remain for general sale. You may be luckier with some of the less glamorous matches in the calendar — although at the very biggest clubs, your chances may be slim even then.

Road games

If you want to watch your team away from home, tickets can often be equally hard to come by — perhaps even more so. Home teams usually only give the away support a small allocation of tickets: Stadiums holding 20,000-plus home fans may offer their opponents only a couple of hundred seats.

Arrangements for away games vary radically for each team. In MLS, supporter groups often arrange road travel for fans themselves — providing buses for games within driving distance and making tickets available. Sometimes, you may need to be a member of a supporter group to get tickets. Contact your club's front office and ask what the setup is for your team.

You can, of course, attempt to purchase tickets directly from the team you are visiting, but remember that if you buy a ticket in an area of the stadium surrounded by supporters of the other team, you may not receive a very positive reaction when you openly cheer on the visiting team. And be careful not to end up in the designated cheering section for the home team — you may not be welcomed at all if you wear your team's colors.

Luxury seating

As well as standard seating, many stadiums offer premium entertainment. This usually consists of a seat in an exclusive environment, either a luxury seat in a prime section of the stand, or a seat in an enclosed suite. It may also include dinner in the club restaurant, drinks, and a brief introduction to a club legend, usually a former player.

Remember that there are many people in luxury boxes who are not huge fans of the game, and are there as business guests of a corporate sponsor who has rented the box. The dinner, the drinks, and the chance to chat socially with colleagues may be more important to these attendees. So don't expect the sort of intense atmosphere you get in the stands.

International games

The U.S. national teams have no fixed location for home games, playing in stadiums around the country. You can keep abreast of upcoming games and ticket information via the U.S. Soccer Federation website (http://www.ussoccer.com/). If you purchase an official U.S. Soccer Supporters

Club membership, you receive access to presales for select home and away national team games for both the men's and women's teams, as well as other benefits.

Making Your Way to the Game

Please remember that some of the following advice is relevant only if you are traveling to a game away from home — or if you're paying your first visit to your local team's home stadium.

Obtaining your tickets

First things first: Don't forget your ticket. If you ordered online, you may need to pick up your ticket at a will call window if you selected that option — be sure to get to the game in plenty of time in this case because lines can be long.

If you do forget your ticket, all may not be lost. If you're a season ticket holder, some clubs can reprint your ticket for you at the stadium. Check your season ticket benefits booklet or call your ticket representative to see if this is the case for you, and whether any fee is applied for this service.

Making travel arrangements

If you're headed to one of your club's games on the road, you should make your plans as far in advance as you can. Flights and hotels are usually cheaper the further ahead you book.

If you're making it to a game under your own steam, first check the details of the stadium's location. Sometimes the venues are not even in the city the club calls home. For example, the Philadelphia Union's stadium is actually in Chester, about 15 miles outside of the city. Check the club's website for directions to the stadium — and remember, you may have to drive if the stadium is not easily accessible by public transit. Not all stadiums are as accessible as Arsenal's Emirates Stadium in London (see Figure 15-1), where the nearby subway stop is named after the team — it's called the Arsenal station — and is only a three-minute walk away from the stadium.

Figure 15-1:
A crowd makes its way to a game at Arsenal's stadium in London.

If you are driving, make sure you know the most efficient route, and check on access to the parking lot. Check also to see if there's a fee for parking and if you need to take cash for payment.

Traffic can add another hour to your journey in extreme circumstances, so leave plenty of time. There's no point rushing for kickoff: There have been plenty of tragic accidents involving supporters speeding recklessly to make it in time for the game.

Dressing for the occasion

Sports fans so often forget that they'll be sitting outside exposed to the elements for a lengthy period of time, and fail to take account of the weather. Check the forecast, and dress appropriately. If it's going to be sunny, apply sunscreen; if it looks like rain, take a hat and wear a jacket. (Don't take an umbrella, because these aren't usually allowed into the stadium.)

In the height of summer, be sure to stay hydrated before and during a game, especially if you plan to tailgate for a long time. During heat waves, clubs often let fans bring in unopened bottled water. Check for an announcement on the club's website or social media to see if this is the case on a very hot day.

Taking a look round the city

If you've given yourself plenty of time by arriving early or staying in a hotel the night before, take the opportunity to have a look around the city you're visiting. It's a great opportunity to take in some sights and places of interest. There's plenty of time to have a few drinks with fellow fans after the game.

Checking out the stadium

If you have time, take a wander around the stadium and its immediate environs. Some stadiums have a Hall of Fame with memorabilia from the club's achievements, an interesting statue honoring a club legend, or game day activities; most arenas have an area for families to gather and keep the kids entertained.

Even if the stadium you're visiting seems at face value to be a bit of a ramshackle affair, it's worth having a quick look around: There's not a stadium on the planet that doesn't have some character, a lot of history, and a few redeeming features somewhere.

The club store

It's perhaps not going to be on your checklist if you're visiting a team you don't particularly like, but having a look around the club store to see what is on offer can while away the time before a game. They are, naturally, full of home fans — and can get terribly busy on game days.

If you're a home supporter and live relatively close, it may be better to come to the stadium on a nongame day. The stores are usually open during normal trading hours, but be sure to call first to check.

Although it's nice to have the latest official merchandise, don't feel you need to buy any of it to prove yourself a proper fan. Some of the items on offer can be expensive — and sometimes amazingly overpriced. On the other hand, club stores often stock club-related items that are hard to find elsewhere — from replica jerseys to collectibles and DVDs.

Tailgating

It's an American sports tradition to *tailgate* at the stadium before a game, though it's not possible at every venue — check the parking lot rules before heading out.

If you're allowed to tailgate, pack a cooler with drinks and take a portable grill — and don't forget to bring some food to cook on that grill. You can keep it simple with burgers and hot dogs, or go a bit more adventurous with kabobs . . . and even whole turkeys.

If you're using a charcoal grill, make sure you dispose of your coals in a designated receptacle. Portable gas grills, although more expensive, make tailgating easier because they start up right away.

If you're old enough to have an adult beverage, you have a couple of options before the game. If you're tailgating, you're probably allowed to have an alcoholic drink or two. Check the parking lot regulations before you imbibe, however, because they may not allow glass bottles — or kegs, if you're planning a big party.

If you don't want to bring your own drinks and food or tailgating isn't allowed, you can see if there's a bar or restaurant near the stadium, or even at the stadium, for that matter. If there's nowhere to have a beer or a bite to eat near the stadium, you should be able to find somewhere to stop in the downtown area.

Never, ever drink and drive. If you're drinking before, during, or after the game, make sure someone in your vehicle is a designated driver whose job it is to stay sober and get everyone home safely, or take public transit.

Some stadiums have plenty of parking lot space, and you may find a big tailgate organized by a supporter group you can join. They may have both food and drinks available for a small donation, though you should check whether they allow nonmembers to participate or not. Some tailgates run by home team supporters welcome fans of opposing teams to join them for a bite to eat or a drink, whereas some don't. Be sure to contact the group in advance via their website.

Refreshing yourself inside the stadium

Most stadiums offer a good selection of food and drink inside at the concession stands. Don't expect to eat for cheap, though. Stadium fare can be pricey, as a burger and a beer may set you back over $20 in some places. You can likely find variety, so don't just settle for the first stand you find. Walk around the concourse and see what options are on offer. Plenty of different beverages are also available, from soft drinks to mass-market beers and sometimes, a local craft brew or specialty mix drink. Again, take a walk around to find something that tickles your fancy.

Some of the most modern stadiums even offer delivery service to your seat if you order by smartphone from a designated area.

Getting into the game

Before you eventually make your way to your seat, you have a decision to make: Do you go to it in plenty of time, or just before kickoff? If you enjoy getting into the atmosphere with your fellow fans, you may want to arrive a bit earlier, perhaps joining in some chants for your team in the supporters' section. You may also want to take in the general ambience before the game, watch the teams warm up and then run out from the tunnel for the game — all of which heightens the anticipation.

If you do head in early, the chances are you may find yourself being offered something for free — clubs regularly offer commemorative items to the first X number of fans to enter the gates, such as a bobblehead of a club's past or present star, a scarf, or another collectible item. These are usually sponsored by a corporate partner of the club, so you may find a logo plastered on your giveaway item.

Don't wait too long to get into your seat. There's nothing worse than missing a goal, so make sure you're comfortably in place before the game kicks off.

If you're not familiar with the stadium, make sure you know which gate or entrance is closest to your seat. Few things are more frustrating than finding out you are all around the other side of the stadium with seconds until kickoff. Also, don't assume just because you're close to the entrance that you are able to directly walk there. Depending on stadium geography, there may be something blocking your way, such as a large parking lot or practice field — and you can end up having to circumvent almost the entire stadium to get to your destination.

Kickoff

The moments before kickoff are perhaps the sweetest for a soccer fan: Nothing has yet gone wrong, and everything is possible. As the excitement builds, the teams trot out of the tunnel to cheers.

The stadium announcer reads out the team lineups over the public address system, and the players' pictures and number are usually shown on Jumbotron (those giant TV screens placed high up in the stadium) so you can familiarize yourself with who is who. Often, a piece of energetic music is played over the PA system either as the teams run out, or just before the game begins. A video may also play on the Jumbotron.

Just before kickoff, your team may embark on a final pre-game routine, such as a group huddle. In the seconds before the referee blows his whistle to set the ball rolling, there's suddenly a swell of noise. Feel free to scream and shout as loudly as you want — you're not at a library.

Shouting, screaming, and other matters of general etiquette

Soccer games — like most sporting events — straddle a fine line between family and grown-up entertainment. Although most areas of the stadium are friendly to kids, you should be aware that emotions run high and you will often hear more than one curse word spoken out loud by someone in your vicinity. Fans often like to let loose by making their voice heard about the referee, the opposition, or even the failings of players on their own home team. It's usually all in fun, but expect to hear adult language at times.

If you're not the gregarious shouting, screaming, and singing type, don't feel pressured to join in. Many fans inhabit a world of their own as they quietly — and perhaps nervously — watch the game unfold. There isn't any one way to act at the game; if you want to sit quietly minding your own business, that's exactly what you should do. Let others do the shouting for you.

Supporter groups

If you're the sort who may like to mix with the rowdier fans, then joining a supporter group may be for you. These groups are usually easy to spot at any game, distinguished by loud, organized chants and songs, flags, and banners. They are sometimes called *ultras*, named after the European word for fanatical groups of fans. These groups often create choreographed *tifo* displays to show support for their team — usually large, elaborate, homemade banners.

Joining in with a supporter group's songs means learning the words, but these are usually simple and you can usually find them listed on a club's website or supporter group home page. Most of the songs and chants are family friendly, but that's not the case 100 percent of the time.

If you want to join in with a supporter group's activities, which can include organized tailgates and road trips, most are welcoming to newcomers, and a good way to familiarize yourself with them is through the group's website.

Half-time

At half-time, a variety of entertainment unfolds on the field — kids may play mini-games, mascots may race, or fans may take part in elaborate games. Meanwhile, you have 15 minutes to get something to eat or drink, and visit the bathroom. Be quick, though, because you don't want to miss the second half kickoff.

Full-time

After 90 minutes (plus a little stoppage time), the referee blows his whistle for the last time, and the game ends — unless extra time is needed to break a tie. Some fans head out before the whistle blows in an effort to jump in their cars and beat traffic, but this is often a bad idea; you may miss a goal because you never know what can happen at the end of a game. Many players also circle the stadium thanking the fans, so stick around for that before exiting the stadium, and give them a clap in return.

Chapter 16

Compelling Viewing: Soccer on Screen

*P*eople have been catching soccer on camera ever since the early days of moving pictures: Plenty of grainy, old black-and-white footage is in existence from the early 1900s that shows men in long shorts chasing around after a ball. Cinema newsreels soon featured clips of big games, television got in on the act in the 1930s, movies were made, and videotapes and DVDs released for posterity.

Nowadays soccer onscreen is a multibillion-dollar industry, with something for everyone to watch. It's never been a better time to be an armchair fan, and in this chapter I search out all the places you can find the game on a screen. Settle back, there's a lot on . . .

Watching on Television

Worldwide, soccer has been on screen since the 1930s — but America took a little while to catch up because the game didn't reach the small screen here until the 1960s. The 1966 World Cup final in London made a splash on this side of the Atlantic — shown on tape-delay on NBC, the audience reaction to England's exciting victory over West Germany prompted promoters to put domestic soccer on TV again.

TV's first-ever live game

The very first live soccer game on TV wasn't much of a spectacle. A trial run in London by the British Broadcasting Company (BBC) at Arsenal's Highbury stadium on September 16, 1937, the game was a practice affair between Arsenal's first team and its reserve team!

"Three cameras will be used, one being on the stands to give a comprehensive view of the ground," previewed the *Manchester Guardian* newspaper on the morning of the big event. "Two others near the goalmouth will give close-ups of the play and players. No film will be used, transmission being by radio direct to Alexandra Palace which can actually be seen from the ground."

Even though the BBC showed only 15 minutes of the game live, the experiment was considered so successful that the broadcaster transmitted the first full game the following April — an England versus Scotland international at Wembley Stadium in London.

The North American Soccer League (NASL) featured a game of the week broadcast on CBS when it was launched in 1968. The Soccer Bowl championship game and several others were carried on ABC nationally from 1979 to 1981, bringing the likes of the New York Cosmos prominently into America's living rooms. But with the demise of the NASL in 1984, outdoor soccer disappeared from screens with the exception of a show called "Soccer Made in Germany," a weekly slot on public television that showed a small but curious audience footage from European soccer between 1976 and 1988.

Soccer next made a big splash when the biggest show in world soccer — the World Cup — came to the United States in 1994. All 52 games were broadcast live, with 11 of those on network television. The final between Brazil and Italy attracted almost ten million viewers, a record for a soccer game on television at the time.

It was a record that did not last for very long — just five years later, the growing popularity of soccer was demonstrated by the ratings for the Women's World Cup, held in the United States. The final between the host nation and China was shown live on ABC, with an estimated 40 million Americans tuning in to watch the United States win the title.

In the meantime, outdoor professional soccer began broadcasting regularly again, with the establishment of Major League Soccer (MLS) in 1996. MLS has featured on numerous different networks and cable outlets both nationally and locally, with the final — MLS Cup — currently shown nationally on NBC.

Even though MLS is gaining in popularity, the biggest television audiences for league soccer in the United States aren't for its domestic competition, but for international leagues. Since it began appearing regularly on obscure cable channels in the early 2000s, the English Premier League (EPL) has become very popular. Other European leagues such as Spain's La Liga or Germany's Bundesliga are also shown regularly on cable outlets, whereas the Mexican league is extremely popular on Spanish-language channels.

Network television

You won't find a great number of soccer games on nationally broadcast network television. Soccer remains in a niche on TV compared to the NFL, though a broadcasting agreement signed in 2012 between NBC and MLS means that two regular season games, two playoff games, and two United States national team games are planned for each season on the NBC network.

As international soccer leagues grow in popularity, games from overseas are also beginning to pop up on network television. In early 2012, a game between Arsenal and Manchester United was the first Premier League broadcast to be shown live on a major network (Fox).

Network television loves a ratings winner, though, so when the biggest show in world soccer rolls around — the World Cup — the final and one or two other games are usually shown by the major network that owns the rights to the competition (ABC for the 2014 World Cup; Fox for the 2018 and 2022 World Cups). The same goes for the Women's World Cup.

Don't sleep on soccer broadcasts! International games are often shown at odd hours of the day due to time zone differences. A Premier League game kicking off in England at 1 p.m. means an early rise at 5 a.m. for fans on the West coast of the United States.

Set your DVR!

A little over a decade ago, it was almost impossible to watch live international soccer in the United States on a regular basis. Nowadays, you can find action 24/7 on multiple channels carried by most major satellite and cable carriers. There are four dedicated soccer channels currently available in English — Fox Soccer, Fox Soccer Plus, BeIN Sport USA, and GOL TV.

Each of these channels shows a variety of action from leagues all around the world, from the best known in Europe to the more obscure. They also regularly carry international games and major international tournaments such as the Copa America and the Confederation of North, Central American and Caribbean Association Football (CONCACAF) Gold Cup.

Many games can also be found on general sports' channels that are increasingly showing soccer as part of their regular programming. ESPN broadcasts every game at the 2012 European Championships and shows a Major League

Soccer game almost every week. Local MLS broadcasts are also often found on regional sports channels — check your local listings or the club website of your local MLS team for details.

Websites such as www.livesoccertv.com can be a big help as they list which soccer games are scheduled to be broadcasted across all the channels.

The availability of soccer channels varies by carrier and may be part of premium subscription tiers. Check with your cable or satellite company to see if they offer the channel you want to see.

Essential channels

Being a soccer fan in the United States means keeping up with a sometimes confusing array of channels that show the beautiful game from around the world. The following sections try to cover everything that's currently available, but remember to check your local listings as broadcasting rights frequently change hands.

Fox Soccer and Fox Soccer Plus

Since 1997, Fox Soccer — originally known as Fox Sports World — has shown a wide variety of international soccer and is best known for its focus on the English Premier League. Fox Soccer shows multiple games from the EPL each week, along with roundup highlights shows *Premier League Review* and *Goals on Sunday.* A weekly magazine show, *Premier League World,* and a preview show, *Premier League Preview Show,* add to the comprehensive EPL coverage on Fox Soccer. However, Fox Soccer failed to win the rights to show the EPL beyond the 2012–2013 season, so it won't be showing any action after that season.

The channel also shows international action from countries such as Australia and Japan, along with international exhibitions and tournaments, and lower division American soccer from the United Soccer Leagues.

Fox Soccer Plus is a premium channel that shows exclusive games not carried on Fox Soccer, and is only available by paying an additional monthly fee to your satellite or cable carrier.

Much of this action is also available live online, with a subscription to the FOXSoccer2Go service.

ESPN, ESPN2, and WATCHESPN

Since it launched in the 1980s, ESPN has featured patchy coverage of soccer, mostly sticking to its mainstays of football, baseball, and basketball. But in recent years, soccer has become increasingly prominent on the (now multiple channel) ESPN network, especially during major championships.

ESPN and its sister channel ESPN2 showed almost every game of both the last World Cup and European Championship, and feature a weekly game from Major League Soccer throughout the season. Dozens of English Premier League games are also currently shown. Online, ESPN's streaming service — WATCHESPN — shows even more live soccer, especially international action, though you need to have a cable subscription to be able to watch much of the action when it happens.

BeIN Sports USA

A newcomer to American television in 2012, BeIN Sports USA is owned by Al-Jazeera, and the channel made a splash in its first season by snapping up broadcasting rights to major European leagues including Spain's La Liga, Italy's Serie A, and France's Ligue 1. BeIN is also busy buying up rights to other games, such as World Cup qualifiers and England's League Cup. It's not yet carried as widely as Fox Soccer, so check with your local cable or satellite company on availability.

GOL TV

Most soccer channels in the United States are dedicated to either English-speaking or Spanish-speaking fans, but GOL TV is unique with bilingual broadcasts of most games (depending on your carrier, you may be able to switch between languages using the SAP feature on your remote). Unfortunately, after it recently lost the rights to show Spain's La Liga to BeIN Sports, GOL TV does not have a whole lot of soccer to show — its current mainstay leagues are the German Bundesliga, Brazil's Série A, and Argentina's Primera División.

NBC Sports Network

One of the most widely carried of the cable networks listed here, the NBC Sports Network (formerly Versus) is well-known for its coverage of the NHL and Tour de France. In 2012, the network began showing Major League Soccer with a deal to broadcast over 30 live games per year through 2014. The network also shows United States national team games, and its broadcast of the 2012 Women's Olympic gold medal game between the United States and Japan attracted a record audience for the channel of over four million viewers. In late 2012, it was announced that NBC had won the rights to show English Premier League soccer starting with the 2013–2014 season, so expect to find most of those games on the NBC Sports Network channel.

Univision, Telefutura, and Galavision

Spanish-language network Univision and its subsidiary channels Telefutura and Galavision are the homes for a large amount of action from Mexico's Liga MX, attracting sizeable audiences among the fast-growing Mexican-American population in the United States. The league's mainstay is the top Mexican league, currently known as Liga MX. One MLS game a week is broadcast on Galavision, and exhibition tournaments such as the World Football Challenge are also screened on these networks.

Live Streaming

Many television channels now also offer live streaming of games, but be aware that there are often restrictions on who can access these broadcasts. You may have to authenticate yourself as a subscriber with a cable carrier showing the channel, or purchase a separate online streaming subscription. MLS offers an annual subscription package for online access to most games for a reasonable price, but note that games from the home team in your market may be blacked out due to agreements with television broadcasters. Territory rights are a thorny issue — if you're overseas, you may not be able to access streams from back home because broadcasters from other countries may hold exclusive rights to screen games.

The Internet also offers options that are legally dubious to say the least: live streaming through third-party sites. Judicious searches on Google can unearth feeds, not that I'd recommend them. As well as technically breaking the law, they're usually of extremely poor quality and the action often seizes up at inopportune moments. Even when the feeds work they usually fall at least a couple of minutes behind real time.

Recent action

Many video-sharing sites such as YouTube feature up-to-the-minute action or crucial clips from recent games. You can also find clips on many official websites — extensive highlights of MLS games are usually available almost immediately following games at www.MLSSoccer.com.

You can always find clips of goals of the day from all leagues somewhere on the Internet. Clips of particularly good goals, vicious fights, or outrageous fouls often become widely disseminated online.

Classic clips

Video-sharing sites can be a treasure-trove of classic soccer action, with fans worldwide posting snippets from their favorite videotapes and DVDs on the Internet. Unfortunately, much of the content posted has technically violated someone's rights somewhere down the line, yet thousands of hours of classic action have been left up on sites with no one taking action.

It's worth searching around because hours of old games, clips of famous players from the past, and long-forgotten shows are now floating around somewhere in the ether. YouTube is a good place to start.

Listening to Audio

Technically not onscreen, of course, but while I'm discussing broadcasting it's only right that I should touch upon one of the oldest — and still one of the best — ways to keep up with the very latest soccer talk.

You're not likely to have a lot of luck finding coverage of soccer on your local AM and FM radio stations in the English language, with the occasional local exceptions. However, thanks to the Internet, you can easily find enough audio to tune into via your computer, tablet, or smartphone to keep you listening around the clock.

Live audiocasts

Because the medium lacks a visual aspect, announcers with only audio to work with are more descriptive and voluble than their TV counterparts.

English-language audiocasts are found rarely on broadcast radio, but are sometimes offered by MLS clubs online, especially if a video stream of a game isn't available. Spanish-language audio broadcasts are much more common on major Spanish radio stations.

Via satellite radio and the Internet, it's also possible to tune into commentaries from games overseas, especially those from England. Sirius/XM satellite radio offers live audio of English Premier League games, and online, UK-based TalkSport covers every game. You won't often have much luck trying to tune-in directly to English broadcasts from other UK-based websites such as the BBC, though — these are usually blocked from transmission overseas due to rights restrictions.

Podcasts

You can download or stream hundreds of soccer shows — mainly reviews, magazine shows, and call-ins — as podcasts from websites or by subscribing on iTunes or other online audio services such as Stitcher Radio. These range from professional offerings by official entities such as clubs, leagues, and governing bodies, to sometimes idiosyncratic productions by individuals. Major newspaper websites from the UK such as the *Guardian* and *The Times* also offer excellent weekly or biweekly podcasts, as do numerous specialist blogs.

Focusing on Soccer Films

On the whole, soccer has been badly served by the silver screen. Nobody seems to know exactly why sports such as baseball, golf, and even dodgeball have cinematic classics to their name, but soccer doesn't have a single flick worthy of legendary status.

The reasons for this have long been debated. The main argument is that soccer generates such unbelievable dramatic tension in real life, it simply doesn't translate when reenacted in a work of fiction.

There have been some good efforts, though some of the very best are only about the sport in the loosest sense.

Victory

Set during World War II and released in 1981, this is the most famous soccer movie of all time; it's known in the United States as *Victory* and elsewhere as *Escape to Victory*. Michael Caine and Sylvester Stallone star in a prisoner of war caper which sees an Allied soccer team take on a team made up of Nazis in a propaganda game, with the Allies' ultimate intent to escape from imprisonment. There's a star-studded cast of soccer extras from players including Pelé, Bobby Moore, Ossie Ardiles, and, er, former Ipswich man Russell Osman. A schmaltzy tale, but good fun.

The plot of *Victory* isn't as ridiculous as it may seem. It's loosely based on games between Russian POWs and Nazi soldiers in 1942. The POWs, formerly professionals with FC Start, repeatedly thrashed the German teams despite being warned of severe repercussions should they win. Unlike the film, there was no Hollywood ending: Several members of the Russian team were eventually tortured for their insolence and then shot.

Zidane: A 21st-Century Portrait

Simple and atmospheric, *Zidane* tracks — guess who? — Zinedine Zidane as the Real Madrid midfielder plays in a league game against Villarreal in 2005. Seventeen cameras track his movements on the field, which are shown in real time. Scottish art-rockers Mogwai provide the soundtrack for the film.

Toward the end of the game, Zidane is involved in a brawl and sent off, a serendipitous climax to the film.

The Damned United

David Peace's superb novel *The Damned Utd* fictionalized the story of Brian Clough's doomed 44-day reign as coach of Leeds United in 1974. This 2009 movie, *The Dammed United,* starring Michael Sheen as Clough, isn't quite as hard-hitting as the book — it's at times an almost comedic take on events — but it's still an evocative snapshot of life in 1970s England: preposterously muddy playing fields, cigarette smoke, brown wallpaper, and all. Oh, and Sheen's impersonation of Clough is *priceless.*

Green Street Hooligans

Movies based on *hooliganism* (disruptive or unlawful behavior such as rioting, bullying, and vandalism) in England are popular, though most have an unfortunate — some would say unpleasant — tendency to glamorize fighting between rival gangs known as *firms. Green Street Hooligans* attempts to offer an outside perspective on the violence with the main protagonist Matt Buckner, an American Harvard dropout played by doe-eyed Elijah Wood (of *Lord of the Rings* fame). In slightly unbelievable fashion, Buckner ends up joining up with West Ham United hooligans, and becomes caught up in some very graphic violence. The movie treads a fine line between trying to show the consequences of said violence while also reveling in it to some degree.

Pelada

Soccer is the most popular sport in the world — not just at the professional level, but as a recreational pursuit. In this documentary, two Americans who loved the game but did not make it as professionals themselves decide to trek around the world and find out how pickup soccer is played in places as diverse as France, Brazil, and Iran. The result is a well-told tale of how soccer is weaved into ordinary life in so many different ways — from prison games to Iranian women finding places to play under a disapproving regime.

Gregory's Girl

A gentle romantic school comedy, *Gregory's Girl* tells the story of a goal-keeper in a terrible school team who falls in love with the team's new striker and star player — a blonde girl named Dorothy. Considered one of the best British movies of the past 30 years — it was released in 1981 — it admittedly has a tenuous link with the sport, but the film did earn the actor who played Gregory, John Gordon Sinclair, the chance to sing the lead on the 1982 Scotland World Cup team's top-ten single, "We Have a Dream."

Looking for Eric

Looking for Eric, a 2009 movie by the British director Ken Loach, is the only feature film to star a former world-class professional soccer player in one of the lead roles. The former Manchester United and France striker Eric Cantona plays himself, offering philosophical advice to a troubled mailman. Cantona also had a cameo role in the 1998 movie *Elizabeth* alongside Cate Blanchett.

Cantona isn't the only player to cross over into acting. The former Rangers striker Ally McCoist starred alongside Robert Duvall in the 2001 flick *A Shot at Glory,* and Graeme Souness, then playing for Liverpool, took a cameo role in the acclaimed 1980s British BBC drama *Boys from the Black Stuff.* Midfield enforcer Vinnie Jones, too, has become as well-known for his portrayals of hard men off the field as for his role as one on it.

Bend It Like Beckham

There isn't a whole lot of David Beckham in this 2002 comedy — he does have a very brief cameo role — but there's an enjoyable story of two young female soccer players from London trying to make their way in pro soccer. The story revolves around the difficulties faced in achieving this by the central character, Jess, whose Sikh family is disapproving of her ambitions. But she is encouraged by her friend Jules, played by Keira Knightley, and the quick pace of the story is engaging, if not incredibly insightful.

Discovering DVDs

You can find plenty of action and documentaries on DVD, though the quality varies wildly. Try to look for reviews or rely on friends' recommendations before buying a new release — an awful lot of poor-quality productions are kicked out every year just to make a buck.

General history

If you have plenty of time to brief yourself on the entire history of soccer, the seven-disc series *History of Soccer: The Beautiful Game* is well worth digging into. Narrated by Terence Stamp, it tells the global story with plenty of highlights and interviews with key figures. A more idiosyncratic and shorter intro to soccer on DVD is John Cleese's *The Art of Soccer,* with the former Monty Python star covering the basics in typically amusing style.

Reviews

There are few greater pleasures following a successful season by your club than settling down and enjoying a recap of it all. Season reviews usually show all the goals and other key highlights, with production quality depending on the team budget. The bigger clubs may offer reviews just for specific tournaments, with extensive highlights and interviews — Barcelona, for example, regularly does this for their Champions League runs.

Club histories

Most clubs around the world have released an *official history* at some point over the last few seasons. They're usually pretty comprehensive DVDs, detailing the club's progress from its earliest days and using as much old footage as exists. Most discs are inevitably skewed toward more recent times, where more television footage is available, but nevertheless the discs are usually scrupulously compiled and produced with knowledgeable fans in mind.

These histories are less common in Major League Soccer because none of the clubs are old enough to be out of their teens yet.

Country histories

Just as clubs release histories, so too do countries. England, for example, boasts many different DVDs: an overall history, great goals, great players, and great games. The 1966 World Cup final is a big seller, and worth watching in its entirety to see how different soccer was back then and to appreciate what a sudden shock West Germany's last-minute equalizer would have been at the time.

As ever, the Brazilians are the big draw here, with a superb DVD called *The Boys from Brazil* charting the team's history. A BBC production, it's been out for the best part of two decades — it was first released on video — and only goes up to 1986, but it's a real bargain if you can find a copy to purchase online. The soccer is *fantastic.*

Player histories

These are often a mixed bag, with quality varying wildly. DVDs about a specific player often disappoint, with too much emphasis placed on interviews and clips of the player going about his everyday business, in lieu of proper action. Choose wisely.

It's by no means a guarantee of quality, but a general rule of thumb is this: The longer a player has been retired, the better the player history. Put another way, if the player is 23 years old, the chances of an hour-long DVD being captivating all the way through are very slim indeed, no matter how many trophies they've already won.

Tournament histories

Most major tournaments now have superb retrospectives on DVD, including the World Cup, the European Championship, the MLS Cup, and the Champions League. Each disc has every goal from the tournament, plus extended highlights of major games and incidents.

In addition to all-the-goals-in-the-tournament retrospectives, each World Cup has an official FIFA film — the 1966 film, *Goal!*, is widely considered to be one of the most evocative of its time — but nearly all of them are currently unavailable.

Chapter 17

Reading All About It

. . . .

. . . .

*P*ut all the other sports in the world together, and still they wouldn't have as many words written about them as soccer. From up-to-the-minute websites containing the latest breaking news to huge tomes full of statistics of every game played by every team under the sun since the late 1800s, everything is covered somewhere online. You just have to know where to look . . .

Following the News

The back pages of American newspapers rarely take notice of the beautiful game. Football, baseball, and basketball dominate the column inches. Still, as long as you have Internet access, have no fear — there is more soccer news to read about than you have time in a day for, both domestically and internationally.

What to find in press coverage

There are many angles to the coverage of world soccer. In countries where soccer is the number one sport, salacious gossip is as prevalent as serious analysis. In the United States, most media outlets offer straight coverage of local and national soccer. Here's what you can expect to find.

Game reports

This is a description of how the game unfolded. Game reports are usually — whatever fans believe — written from as neutral a perspective as possible. They describe all the major incidents, offer mild opinion on them — whether a referee's decision was justified or not, for example — and add some post-game reaction from players and coaches.

Reports in the local press are usually weighted with the local favorites in mind.

Latest news

This is a selection of the latest stories from the world of soccer. In lieu of big stories — such as a coach getting fired, a player being banned for bad behavior, or a war of words between two stars, coaches, or club officials — these concern player injuries, upcoming team selection decisions, and choice quotes made by players and coaching staff.

The rumor mill

One of the biggest drivers of eyeballs on stories is gossip about player moves from club to club. Every day the news links different clubs with high-profile (and not so high-profile) players. A lot of the gossip is genuine, even if the moves don't always end up happening. However, sometimes the gossip is clearly fabricated in order to generate some excitement and clicks on a website.

Fans are aware of the idiosyncratic nature of this gossip and take it all with a pinch of salt. Most consider weighing up the chances of a story being true or not to be one of the simple pleasures of soccer fandom, though the sheer volume of stories can become tiresome.

Opinion pieces

Every major website has at least a couple of big-name columnists whose job it is to opine about the latest action and news. Often these columnists simply look for a controversial angle on events — but right or wrong, most fans agree that columns are rarely boring.

Often columnists generate controversy for its own sake, spinning a quote into a controversial top line or dragging out an incident from a game — perhaps a bad foul or a dive — for as long as possible. Keep this in mind because although there'll be thousands of news stories and opinion pieces over the season, people will probably only remember one or two for much longer than a week.

Breaking news

Sports news is now a 24-hour business and all the top sites offer the latest breaking news on rolling tickers. Some sites are faster than others to put up fully written-up stories — both ESPN and the BBC use their extensive networks to break big news quickly. Official club sites are also increasingly quick on the draw to release news that you can actually (usually) take as gospel.

Live scores and minute-by-minute reports

Most major news and sport sites offer a live score service. Some sites, such as www.MLSSoccer.com, provide up-to-the-minute details of latest scores, scorers, red and yellow cards, injuries, and attendances from Major League Soccer (MLS). One of the newest and most popular methods of following games online is the live minute-by-minute text report. These are running text commentaries that describe events as they unfold, adding some color and description to bare statistical analysis. These reports often editorialize, adding comment, opinion, or humor to the basic description of events.

Breaking opinion

In the old days, considered opinion on noteworthy sporting events often didn't appear in newspapers until a couple of days after the events had occurred. Nowadays, the turnaround is much quicker, with discussion points often identified within minutes of the final whistle and brief opinion pieces published not long after. These are usually put up as blogs, with readers invited to respond and generate debate in the comments.

The mainstream media online

The major Internet sports websites in the United States — indeed around the world — are run by major media companies, mainly television broadcasters and newspaper companies.

In the U.S. the sports market leader is ESPN FC, whose soccer coverage offers an up-to-the-minute breaking news service, live scores, and news and columnists on soccer around the world. This coverage is centered on www.ESPNFC.com, with a mobile app also available.

Several other major outlets also have sites with up-to-date news and opinion, including Sports Illustrated, Fox Soccer, and NBC Sports. *The Guardian,* though a British newspaper, has a dedicated North American outlet with regular roundups and minute-by-minute reports on MLS and other big American soccer games. *The New York Times* has a dedicated soccer blog, *Goal,* covering domestic and international soccer extensively, and the *Washington Post*'s soccer reporter, Steven Goff, provides excellent coverage on his Soccer Insider page.

If you're interested in European soccer, British newspapers offer comprehensive coverage that you can access. The *Guardian*'s site (www.guardian.co.uk) has become the biggest and most successful in recent years, though the *Daily Telegraph* (www.telegraph.co.uk) and the *Independent* (www.independent.co.uk) all now offer similar services. Outside the U.K., there are plenty of websites to dig into in just about any country you can name, but obviously you need foreign languages skills to follow the game closely in most countries where English isn't the first language.

Blogs and other websites

Although the mainstream media covers top-level soccer in depth, it doesn't touch upon every aspect of the game. But thanks to the Internet, experts in specific fields are able to maintain sites and blogs on subjects widely ignored by the usual media outlets. A few of the best independent sites are In Bed With Maradona (www.inbedwithmaradona.com), covering world soccer; American Soccer Now (www.americansoccernow.com), offering news and features on the United States national teams; and Zonal Marking (www.zonalmarking.net), which provides a ton of analysis on tactics.

You can also find an almost endless amount of new material about soccer on popular social media websites such as video highlights and interviews on YouTube and streams of visual material (photos and illustrations) on social media sites like Tumblr and Pinterest. Dig in, and you may soon get addicted.

It's worth using search engines to hunt for subjects you're interested in, no matter how niche you think they may be — because chances are someone has set up a site or blog to cover those specialist subjects you love.

Making the Most of Magazines

Soccer hasn't always been well served by magazine publishers, though in recent years this has changed, with the advent of several well-written and thoughtful publications to which you can subscribe from both the United States and the United Kingdom.

Most magazines have some presence on the Internet, posting a taster selection of their articles online, as well as offering additional content such as blogs by their editors and writers.

Soccer America

The longest-running soccer magazine in the United States, *Soccer America* was founded in the 1970s and was for a long time the best way to keep up with the game at all levels nationally. Before the advent of the Internet, *Soccer America*'s print edition was an invaluable source of information. But with the arrival of the Internet, providing timely news via print became less useful, and the majority of *Soccer America*'s content is now delivered via e-mail and the web (www.socceramerica.com). Quarterly special editions are still available via print subscription and on newsstands.

XI Quarterly

I can't write too objectively about this new North American soccer quarterly, as yours truly is one of the founding editors. The aim of *XI Quarterly* is to explore North American soccer in a print edition produced four times a year, each one themed around one particular topic of the game. Long-form essays, illustrations, and photography form the content, with 11 different pieces in each issue. It's available via mail order at www.xiquarterly.com.

The Howler

Like *XI Quarterly,* another quarterly print publication was launched in 2012 — *The Howler,* named after the English word used when a player makes a howling mistake. Glossy, richly illustrated, and elaborately designed, *The Howler* covers both domestic and international soccer in depth. It's available via mail order and in some specialist stores; check www.howlermag.com for details.

The Blizzard

Founded by Jonathan Wilson, *The Blizzard* was launched in 2011 as a groundbreaking alternative to other current soccer periodicals in the English-language — stories are long-form and less dependent on recent news, and the magazine proudly states it has no editorial line. *The Blizzard* is available via mail-order subscription to the United States, and also offers a digital edition on a pay-what-you-like basis at www.theblizzard.co.uk.

FourFourTwo

The biggest monthly soccer magazine in the UK, *FourFourTwo* includes big-name interviews, extended features on the pressing issues of the day, historical pieces about old players and teams, and a world soccer roundup. *FourFourTwo* is editorially mainstream, offering something for every type of fan. It's aimed for the UK market, so don't expect to see more than very occasional coverage of American soccer, and most of the content covers soccer in the British Isles.

Champions

This is the official magazine of the UEFA Champions League. It contains interviews with players and coaches who feature in the current Champions League, plus statistics, photographs, and reports from the competition. However, *Champions* also features a range of historical articles about players and clubs who have made their mark on the European Cup since 1955.

When Saturday Comes

Launched in the mid-1980s, London-based *When Saturday Comes* started off as a non-club-specific fanzine and quickly grew into one of the biggest and best soccer magazines in the UK. Giving a voice to fans of clubs across the United Kingdom — not all of the writers in the mag are professional journalists — *WSC* is the most eclectic magazine out there, offering a mix of politics, humor, and considered opinion. Most of the content is directed at a UK readership, but there are regular columns about soccer around the world as well.

World Soccer

As its name suggests, UK-based *World Soccer* is a digest of the game around the world that has been running since 1950. World Soccer is comprehensive in its coverage and offers plenty of intelligent analysis from top international soccer writers, though much of the information the magazine reports (such as scores and league tables) can now be found more quickly on the Internet.

France Football

This magazine is not easy to get hold of in the United States, and isn't much good to you unless you speak French. However, I mention it because it's without doubt the most famous magazine in world soccer. It's noted as well for its in-depth take on the sport as for the Ballon d'Or, its prestigious annual award to the best player in the world — recently merged with the official FIFA (Fédération Internationale de Football Association, or International Federation of Association Football) World Player of the Year awards.

Hearing the Official View

All clubs, from the very top of the league pyramid to the very bottom, have an official website, and these sites are now the primary sources fans turn to for information from upcoming games and roster updates to news articles and sometimes even live video broadcasts. Leagues such as MLS, and governing bodies such as FIFA and the U.S. Soccer Federation, also spend plenty of time polishing their websites into useful resources.

Club websites

Almost every club in the world, from the smallest up to the likes of Manchester United, now has an official website that serves as the starting point to learn about the team and to stay up-to-date on the latest news. Most club sites offer a mix of news, videos, photos, and a history of the team, along with information on how to get tickets to games and find broadcasts.

Governing body websites

Communication to fans across a country the size of the United States isn't easy, especially when the mainstream media often still treats even the biggest soccer league in the country — Major League Soccer — as an afterthought on news roundups. So as the Internet took off, leagues such as MLS benefitted greatly because fans could check on the latest standings or upcoming games simply with the click of a button, wherever in the country they were.

In the past few years, the advance of web technology and the growing demand for more news has meant that portals such as www.MLSSoccer.com have become ever more extensive. Along with the basics such as statistics, the site offers tons of video highlights from games, live streams of games (for a fee), a variety of podcasts, games such as fantasy soccer, a blog with multiple columnists, and an online store selling every trinket you can want.

Similarly, the U.S. Soccer Federation — which runs the men's and women's national teams — uses www.ussoccer.com to keep fans informed of the latest news and offers an array of video updates and merchandise. The world governing body of soccer, FIFA, offers a stream of news and features at www.fifa.com, and extensive, dedicated sites for the major tournaments it oversees such as the World Cup, including video highlights of games.

MLS is a multilingual league. Though www.MLSSoccer.com defaults to English, there is also a Spanish-language version. And with the recent expansion of MLS to Montreal, there's a French-language podcast, too.

Signing up for e-mail lists can be the best way to ensure you don't miss important announcements.

Social media

Websites generally keep you up to date on a daily basis with the latest news; social media outlets like Twitter and Facebook allow clubs to offer up-to-the-second updates, as well as give you a chance to directly interact with them. Team lineups are often announced first on Twitter, with many clubs also offering streams of updates during games covering the action. On Facebook, official club pages often offer updates, prize contests, and photo galleries.

Twitter also offers a unique way to follow along with club staff, supporter groups, and even players. If you've ever wondered what your favorite striker is having for breakfast, his or her latest tweets may allow you to find out.

There are a lot of fake Twitter accounts out there run by people purporting to be celebrities such as professional soccer players. Look out for a blue tick next to a Twitter account name for official confirmation that a player is who he or she claims to be — it means the player's identity has been verified by Twitter.

Finding the Fans' View

Almost since club soccer began back in the late 1800s in Britain, it was argued that neither professional journalists nor club employees reported on the sport from the viewpoint of the paying spectator. It was a rational argument — writers on club publications were hardly going to bite the hand that feeds, and journalists from newspapers, either regional or local, had to maintain relationships with coaches and players if they wanted continued access and a steady flow of quotes and insider stories.

In the 1980s, though, supporters in England and elsewhere in Europe began to get their act together. Working on the do-it-yourself principles of the self-published fanzines that sprang up in the wake of punk music in the 1970s — when the major music papers were slow to report the new music — supporters began to write their own reports on what was going on at the club. In the 21st century in the United States, that has translated into an ever-exploding number of blogs on the Internet written from the fans' perspective. Take alook back at the inspiration for those sites.

Fanzines

Since the 1980s, fans of hundreds of clubs from the top divisions in England down to the nonleagues have produced fanzines. They vary widely in quality — some are little more than pamphlets and others are professionally produced color magazines — but all are concerned with issues rarely covered by the mainstream media.

Fanzines usually make an effort to avoid being too serious, however, leavening the mix with irreverent humor, jokes, and cartoons that poke fun at both their rivals and often their own club and players too.

Few American clubs have fanzines, though in a few places you may be in luck — Portland Timbers' fans, for example, produce an excellent independent fanzine called *Whipsaw*.

The website of magazine *When Saturday Comes* — which started out as a fanzine in the mid 1980s — has a list of links to fanzines (www.wsc.co.uk).

Fan Blogs

American fan culture is based around the web, where an online presence is cheaper and easier to maintain than in print. The Internet also has the added advantage of being instantly reactive, unlike periodical fanzines.

Almost every club has at least one fan-run blog attached to it that offers features such as game reports, previews, tactical analysis, opinion pieces, and interviews. Some of these are part of larger networks of blogs, such as SB Nation, which covers every team in MLS. Independent fan-run blogs tend to come and go as writers move to new pastures, so look for those run by a team of bloggers instead of a single writer because there's a greater chance for longevity in the blog.

Forums and message boards

Most clubs in the world have at least one online forum that fans can visit and on which they can have their say.

These are often independently run by fan groups, though many are part of the biggest network of message boards in North America, BigSoccer (www.big soccer.com).

Each discussion topic is called a *thread* or *topic.* You can either start one yourself (by clicking a new thread or new topic button, giving it a title, and posting a first entry) or reply to one that's already been started — you should be able to see a list of topics, click the one that interests you, and post a response.

These forums can be quite addictive because fans usually have a lot to say about what's going on at their club at any one time. As you can imagine, passions can sometimes run high; try to keep calm and address other posters as you would if you were talking face to face with a friend.

Some people post entries simply in order to provoke other users and start arguments; they may not even be fans of the club. (Such people are known as *trolls.*) This is sadly part and parcel of the medium, though the folks in charge of managing forum discussions (known as moderators) often ban particularly offensive trolls.

Branching Out into Books

Soccer books are still very much a niche topic in American publishing. Though more books have come out in recent years, there is much more to read about the global game than soccer in North America itself. But there is certainly a huge range of well-written histories of clubs, countries, and players from across the world of soccer well worth dipping into.

The turning point — so the popular theory goes, anyway — was the publication in 1991 of a book called *Fever Pitch* by Nick Hornby (see the "Literature" section below for more on this great book). Treating the sport and its fans with intelligence, it sold by the truckload, proving that books about football needn't be the lowest common denominator.

The following list is by no means definitive — you can choose among hundreds of fantastic soccer books at online outlets like Amazon — but my selection forms the basis of a very decent soccer library.

Most of the following books are still in print; you can easily and cheaply source the few that aren't at Internet secondhand bookstores.

General history

Soccer has a rich history, and you can use the books in this section to round out your knowledge of the game's past — and maybe get a glimpse of the future — as a cultural, social, and economic phenomenon.

The Ball Is Round: A Global History of Soccer (David Goldblatt)

From the birth of modern soccer in nineteenth-century Britain to the game under the auspices of Latin American generals, this is the definitive history of how soccer spread across the globe. This is a huge tome — over 900 pages, with no illustrations. But don't be intimidated by its size and scope: It's a breezy read, its 20 chapters easy to dip in and out of.

Inverting the Pyramid: The History of Football Tactics (Jonathan Wilson)

The is the story of how soccer progressed from disorganized park games, with seven players up front, to the highly strategic games of today. This wonderful book is effectively a brief history of soccer, as well as being superbly insightful into the minds of some of the greatest coaches and tactical thinkers the sport has known.

Soccer against the Enemy (Simon Kuper)

In this 1990s book, Simon Kuper travels to 22 countries to see how soccer is played and viewed across the world. An enlightening and witty book, among many observations Kuper notes that Britain is the only country that produces soccer players willing to continue playing even if they've broken their heads.

How Soccer Explains the World (Franklin Foer)

Almost two decades on from Kuper, journalist Franklin Foer goes on a similar traveling adventure to explain connections between soccer and society in a variety of exotic locales. His book discusses globalization and its connection to the sport's status around the world.

Soccer in Sun and Shadow (Eduardo Galeano)

Soccer is a beautiful game, but it can be hard to show that via the written word. Uruguayan writer Eduardo Galeano's lyrical prose does better at illustrating the game's poetic appeal than anyone else's, drawing short portraits of virtuous players, games, and the culture of soccer from throughout its history. Though written originally in Spanish, little is lost in the English translation.

100 Years of Football: The FIFA Centennial Book (various)

Produced to celebrate the centenary of the world governing body, this is a comprehensive, if fairly straightforward and uncontroversial, history of the game. It is, however, a gorgeous coffee-table tome, with hundreds of glossy color photographs of famous players, events, places, and artifacts. A superb snapshot of a soccer century.

Books about players

There are literally hundreds of autobiographies and biographies of famous players past and present, and these can be variable in quality, particularly if they're written to cash in on temporary fame or notoriety. There are plenty of good ones, however.

Keane: The Autobiography (Roy Keane with Eamon Dunphy)

Former Manchester United star Roy Keane got in a lot of trouble when this book was released because he admitted to deliberately fouling Manchester City rival Alf-Inge Haaland during a tempestuous Manchester derby. But Keane was nothing if not honest, and he also lifted the lid on the infamous row with Republic of Ireland coach Mick McCarthy that saw him sent home from the 2002 World Cup. A real page turner, and a must for Manchester United fans.

Solo: A Memoir of Hope (Hope Solo with Ann Killion)

Perhaps the greatest female goalkeeper of all-time, the United States' star goalkeeper Hope Solo has never been known to be shy about expressing her true feelings, and that trend continues in this memoir published in 2012. Solo refuses to pull her punches whether she's discussing the inner workings (and dysfunctions) of her family life or the national team.

Out of His Skin: The John Barnes Phenomenon (Dave Hill)

The story of how John Barnes signed for Liverpool in 1987 and quickly became the main man in the most attractive team the club had ever fielded. But the book is a social history as well because Barnes was the first-ever black player to become a first-team fixture at Anfield — causing racial tension to rise to the surface on Merseyside.

The Beckham Experiment (Grant Wahl)

David Beckham's arrival in Major League Soccer to play for the LA Galaxy in 2007 was arguably a key moment in the rise of the league's profile — at least from a show-business standpoint. Wahl examines the inside story of

Beckham's arrival in the United States, using excellent access to both those close to the Englishman and the main movers at the Galaxy.

Club-specific books

Although each of the following books is about a specific club, I chose them because they're just as interesting for nonfans — and are in no way as blindly biased as some club-specific books can be!

The Glory Game (Hunter Davies)

During the 1971–1972 season, the writer Hunter Davies was given unprecedented access to the inner workings of a top soccer club. Allowed behind the scenes at Tottenham Hotspur for an entire season, he showed how the coaching staff and players in a professional team interact with each other. Highly revealing.

Barca: A People's Passion (Jimmy Burns)

The story of how Barcelona became one of the most important clubs in the world, and a shining example for Catalan identity and nationalism. Some of the biggest names in soccer have played for the club, from Johan Cruyff to Diego Maradona — though not always successfully.

Once in a Lifetime (Gavin Newsham)

New York in the 1970s was a wild place, but perhaps few things were more unexpected than a soccer team in the city capturing the world's attention. That's exactly what the New York Cosmos achieved, backed by serious funding from the Warner Brothers and most famously bringing Pelé to the Big Apple. Gavin Newsham tells this fantastic story in a compelling way.

Country-specific books

Soccer is a world game, so broaden your horizons by reading up on the sport's development around the globe.

Winning at All Costs — A Scandalous History of Italian Soccer (John Foot)

Few countries have as glamorous — or controversial — a history as Italian soccer does. This comprehensive book tells the story of the style, the success, the teams, the players, the scandals, and the tragedies that have shaped one of the most famous soccer nations in the world. A very easy book to dip in and out of.

Futebol: A Brazilian Way of Life (Alex Bellos)

Soccer in Brazil is totally chaotic, yet this country's team is the most successful in the world. This book charts the history of the nation that gave us Pelé, Garrincha, Zico, Ronaldo, and Kaká, explaining how failure at the 1950 World Cup made every Brazilian determined to reach the pinnacle of the sport.

Soccer in a Football World (David Wangerin)

This book tells the fascinating story of aborted launches in the 1920s; of the failure of world stars Pelé, Cruyff, and Beckenbauer to establish soccer in the 1970s; and of a renewed push in the 1990s with the foundation of Major League Soccer. A must-read for American soccer fans who want to understand that the game's roots here run deeper than most realize, and an entertainingly told story.

All Played Out (Pete Davies)

The writer Pete Davies traveled to the 1990 World Cup, talking to both the England national team and its fans, at a tournament from which nothing was expected. But England reached the semifinals, changing the mood of a nation. Davies captures this perfectly.

Brilliant Orange (David Winner)

What does the unique nature of Dutch architecture — a country stuffed into a tight space — have to do with the brilliance of Dutch soccer since the 1970s? David Winner connects the Netherlands' sporting development to the unique nature of Dutch design, culture, and society in an ambitious but compelling argument.

Offside: Soccer and American Exceptionalism (Andrei S. Markovits and Steven L. Hellerman)

This isn't a light read, but if you want to dig into why the rest of the world became obsessed with soccer in the 20th century while Americans instead followed other major sports, then this work by Markovits and Hellerman offers plenty of solid reasoning to help you understand.

Reference

Facts and figures are part of soccer's lifeblood. You need to be able to reach for a range of authoritative tomes if you're going to get to know the game in detail.

The Story of the World Cup (Brian Glanville)

Brian Glanville is one of the longest-serving soccer writers in the business, and his deep knowledge and recollections of the World Cup informs this narrative account of the biggest tournament in the world. More than just dry statistics, Glanville gives insight into the character of each event and the key men who became stars through the World Cup.

The Soccer Book (David Goldblatt)

Want to know more about the competitions, tactics, and rules of soccer? David Goldblatt provides a superbly illustrated guide to the game for those who want to dig into all the details in some depth. An entertainingly presented reference book covering all the basic details of the world game.

The Encyclopedia of American Soccer History (Roger Allaway, Colin Jose, David Litterer)

American soccer has a far longer and richer history than even fans of the game in the United States realize, and this encyclopedia — by three of the leading historians of the game in North America — provides an immense amount of detail on hundreds of players, coaches, teams, and leagues who toiled to grow the game in America from the 1860s to today.

The Complete Encyclopedia of Soccer (Keir Radnedge)

The entire history of the world's game is referenced in this extensive work by a longtime contributor to _World Soccer,_ Keir Radnedge. From the World Cup and all the major championships to notable players and coaches from throughout the sport's history, this is one of the most comprehensive guides you'll find.

Literature

For a subject which means so much to so many, soccer isn't that well served either by fiction or more literary memoirs. Some gems exist, however, and this section leads you through them.

Fever Pitch (Nick Hornby)

Arguably the most famous book ever written about soccer, _Fever Pitch_ is the autobiographical story of an Arsenal fan's devotion for the game, though it's about much more than the action between the lines. The book is written as a diary, each entry referring to a specific game between the late 1960s and early 1990s and touching on a different aspect of being a supporter. A classic in the genre, it's sold over a million copies.

The Damned Utd (David Peace)

Peace, a novelist who'd previously written several bleak novels about life in 1970s Yorkshire, England, returned to the area to retell the story of Brian Clough's ill-fated 44 days as coach of Leeds United in 1974. A work of fiction based on fact, it caused some controversy — Clough's family denied he used to drink as heavily at the time as he did in the book — but it is a gripping, brilliantly told story.

A Season with Verona (Tim Parks)

Novelist Parks goes around Italy, traveling with fans in support of Hellas Verona. Like *Fever Pitch,* this book shines a light on how soccer fans think and act, though this time as part of a totally different culture. A superb take on what it's like to be a supporter in one of the most passionate soccer countries in the world.

Chapter 18

Finding Other Soccer-Based Pastimes

So you've been to the game, eaten a hot dog, joined in a chant, switched on the TV, bought a bunch of DVDs, played a quick game of Cuju, committed the offside rule to memory, raised a glass to Pelé, Diego Maradona, and Lily Parr, got in shape, joined a team — and practiced the Cruyff Turn, no doubt stepping on the ball accidentally and falling flat on your face.

And yet you've only just scratched the surface. You can get involved with soccer in hundreds, maybe thousands, of other ways. This chapter looks at just a few more ways to spend your time supporting the beautiful game.

Taking Control with Fantasy Soccer

Fantasy sports boomed with the Internet, making it easy to take part and control your own imaginary team based on the performances of real-life players. Baseball has led the way in the United States, but you can now run a fantasy soccer team based on dozens of real soccer leagues around the world from your computer (or even your smartphone).

The rules

The idea behind fantasy soccer games is a simple one. A fantasy head coach — that's you — gets a fantasy budget to spend on 11 players. From a list of current stars — usually a complete list covering all teams from a specific league — the fantasy coach has to compile his team within his set budget.

Points are then accrued after each game, based on what happens to each player in the actual games. Totals are added up and the fantasy coach's team is given a place in an overall league of all entrants.

Most games are offered free of charge.

In addition to entering the main competition, players can enter into *mini-leagues* consisting solely of their friends and work colleagues.

With so many different types of game now available, many add additional rules to the basic setup in order to differentiate them from competitors. For example, the official Major League Soccer (MLS) game allows you to select a team captain among your 11 players — and his score counts double that of anyone else on the team. The following advice covers the basic principles that apply to most games.

How to choose your players

You must choose 11 players. You can't go over your budget, but you don't have to spend it all. You usually have to pick one goalkeeper, four defenders, four midfielders, and two strikers. Sometimes you're allowed different tactical combinations, the most common being an option to select three midfielders and three strikers.

Some games now are roster based, which means you also have to pick a substitutes' bench.

You can make changes — transfers — to your team or roster as the season progresses. Most games limit you to one or two trades per week, and you must stay within your budget.

You won't be able to pack your team with 11 star players — the budget and player list has been worked out so it's impossible to do that.

Most players decide to choose one or maybe two big name players. These eat up a vast proportion of your budget, so it's best to decide on them first and then fill in the other positions. The more big name players you buy, the more cheaper players you need to select to balance your budget. It's a tricky balancing act: Your team selection can take many drafts before you decide who to select.

Scoring points

Details vary considerably among formats — you have to read the scoring rules of any game you play carefully — but on the whole points are scored when players:

- ✔ **Play in a game.** Sometimes points are docked if players are substituted or go off injured.

- ✔ **Score a goal.** Goals scored by defenders are sometimes worth more than goals scored by forwards.

- ✔ **Make an assist.** If a player sets up a goal — the pass leading to the goal — they're rewarded.

- ✔ **Shut out the opposition.** Points are awarded when goalkeepers and defenders keep opponents from scoring. Sometimes goalkeepers win extra points.

Depending on the game, players also pick up points if they save penalties or play a certain proportion of a game (such as 60 minutes or more).

Points are docked from player totals if they:

- ✔ **Concede a goal.** This usually covers only goalkeepers and defenders.

- ✔ **Receive a yellow or red card.** The penalties for a straight red, as opposed to two yellows, may be harsher.

Players may also lose points if they miss penalties or score their own goals.

Collecting Memorabilia

Like most sports, soccer generates an awful lot of memorabilia and ephemera along the way. Keeping mementos from games not only can preserve memories or give you something unique to pass on to future generations, but may also become valuable in the future.

Trading cards

Small cards with a picture of a player on the front and statistics and biographical information on the back have been produced for soccer since the late 19th century in England. Although they are not as popular as baseball trading cards in the United States, you can collect sets of cards for Major League Soccer or from overseas for most of the major leagues around the world.

Stickers

Not unlike trading cards, stickers of players can be traded to complete sets. Unlike trading cards, stickers are collected and stuck into organized album books — a sticker book for a major tournament such as World Cup will have empty spots for the complete rosters of every individual team taking part, and it's your job to buy and trade the right stickers to complete each team. Sticker books are usually inexpensive — a Euro 2012 book made by the company best known for producing soccer stickers, Panini, was sold for just a couple of dollars.

Programs

Game day information is commonly released in a game day program. In Major League Soccer, programs aren't particularly extensive and are usually given away for free. Overseas, programs are often sold for a few dollars and can become valuable over time for their collectible nature — in England, programs from before World War II, for example, fetch at least $50, no matter what team is involved. Extremely rare editions, before or after the war, can be worth thousands of dollars.

One of the most expensive programs is for the game between Manchester United and Wolverhampton Wanderers on Saturday, February 8, 1958. The game was never played because the Munich air disaster occurred two days previously — but although most of the programs, already printed, were pulped, some remain. The program is now worth over $8,000.

Newspapers

It's always worth keeping a scrapbook, or a folder, containing newspaper clippings — even in today's digital age. Although nowadays you can source an old soccer report on the Internet, there's still something special seeing it printed next to the rest of the day's news.

So if your team registers a memorable result — an MLS Cup win or maybe even an everyday league result you always want to remember — it's worth making a wise investment the day after by purchasing a newspaper or two (or three). It may not seem like it now, but in a few years you'll love flicking back through those papers.

Old jerseys

If you have any old replica jerseys lying around and you don't wear them any more, don't throw them out. Wash them, fold them up, and store them somewhere the moths won't get to them — because in 10 or 20 years you'll look back on them with misty eyes.

It's common practice to frame jerseys and hang them on walls. If you do this — especially if the jersey has been signed by a famous player — get sun-resistant glass in the frame so the colors of the jersey don't fade over time.

Autographs

How much an autograph is worth depends not only whose it is — you obviously get more money for 1986 World Cup winning captain Diego Maradona than 2006 DC United midfield stalwart Dema Kovalenko — but also what it's on. A classic jersey is more collectable than a scrap of paper.

However, even combinations of famous players, dead or alive, and classic memorabilia may not fetch as much as you think: A lot of famous players have signed an awful lot of autographs over the years.

The best autographs, anyway, are personal, and have a dedicated message to you. Some things are worth more than money, especially if it's the player you idolized as a child.

Scarves

A lot of soccer fans love wearing a scarf to a game, and the scarf itself — traveling with you through good times and bad — can become a memento of days gone by and something you may want to hang somewhere prominent in your den. Commemorative scarves are often produced for special exhibition games or cup finals — these official or unofficial products may feature the unusual combination of rival teams' colors and badges on the same scarf, a rarity in itself.

Visiting Stadiums

If you can visit a church or a cathedral to admire the architecture, why can't you do the same with a soccer stadium? Many of them around the world either have over a century's worth of history behind them or are shining new monuments to the beautiful game.

Even if a game isn't on the day you're visiting Madrid or Manchester as a tourist, it's worth taking a look around. You can usually find something soccer-related in the immediate environs — a statue, a plaque, a memorial, or even a famous pub or meeting room — and there's a good chance a bigger stadium will offer guided tours or feature a museum full of collectibles worth checking out. And then there's always the gift shop . . .

Playing Video Games

Soccer was badly served on home computers during the 1970s and 1980s because the game was too complex to render on machines with small chips and slow processors. In the early 1990s the advent of comparatively powerful gaming machines like the Sega Genesis and the original PlayStation allowed computer whizzes to develop more advanced soccer games. Soon enough there was an intense video-game rivalry to match anything Real Madrid and Barcelona could manage . . .

FIFA

The biggest selling soccer action game is Electronic Arts' (or EA Sports') FIFA series. It has been released on an (at least) annual basis since 1993 on various platforms.

You can compete on your own — playing against the computer controlling a single player or controlling a whole team, also managing their trades and team selection if you want — or with friends at home (or online against one of millions of people playing worldwide).

Championship Manager and Football Manager

For years the most popular strategic soccer game was Championship Manager. Essentially a more in-depth version of fantasy soccer games,

Championship Manager — first launched in 1993 — allowed you to take over a team and try to lead it to glory over a series of seasons, by acting as the general manager in charge of all the big roster decisions and as coach by running the team's selection and tactics.

In England during the 1990s, the game developed first into a huge cult hit, then a mainstream smash. A notoriously addictive game, managerial "careers" on Championship Manager could cost players hours, days, and sometimes many weeks of their lives. The chance to take a small club up from the lower leagues, wheel and deal, set tactics, keep the chairman and media happy, and win first the league championship, then the European Cup, was too good for many to miss.

However, in 2006 the game's creators split from the production company. Since then the company has retained the name Championship Manager while writing a completely new game. Meanwhile the old game is now marketed under the name Football Manager and is available for your PC, Mac, or as a hand-held game on the iPhone.

On the whole, fans of the original Championship Manager express a preference for the new Football Manager.

Joining Supporters' Groups

You may want to meet up with other fans, either supporters of the same club or those with similar interests. Plenty of organizations exist that you can join.

National groups

There are three main groups that operate across the country, gathering together supporters of the United States national teams. Two of them are independently run by the most fanatical supporters. The original and oldest is Sam's Army, founded in 1994 after the World Cup was held in the United States. This group, named after Uncle Sam, aims to promote enthusiastic fans who will participate in organized support — such as chanting throughout the game — at national team games, wherever they take place.

Though founded much more recently, the other unofficial supporters' group for the United States has now grown much bigger than Sam's Army — they're known as the American Outlaws. Founded in Lincoln, Nebraska, they have local chapters organized all across the country. Members wear distinctive bandanas and aim to be more militant in their support than Sam's Army.

Both groups are open to new members — search the Internet and see if there's a local chapter to watch games with at a local bar. There's also an official fan club run by the U.S. Soccer Federation, with a membership fee of around $50 per year that can help get you priority for national team game tickets.

Local groups

At club level, most teams also boast at least one group of supporters who gather together to lead chants and hit the road to follow their team. This is true both at the highest level of Major League Soccer, and all the way down at the semipro level several tiers below.

The standard for supporter groups in MLS was set by DC United's fans in the early seasons of the league, with the Screaming Eagles and Barra Brava visibly active as they jumped up and down on the sidelines of RFK Stadium, with the flags and chants producing an atmosphere reminiscent of hard-core fans in South America or Europe. All MLS teams, and many in the lower leagues as well, now have supporter groups aiming to create those kind of atmospheres.

Joining a group is usually easy — club websites often list links for the homepages of its best-known supporter group, so check there for information on how to get involved.

Displays of support

The most obvious way supporter groups get behind their team are with organized shows of support. This is done both vocally and visually. Songs and chants are led by groups who work to ensure everyone sings the same words at the same time, sometimes meaning thousands of fans are belting out the words (mostly) in sync together. This can have a powerful effect on the atmosphere in the stadium, with each group hoping to inspire the players on the field to greater effort.

Elaborate visual displays are also created by supporter groups to spell out their passion for the team — often known as *tifo* displays (from the Italian for supporter, *tifosi*), these can be something as simple-looking as everyone in the same section of the stadium holding up the same colored card, or as complicated as a homemade, painted banner measuring hundreds of square feet.

Supporter group memorabilia

Creating big banners isn't cheap, so supporter groups often try to raise funds by creating merchandise for sale. This often features the group's logo on items such as scarves, hats, or pint glasses. The work done by American supporter groups is a volunteer effort, and many groups are officially registered as nonprofits in their state, so you can usually be sure you're supporting a good cause by parting with your hard-earned cash in exchange for some cool swag.

Owning Your Own Club

The ultimate dream of many fans would be not just to support a club, but to own it — or at least a small part of it. Of course, you can go the whole hog and run a soccer club yourself. Naturally, the only way this is usually possible is if you have a spare few zeroes on your bank balance. But in many places, fans can do this without breaking the bank — lots of European clubs, even the biggest like Bayern Munich and Barcelona, are actually owned by the members of their club — the fans.

Such opportunities are much rarer in American sports — the Green Bay Packers are an outlier which is run like this in the NFL — but fan ownership is gathering steam in many places, especially England, and may land in the United States some day.

Part V
The Part of Tens

The 5th Wave   By Rich Tennant

"Let's see — I'll need some children's aspirin for my players and some sedatives for their parents."

In this part . . .

Every *For Dummies* book includes a Part of Tens, chapters that each contain ten or so interesting pieces of information. So who were the greatest players of all time? The best teams? The most absorbing game? Not everyone is going to agree with my choices — that's half the fun of choosing — but one thing I think we can agree on is that the ones I've picked are straight from soccer's top drawer.

Chapter 19

Ten Great Players

Ask a hundred soccer fans to draw up a list of the ten greatest players of all time, and the chances are no two lists will be the same. So I don't expect you to agree with the following list . . . but you'll give me Pelé and Maradona, right?

Pelé

Edson Arantes do Nascimento can't remember how he got his nickname. He certainly didn't like it as a child, getting into fights at school with friends who used it. But Pelé would become the most famous nickname in the history of sport. He was barely out of school before, in 1956 and at 15 years of age, he had joined Santos, one of the biggest clubs in Brazil. A year later he was playing for the national team. And another year had passed when he became the most famous player on the planet at the 1958 World Cup in Sweden.

Brazil had failed to impress in the country's two games of the tournament, so in the Brazilians' third game against the Soviet Union, 24-year-old Garrincha (whose given name is Manuel Francisco dos Santos) and the 17-year-old Pelé were both included in the starting lineup for the first time. In the first minute, Garrincha hit the post. In the second, Pelé did the same. And in the third, the trouble the pair were causing gave Vava room to score. Brazil won, allowing Pelé to take center stage for the rest of the competition. He scored the winner against Wales in the quarter-final, a hat trick (three goals) against France in the semifinal and two goals in a 5-2 win over host nation Sweden in the final. Brazil had won its first World Cup. The youthful Pelé, crying with joy at the final whistle, was the nation's hero.

An instant world star, Pelé and Santos toured the globe, becoming World Club champions in 1962 and 1963. The next two World Cups weren't so successful for Pelé: Brazil won in 1962, but Pelé was injured in the first round, and in 1966 the Portuguese kicked him out of the tournament with some vicious tackling. Pelé announced his retirement from international soccer, saying he "didn't want to end his years as a cripple." But he was persuaded to return at the 1970 World Cup, for his — and soccer's — greatest moment: Pelé scoring in the final as the attacking verve of Brazil put defensive tactics, in the shape of Italy's conservative play, to the sword.

This time Pelé really did retire from the international game. By now commonly regarded as the greatest player who ever lived, Pelé's achievements were outstanding: He scored 1,281 goals in 1,363 games, coined the phrase *the beautiful game,* and even caused warring Nigerian factions to call a two-day ceasefire so everyone in Lagos could watch him play in an exhibition game in 1969. But he wasn't finished yet. In 1975 he joined the New York Cosmos in the North American Soccer League, leading his team to the 1977 Soccer Bowl championship while almost single-handedly establishing soccer as a serious sport in the United States. He retired in 1977, and has since become a roving ambassador for Brazil, the United Nations, and UNICEF.

Diego Maradona

So is Pelé the greatest player to have ever kicked a ball? Or is that man El Diego? The debate is likely to rage on for all time, though one thing is certain: Diego Armando Maradona may or may not be a better player than his Brazilian rival, but he's certainly more of a flawed genius.

Like Pelé, Maradona broke onto the international scene early, playing his first game for Argentina as a 16-year-old. He was expected to make the Argentinian roster for the 1978 World Cup, but was left out by head coach César Luis Menotti. The decision angered Maradona at the time — he refused to speak to his national coach for nearly a year — but he calmed down enough by 1979 to win the World Youth Cup with his country.

The 1982 World Cup was a personal disaster for Maradona: The midfielder lost his temper in a second-round game against Brazil and received a red card for crunching his cleats into the groin of Brazil's Batista. He was transferred from Boca Juniors to Barcelona that summer for a world-record $6 million, though his stay in Spain wasn't a success either and ended with a spectacular brawl in the 1984 cup final against Atlético Bilbao; Maradona was swinging haymakers and executing karate kicks in revenge for having his ankle broken earlier that season by Andoni Goikoetxea: the Butcher of Bilbao.

Maradona's excesses put him in danger of becoming a wasted talent, but now his fortunes changed dramatically. He transferred to Napoli for another world-record fee — this time $10 million — in the summer of 1984, and led the southern Italian club to two Serie A titles plus a UEFA Cup. It was an amazing achievement: Napoli had never won a major title before Maradona's arrival, nor have they won one since his departure.

As if that wasn't achievement enough, Maradona single-handedly led Argentina to victory in the 1986 World Cup, inspiring an otherwise average team with some of the greatest personal displays in the World Cup's history. He scored an amazing complicated goal in the semifinals against Belgium, and set up the winner in the final against West Germany. But it's his performance in the quarter-final with England that defines him: a blatant handball goal punched past goalkeeper Peter Shilton to open the scoring, followed two minutes later by his second of the game, a hypnotic dribble from inside his own half, considered by many to be the best goal of all time.

Maradona led Argentina to a runners-up spot in the 1990 World Cup, but then his career went into sharp, self-inflicted decline. He was sent home from the 1994 World Cup in the United States for failing a drug test. His elite career as a player effectively over, his personal life descended into a blizzard of cocaine, though he eventually kicked the habit. He took over as coach of Argentina in 2008, but his spell in charge ultimately ended up in disappointment, as a talented Argentine team crashed out of the 2010 World Cup to Germany 4-0 at the quarter-final stage.

If Maradona wasn't the greatest player of all time — a title he has a claim to — he is certainly the most controversial of the soccer greats.

Franz Beckenbauer

Der Kaiser, as the swaggering, imperious Franz Beckenbauer was known, was captain of the great Bayern Munich team of the late 1960s and 1970s, but it could all have been so very different. Young Franz was a fan of another Munich team, Munich 1860, and planned to join his favorite club in the early 1960s. However, at a youth tournament he was slapped in the face by an 1860 player, and decided to join rivals Bayern instead. It was a brave decision because Bayern was in the second-tier Regionalliga Süd at the time, but within a year of Beckenbauer's 1964 debut Bayern had been promoted to the Bundesliga and a glorious career began.

Beckenbauer was soon picked for West Germany's national team, and in 1966, as a 20-year-old, he helped his team reach the final of the World Cup, scoring four goals from midfield along the way. England beat the Germans in the final, but four years later Beckenbauer — by now bossing the game from central defense with a peerless arrogance born of his comfort on the ball — had his revenge, his long-range effort inspiring West Germany to come from two goals down in the quarter-final against the English to win 3-2. His luck ran out in the *semifinal,* though, as he was forced to play on with a dislocated shoulder as Italy won a classic, 4-3 in extra time.

The 1974 World Cup was his crowning achievement. Now captain of West Germany, the team struggled initially, losing a politically embarrassing game against East Germany in the group stage. Coach Helmut Schön suffered what amounted to a minor nervous breakdown, forcing Beckenbauer to assume full control of the team. Under Beckenbauer's auspices, West Germany became a team reborn, eventually beating the much-fancied Dutch team of Johan Cruyff in the final.

Meanwhile, Beckenbauer led Bayern to three consecutive European Cup wins between 1974 and 1976, four Bundesliga titles and four German Cups. In the late 1970s and early 1980s he spent four years in the United States with the New York Cosmos, winning a championship alongside Pelé, before coming back to Germany for a last hurrah — and a final Bundesliga title — with Hamburg.

As if that wasn't enough, Beckenbauer became only the second man after Brazil's Mário Zagallo to win the World Cup as player and coach, leading his country to victory in 1990. And never once, in all those years, did he appear to break sweat.

Johan Cruyff

Although Beckenbauer was the most decorated of the great 1970s players, the Dutch legend Johan Cruyff — in his native language, Johannes Cruijff — remains the most celebrated. Dutch soccer in the 1960s and 1970s was famous for Total Football — the idea being that every player on the field could do each other's job, switching around as the game went on — and Cruyff was the concept's icon.

Cruyff was a center-forward by trade, but as a Total Footballer he spent many a game on the left wing, or the right, or deep in midfield — wherever he chose. He broke into the Ajax team as a 17-year-old in 1964; within seven years the team had become the greatest in Europe, winning three consecutive European Cups between 1971 and 1973. After Ajax's third European Cup, Cruyff moved to Barcelona for a world-record $2 million, instantly inspiring a struggling mid-table team to a 5-0 win over the Spanish team's arch rivals

Real Madrid, and leading Barcelona straight up the table and to a first championship title since 1960.

Meanwhile, with the Netherlands Cruyff was setting the 1974 World Cup alight with some majestic displays. The tournament showcased his brazen individuality. A piece of skill down the wing against Sweden — sending the ball back between his legs with his instep and then changing direction in an instant to scamper off — became known as the Cruyff Turn. And while his team mates all wore the trademark three stripes of uniform manufacturer Adidas on their jerseys, Cruyff had a custom-made jersey with only two stripes — because he had a personal deal with Puma!

The Netherlands failed at the last hurdle in the final that year, surprisingly losing to hosts West Germany, but in many eyes the Dutch were the moral victors of the championship. Cruyff refused to play in the 1978 World Cup, then began a new career in the United States with the LA Aztecs and the Washington Diplomats, before heading back home to the Netherlands where he won another couple of titles with Ajax. In a final flourish, after arguing with Ajax over the terms of an improved contract, he joined the Amsterdam club's arch rivals Feyenoord in a fit of pique and won one last title at the age of 37. Few players have been so individually determined as this Dutch master.

Zinedine Zidane

For a while it looked like Zinedine Zidane, despite his rich talent, wasn't going to make it to the very top. The midfield playmaker had already been anointed as the greatest French player of his generation by the time of Euro 96, that summer securing a move from Bordeaux to Italian giants Juventus. But the great tournament people expected him to have didn't materialize. Two Italian titles in the following two years with Juve gave him his first medals of note, but even those achievements were tempered by high-profile failures in the 1997 and 1998 Champions League finals.

But then it all suddenly took off. In the 1998 World Cup finals Zidane went from zero to hero — and how. Against Saudi Arabia he was sent off for stamping on an opponent. Zidane was suspended for two games, and France struggled and nearly went out. They hung on in there, though, and Zidane's return was the catalyst for an upturn in form that culminated in a 3-0 win in the final over Brazil, with Zidane heading home the first two goals. As well as being the star player, Zidane — born to Algerian parents — became the symbol of France's multiethnic team. (The French projected *Merci, Zizou!* onto the Champs Elysées the night of the 1998 win.)

Zidane's career then went stratospheric. He was the star of the tournament at Euro 2000, as France added that trophy to their roll of honor. He then moved to Real Madrid, becoming the world's most expensive soccer player as the Spanish spent almost $100 million to acquire him — and he repaid the club by scoring the greatest-ever goal in a Champions League final: an unstoppable volley against Bayer Leverkusen in 2002.

Zidane had one last hurrah in 2006. Almost single-handedly, the 34-year-old dragged France to the nation's second World Cup final with a series of performances that rolled back the years. After scoring the opener against Italy with the cheekiest of chipped penalties, he was sent off in extra time for headbutting Marco Materazzi in the chest. It was his last act on a soccer field, a bittersweet one that symbolized the yin and yang of his temperament: The most aesthetically beautiful player of the 1990s and 2000s, he was sent off 11 times for violent conduct.

Alfredo di Stéfano

No transfer has been as controversial or changed the course of soccer history as much as the one that brought the Argentinian midfielder Alfredo di Stéfano to Real Madrid in 1954. It was complicated, too, and steeped in political intrigue.

In 1949 di Stéfano was playing for River Plate of Buenos Aires when all professional players in Argentina went on strike. The clubs decided to use amateur players to complete the season, so the talented di Stéfano joined Bogota team Millonarios in a fit of pique. The problem was that the Colombian league was at the time outlawed by the world governing body, FIFA (Fédération Internationale de Football Association, or International Federation of Association Football). So when Real Madrid bought di Stéfano from Millonarios in 1954, FIFA pointed out that the player was still — in their eyes — owned by Boca Juniors. Who had just sold him to . . . you guessed it, Real's arch rivals, Barcelona.

The matter was eventually settled in the Spanish courts. In a decision heavily weighted in Real's favor — the Madrid club's biggest supporter being Spanish dictator General Franco — the court ruled that Barcelona and Real should take turns with di Stéfano each season. Barca flounced off, leaving di Stéfano to move to Madrid, and the player went on to star in all five of Real's winning European Cup finals between 1956 and 1960.

Alfredo di Stéfano was a tireless midfielder who could defend as well as he could attack, and many old-timers (including Manchester United legend Bobby Charlton) would tell you he was better than both Pelé and Maradona. But despite playing for both Argentina and Spain, di Stéfano never featured in the World Cup finals, a fact that counts against him in some eyes to this day.

Ferenc Puskás

When Hungary visited Wembley Stadium in 1953 to play England, one member of the home team pointed to a small, slightly podgy inside-left in a red Hungarian jersey during the warm up. "Look at that little fat chap!" laughed the unidentified English international. "We'll murder this lot!" Ninety minutes later, England had been thrashed 6-3, the nation's first defeat at Wembley by a team from outside Britain. And, of course, the little fat chap — Ferenc Puskás — was the architect of Hungary's triumph, one that would go down in history as one of the most famous games of all time.

Puskás gave that game its defining moment, too, pulling a ball back with the sole of his shoe to send England captain Billy Wright sliding off the field while his tormentor simply changed feet and hammered the ball into the roof of the net from a tight angle. In one of the most famous lines in the history of soccer journalism, London's *Times* newspaper described Wright as "like a fire engine speeding off to the wrong fire."

Hungary had already won the 1952 Olympics, with Puskás the star of a team that would become known as the Magical Magyars. The Hungarians followed up that 6-3 win in England with a 7-1 victory over the same opposition in Budapest, and Puskás' team was a huge favorite to win the 1954 World Cup. But Puskás was injured as Hungary beat West Germany 8-3 in a group game in the first stage of the competition, and his tournament went from bad to worse. First, after Hungary beat Brazil in the quarter-final, an opponent accused the nonplaying Puskás of smashing a bottle over his head during a locker-room brawl between the two teams. Then, returning from injury in the final against the rejuvenated West Germans, he scored the opening goal only to see his team lose 3-2. Even then, the hobbling Puskás had scored an equalizer in the dying seconds only to see the referee rule it out for a very dubious offside.

The Hungarians had been denied the prize the world had thought was theirs for the taking, but Puskás still had personal glory, and his greatest triumphs, to come. He defected from the East after the 1956 Hungarian revolution (at one point he was reported to have been killed in fighting on the streets of Budapest), and after serving a suspension ordered by FIFA for absconding from his former club team Honvéd, eventually signed with Real Madrid. He formed an instant understanding with Alfredo di Stéfano, one which peaked in a famous 7-3 win over Eintracht Frankfurt in the 1960 European Cup final; Puskás scored four times (a feat unequalled to this day). Puskás went on to play for Spain — in those days you could switch countries after a certain period of residency — but he never reached the heights of his Hungarian pomp when he scored an amazing 83 goals in 84 games.

George Best

The greatest British player of all time, George Best was the first player in Europe — and arguably the world — to become a celebrity as well as a soccer star. This would be both the making of him, and his ruination.

Best broke into the Manchester United team at the age of 17 in 1963, and by the time he'd completed his first full season he'd won the league title. In 1966 he scored two goals in a European Cup quarter-final tie with Benfica; the press in Lisbon gave him the nickname El Beatle thanks to his good looks and mop-top hair.

Manchester United couldn't get past the semifinals of the European Cup that season, but won the league again in 1966–1967 and reached the final of the 1968 European Cup. Best proved to be the star of the show, walking in what was effectively the decisive goal in a 4-1 win over Benfica.

Having won the European Cup, many older players at Manchester United felt their job was done. Best, however, was only 22, and he became frustrated and disillusioned as the club drifted. His glitzy personal life didn't help: He began drinking heavily and spending more time in nightclubs with various models and Miss Worlds than on the practice field. On New Year's Day 1974, an overweight Best played his last game for the club at Queens Park Rangers. Newspapers reported that he was "a sad parody" of the player he'd once been. Come the end of the season, Best was turning out for semipro team Dunstable Town. He was still only 27.

Best's later career was a slow decline: an entertaining if directionless stint at Second Division Fulham, followed by spells in the United States with the Tampa Bay Rowdies, Scotland with Hibernian, and back in England with Bournemouth. Best's high living eventually caught up with him, first as he went to jail in 1986 for drunk driving and then tragically in 2005 when, despite a liver transplant, the booze ultimately killed him. Few players wasted their talent like Bestie — but then precious few players have had talent like his to throw away.

Gerd Müller

Without question, the Bayern Munich and West Germany striker Gerd Müller is the least spectacular player on this list of ten, and probably the least technically talented. That, however, matters little — because Müller was almost certainly the most lethal goalscorer in the history of the sport.

To quote the German soccer writer Uli Hesse-Lichtenberger, "Müller scored with his shin, his knee and his backside, and sometimes even with his feet . . . he scored in cup games against lowly opposition and on the world stage marked by the best defenders there were." And sure enough, his record stands up to scrutiny: In 427 league games he scored 365 goals. He scored 62 goals in 68 German Cup games and netted 66 times in 72 club appearances in Europe, and in 62 appearances for the West German national team, he scored an unbelievable 68 times.

"I am not putting that little elephant in among my string of thoroughbreds," the Bayern Munich coach Zlatko ⬚ajkovski said upon first clapping eyes on Müller in 1964, when the club was still in the regional leagues. But he eventually relented and Müller's goals took Bayern first to promotion, then victories in the German Cup and the European Cup Winners' Cup within three seasons. Two more seasons passed and Bayern won their first-ever Bundesliga title. Then in 1974 came the club's first European Cup win.

In 1974, Müller retired from international soccer — at the very top. His final meaningful act in a West German jersey was to twist on the spot and hook home the winning goal in the World Cup final. Müller went on to win two more European Cups with Bayern before enjoying a stint in the United States with the Fort Lauderdale Strikers. Since his retirement in 1982, nobody in men's soccer has scored goals with such intense regularity. But then again, nobody did before Müller started out either.

Mia Hamm

It would seem unlikely that the player who has scored the most international goals in history (male or female) could have been born with a club foot. But with the help of corrective footwear in childhood, Mia Hamm was able to overcome that start to score a record 158 goals in 275 appearances for the United States women's national team.

Hamm's list of honors are almost too long to list in this space. Her team honors include winning the National Collegiate Athletic Association (NCAA) championship four times with University of North Carolina between 1989 and 1992, in the middle of which she won the inaugural Women's World Cup, scoring twice in the competition for the United States aged just 19. She followed that with Olympic Gold on the American team at the 1996 Games in Atlanta; then another Women's World Cup winner's medal on home soil in 1999, again scoring twice in the competition. Hamm won a professional championship with the Washington Freedom in 2003 in the short-lived Women's United Soccer Association (WUSA) and then capped off her career with another gold at the 2004 Olympic Games in Athens — retiring shortly after.

Hamm was more than a winner and a goalscorer, though; she was the signature face of American women's soccer as it broke into the mainstream, a household name in a country that had few soccer heroes. Recognition of her individual achievements came worldwide, too: She was named as the women's FIFA World Player of the Year in both 2001 and 2002 (the first two years the award was given).

Chapter 20

The Ten Greatest Teams of All Time

Throughout history hundreds and hundreds of teams have made their mark on the game. Here are some of the greatest, but when you can only pick ten, some famous ones miss out. So, with a heavy heart, I've no room for some truly great teams. Still, these guys are pretty good . . .

Preston North End (1881–1890)

In Victorian England in 1881, a Preston cotton mill administrator called William Sudell joined the board of a newly founded local soccer team called Preston North End and soon became the team coach. Between them, club and Sudell spent the rest of the decade making headlines and shaping the future of a sport still in its infancy.

His first job was to assemble a team. Most clubs at the time picked their team from amongst the local youth, but Sudell decided that wasn't the best way to go. Noting that Scotland's national team kept giving England's regular beatings — between 1878 and 1882, Scotland recorded 5-1, 6-1 and 7-2 victories against its southern neighbor — he decided to fill his team with Scots. The problem was, how could they be enticed to uproot their lives and head down to Preston? Soccer was still an amateur sport at the time — professionalism was outlawed by the governing body, the Football Association (FA) — so paying them was out of the question. Sudell simply circumvented this problem by giving them spurious *jobs* at his mill.

This decision inadvertently revolutionized the game. In 1884 the Football Association disqualified the team from the FA Cup, accusing Preston of professionalism. Sudell simply shrugged his shoulders and organized a boycott, telling the FA that if professionalism wasn't legalized, Preston and a coalition of powerful Lancashire clubs would form their own soccer association. The FA crumbled, and amateurism was gone forever.

Preston became the most powerful team in England. In 1887–1888, the club won 42 out of 43 games they played, winning one FA Cup tie 26-0 (against Hyde, still an English record). However, Preston failed in the one game that really mattered. At the FA Cup final, Preston requested their team be photographed with the trophy — before the game had started! 'Hadn't you better win it first?' the referee (perhaps apocryphally) replied. West Bromwich Albion won 2-1.

But the season after saw Preston remembered as one of the most famous teams of all time. Thanks to the goalscoring exploits of Fred Dewhurst, Jimmy Ross, and John Goodall — 54 goals between them in 27 games — Preston won the first-ever Football League championship, going the entire season unbeaten. The club also won the FA Cup, a perfect season that earned Preston the nickname The Invincibles.

The glory days didn't last much longer. Preston won the league again the following year, but have yet to win it since. Meanwhile, four years later Sudell was jailed for embezzling $10,000 from his mill owners to fund Preston's team building.

Austria (1931–1934)

Austria wasn't much of a team at the start of the century — its record defeat was an 11-1 thumping at home by England in 1908 — but all that changed in the 1920s when the team was coached by Hugo Meisl, an administrator at the Austrian Football Association. Meisl was a student of the international game, and particularly liked the Scottish passing style (many teams of the era were either focused solely on running with the ball or punting it long).

Scotland had famously trounced England 5-1 in 1928 (they went down in history as The Wembley Wizards) but the Scots were in turn thrashed by Austria, who announced themselves on the world stage with a 5-0 win in

1931. The team was built around the striking skills of Matthias Sindelar —
known as Der Papierene (The Paper Man) — and quickly became the number
one team in the world. Austria's quicksilver all-out attack proved too much
for Germany (5-0 and 6-0), Switzerland (2-0 and 8-1), Italy (2-1 and 4-2), and
Hungary (8-2 and 5-2).

Austria became hot favorites to win the 1934 World Cup, especially as the
team could now also boast the goals of Josef Bican (who in his career scored
at least 805 times in official games, more than any other player in the history
of the sport). But in the semifinal, a thuggish Italian lineup viciously set upon
the Austrians, who lost 1-0 when the referee, said to have been threatened
by the dictator Benito Mussolini, turned a blind eye when goalkeeper Peter
Platzer was bundled illegally into the goal while holding the ball.

Nevertheless, it was Austria, not eventual world champions Italy, who would
be remembered fondly: known forever more as the Wunderteam, a title that
needs no translation.

Torino (1943–1949)

Few clubs, if any, have dominated a domestic scene like the Torino team of
the mid-to-late 1940s did in Italy. Known as Il Grande Torino, Torino won five
Serie A championships between 1943 and 1949, and would surely have won
more had the league not been suspended for two years towards the end of
World War II. During those seasons Torino scored 483 goals, while letting in
only 165.

The team's star player was Torino's captain Valentino Mazzola, a powerful attacking midfielder who once scored 29 goals from midfield in a single
season — but Torino was far from a one-man team. In May 1947, 10 out of the
11 players who made up the Italian national team against Hungary were from
Il Grande Torino — and coach Vittorio Pozzo only left out goalkeeper Eusebio
Castigliano because he thought it would demotivate players all around the
country if Italy was 100 percent Torino.

Il Grande Torino's attacking style meant Italy — at the time the reigning
world champion — was the favorite to win the 1950 World Cup, retaining the
trophy won twice before the war in 1934 and 1938. But tragedy struck. Flying
back from an exhibition game in Portugal on May 4, 1949, the team's plane hit
a basilica standing on a hill in Superga, near Turin, as it came in to land under
heavy fog. The entire team was killed instantly.

Torino was awarded that year's championship — which the club had been on the verge of winning anyway — but didn't win another title until 1976. Italy, meanwhile, somewhat understandably decided to travel to the 1950 World Cup in Brazil by boat, instead of plane. The trip took two weeks and, unable to practice, an unfit team of Italians were knocked out after their very first game.

Hungary (1950–1954)

The countries from Europe's Eastern Bloc had an added advantage in the Olympic Games during the Cold War: Under communism, all the top players were technically amateur, and so unlike Western professionals were eligible to compete in the Games. That, however, doesn't wholly explain Hungary's gold medal win in 1952, because the team — with its crown jewel Ferenc Puskás as a forward alongside the equally prolific Sandor Kocsis — was exceptional, and had already gone two years unbeaten in exhibition games.

Hungary's performance at the 1952 Olympics earned the country an invitation to a prestigious matchup against England, seen as one of the top teams in the world. The game was played in November 1953 and the Hungarians — now three years into an unbeaten run and with deep-lying forward Nándor Hidegkuti now added to the mix — put England to the sword with a 6-3 thrashing at Wembley stadium in London. At a return game in Budapest the following February, the Hungarians humiliated England even further, winning 7-1.

Hungary had earned the status of a heavy favorite for the World Cup in 1954, and won its group games against South Korea and West Germany 9-0 and 8-3. The Hungarians then beat the 1950 runner-up, Brazil, 4-2 in the quarter-finals, before repeating the same score in the semifinals to eliminate reigning champion Uruguay. But Puskás had been injured, and though he played (and scored) in the final against a rejuvenated West Germany, Hungary's now four-year unbeaten run came to a juddering halt in the biggest game of all. The team threw away a 2-0 lead to lose 3-2, although the ref controversially ruled out a last-minute equalizer.

Hungary went on another long unbeaten run of 18 games, until losing again to Turkey in 1956, but the team was beginning to show its age. Then in 1956 came the Hungarian revolution, and with fighting raging on the streets of Budapest many players defected to the west. The team had failed to win the World Cup expected of it, but would be forever known as *Aranycsapat* — Hungarian for The Golden Team.

Real Madrid (1955–1960)

Real Madrid had only won the Spanish league twice when goalscoring midfielder Alfredo di Stéfano and flying winger Francisco Gento signed for the club in 1953. And those two championships were back in the 1930s. But within a year, the pair had helped Madrid win its first title for 21 years, sparking an unprecedented run of success. By the end of the decade Real Madrid was, by a long stretch, the biggest club in the world.

The team retained the Spanish championship in 1955 and entered into the first-ever European Cup. Madrid reached the final and faced Reims of France. Despite falling 2-0 down in ten minutes, Madrid landed the cup, winning 4-3 after a di Stéfano-inspired comeback. Adding Reims' star player Raymond Kopa to the team, Madrid went on to win the next four European Cups as well. Madrid beat Fiorentina in 1957, Milan in 1958, and Reims again in 1959. At that point Kopa returned to France, but by now his creative genius had been eclipsed by an even greater talent.

Ferenc Puskás had defected from Hungary in 1956, receiving a ban from European governing body UEFA at the request of his former club, Honvéd of Budapest. Madrid showed an interest in signing him, and leveraged the club's political influence — supported by Spanish dictator Generalissimo Franco — to persuade UEFA to lift the ban. Puskás joined, and went on to score 240 times in 260 games, a phenomenal record.

The team had one last European Cup left in them — a fantastic victory in the 1960 final, still considered by many to be the greatest of all time. Puskás scored four, di Stéfano three, as Madrid murdered Eintracht Frankfurt 7-3. It was di Stéfano's crowning glory: All in all, he won five European Cups, scoring 49 goals in the process. Puskás scored another hat trick in the 1962 final, though Real Madrid lost 5-3 to Benfica. Madrid didn't win another European Cup until 1966 — when Gento, the only survivor of the great team of the 1950s, picked up his sixth title.

Brazil (1970)

The Brazilian team that won the 1970 World Cup is probably the most famous, and certainly the most revered, international team of all time. Brazil had won the 1958 and 1962 World Cups playing some exciting and attacking soccer, but had literally been kicked out of the 1966 finals in England, crashing out in the first round after some rough treatment by opposing defenders. Pelé was carried off the field against Portugal that year, vowing to retire from international soccer. "I do not want to end my life as a cripple," he announced afterwards. It appeared the new cynical and defensive style of soccer had triumphed over Brazil's carefree approach.

Brazil's cause — a commitment to attack and free-flowing soccer — looked even more lost in 1968, when West Germany, Czechoslovakia, Mexico (twice), and Paraguay all beat the Brazilians. For a country on top of the world a mere six years earlier, five defeats in a calendar year was a catastrophe. But then, first under new coach João Saldanha and then his replacement Mário Zagallo, Brazil threw caution to the wind with the most attack-minded front line of all time — Pelé, Jairzinho, Tostao, Rivelino, and Gerson — and the decision paid rich dividends.

Brazil won every qualifying game for the 1970 World Cup and then matched the feat in the finals themselves, winning all six games. The Brazilians scored 19 goals while doing so, beating reigning world champion England, the dangerous Uruguayans, and the super-defensive Italians in the final.

But despite those 19 goals, it is perhaps two missed chances that the team is best remembered for. Against Czechoslovakia, Pelé was inches away from scoring from inside his own half, while against Uruguay he famously let the ball drift past one side of an advancing goalkeeper while running round his other side then nearly whipping the ball into the empty net from an acute angle. Brazilians have since longed for a team to play a similar brand of carefree soccer, but apart from their 1982 vintage of Zico, Falcão, and Socrates, none have come close.

Netherlands (1974–1978)

The Netherlands very nearly failed to reach the 1974 World Cup finals. Had the referee not erroneously ruled out a perfectly good goal by Belgium for a nonexistent offside in a key qualifying game, the Dutch team that invented Total Football would never have made it to the greatest stage of all. But the gods smiled on the Dutch, and the team amazed the world with a totally new way of playing.

The principle behind Total Football was simple enough: Any of the players on the field, excluding the goalkeeper, could play in any position during the game, moving around as they saw fit. So, for example, if the left back decided to scamper up the wing, the central defender may drop into the vacant position. In turn, the striker may temporarily play in central defense!

But you needed great players to be able to do this — and the Netherlands had them in abundance. The star man was forward Johan Cruyff, who had helped Ajax of Amsterdam win three European Cups in a row between 1971 and 1973. He was ably assisted by goalscoring midfielders Johan Neeskens and Johnny Rep, defensive lynchpin Arie Haan, striker Rob Rensenbrink, and ball-playing defender Ruud Krol.

The Netherlands ripped through the world's best in the 1974 finals, humiliating Argentina 4-0 and beating reigning world champion Brazil. But the Dutch froze in the final against West Germany, despite taking a 1-0 lead right at the start without the West Germans even touching the ball, losing 2-1. Nevertheless, the Dutch are remembered as one of the all-time classic teams.

The Netherlands reached the final again in 1978, despite Cruyff having retired from international soccer. The Dutch were the width of a post away from beating the host nation Argentina and winning the trophy, with Rensenbrink rolling the ball onto the woodwork in the dying seconds of normal time with the score 1-1. The ball bounced clear and Argentina won in extra time.

Milan (1987–1994)

One of Italy's biggest clubs, Milan was at the lowest point in its history during the early 1980s. Implicated in a match-fixing scandal, the club was demoted to Serie B — the Italian second division — for the very first time in its history. If that wasn't shameful enough for the proud giants, after winning immediate promotion back to the top division, Milan was relegated again — though this time it was simply because the team wasn't good enough. Milan bounced straight back to the top flight again but drifted aimlessly — and then in 1986 local businessman and future Italian prime minister Silvio Berlusconi bought the club.

Berlusconi's first act was to employ little-known Parma coach Arrigo Sacchi, whose Serie B team had knocked Milan out of the 1986 Coppa Italia. Sacchi brought in some rising Italian stars — midfielders Roberto Donadoni and Carlo Ancelotti — and more importantly three Dutch players, Ruud Gullit, Marco van Basten, and Frank Rijkaard. The team won the Italian championship in 1988 and then the European Cup in 1989, beating Real Madrid 5-0 in the second leg of the semifinal, then Steaua Bucharest 4-0 in the final. Milan retained the trophy a year later with a 1-0 win over Benfica.

But Milan was about to hit even greater heights. Sacchi took over the Italian national team, making way for Fabio Capello. Under Capello, Milan won three titles in succession in the early 1990s, winning the 1991–1992 title without losing a single game. By now attack was less important than defense. Whereas once the Dutch players had been the stars, now it was defenders Franco Baresi, Paolo Maldini, and Alessandro Costacurta who took center stage: In the 1993–1994 title-winning season, Milan only scored 36 goals in 34 games!

Barcelona (2009)

While Real Madrid won the first five European Cups between 1956 and 1960, and added another in 1966, the Spanish club's arch rivals Barcelona sat jealously on the sidelines. It wasn't until 1992 that the Catalan giants finally landed the biggest club trophy of all. The XI that broke Barcelona's (Barca's, as they're known) duck went down in history as The Dream Team. It featured world-famous names such as striker Hristo Stoichkov, winger Michael Laudrup, and the man who scored the winning goal against Sampdoria in the final, defender Ronald Koeman — but the fans' favorite was defensive midfielder Pep Guardiola, a local boy made good.

Guardiola returned as Barca coach in the summer of 2008, and had an immediate impact on the club. He got rid of big-name attacking players who'd helped Barcelona win a second European Cup in 2006 — and placed his faith in the attacking triumvirate of Samuel Eto'o, Thierry Henry, and Lionel Messi. With Andrés Iniesta and Xavi pulling the strings in midfield, and new signings Gerard Pique and Daniel Alves shoring up the defense, Barcelona embarked on the greatest season in perhaps any club's history.

Barca won the Spanish championship with ease, and added the Spanish Cup, securing a domestic double. And after reaching the Champions League final with a spectacular and dramatic stoppage-time winner by Iniesta against Chelsea, the Spanish club added the greatest prize in Europe to a remarkable season tally, rolling Manchester United over in the final.

Barcelona had become the first-ever Spanish team to win a Treble — joining an elite band of clubs who've won a domestic league-and-cup double as well as the European Cup in the same season. To top it off, Barcelona went on to claim the Spanish Super Cup, the European Super Cup, and the Club World Cup before 2009 was over, winning all six out of six possible titles that magical year.

Spain (2008, 2010, 2012)

Spain's success in recent years has been closely tied to that of Barcelona, with players such as Xavi and Andres Iniesta also pulling the strings on the international level. Long known for underachieving on the world stage, Spain went undefeated in winning Euro 2008 held in Austria and Switzerland, defeating Germany 1-0 in the final.

Although Spain switched coaches ahead of the 2010 World Cup in South Africa — Luis Aragonés was replaced by Vicente del Bosque — the Spanish style of play did not skip a beat, with the team's intricate passing (known as *tiki-taka*) and technical skills allowing the Spaniards to dominate possession in every game. Although Spain lost its opening game against Switzerland, six consecutive victories followed including a 1-0 win over the Netherlands in the final. Spain became world champions for the first time.

Spain continued an unprecedented run of success by successfully defending the European title in 2012, with the championships held in Poland and Ukraine. Spain's play was not as dynamic as it had been in South Africa — often playing without a recognized striker — but it all came together in the final, with the Spaniards dismantling Italy in a 4-0 win. Spain become the first team to ever win the European Championship twice and the World Cup once in a span of four years.

Chapter 21

Ten Great Games

*J*ust about anything can make a game live long in the memory: a last-minute goal, a dramatic turnaround, a point-blank save, even the odd controversial refereeing decision. These time-honored classics tick all the boxes . . .

Arbroath 36, Bon Accord 0 (Scottish Cup, 1885)

Even now, well over a century later, Saturday, September 12, 1885, stands without question the most amazing — and as you can see, plain odd — day in the history of soccer. It was the first round of the Scottish Cup, and Dundee Harp recorded a quite outstanding result in a game against Aberdeen Rovers: Dundee won 35-0! The referee was sure the actual score was 37-0, but admitted he may have lost count somewhere along the line. Anyway, the Dundee Harp club secretary sportingly assured him his team had scored *only* 35 goals — and regardless, it was clearly a world-record score, so what difference did an extra couple of goals make? The Scottish Football Association recorded Dundee Harp's win.

It was an especially good result for Harp defender Tom O'Kane, who'd been playing his first game for the club since moving from Arbroath. After the game he sent a telegram to his old team mates, informing them of Harp's world-record feat. O'Kane received an immediate reply, which said Arbroath had gone one better: a 36-0 win in the Cup against another gaggle of Aberdonian half-wits, Bon Accord. O'Kane considered the reply to be a hilarious joke.

He wasn't laughing later, though. Still a resident of Arbroath, he returned home to find that his old team had indeed won 36-0, with an 18-year-old striker having scored 13 goals (a record that has since been equaled, but never beaten). The morning after, O'Kane ran the 18 miles to Dundee to break the bad news to his new club: It was Arbroath who held the world-record score, not Dundee Harp. The club secretary immediately regretted sportingly chalking off those two goals — although it later transpired Arbroath had seen another *seven* goals disallowed for dubious offside decisions, so justice was probably done.

United States 1, England 0 (World Cup, 1950)

England did not play in a World Cup before 1950, the administrators of the sport in the home of soccer feeling the tournament was below them. The public in the United States, meanwhile, knew little about the competition, and even after their country's famous win over the English in Belo Horizonte, Brazil, on June 29, very few newspapers reported it.

The American team was scratched together at a low point for soccer in the country. Although the English team was composed of professionals considered among the best in the world, the United States team was made-up of semipros who made their livings as mailmen, wallpaper strippers, and other occupations. Most were American-born — many from a rare hotbed of soccer in the United States, St. Louis — though the roster also included Haitian-born forward Joe Gaetjens.

Before defeating England, the United States almost upset Spain in its first game at the 1950 World Cup, leading for the first hour before succumbing to three late goals for a 3-1 defeat. Against England, a treacherous field and some poor shooting by the English aided the Americans, but it was still a bold and brave display by all accounts — and a remarkable upset was achieved when Gaetjens glanced in a goal via his head after 38 minutes. England could not break a determined American defense down, and local fans rushed the field in celebration at the final whistle.

The Americans did not play another game — Spain advanced from the pool having also defeated England — and there is a sad postscript for the hero of the day, Gaetjens, who disappeared and was likely murdered in Haiti in 1964 by the regime of Papa Doc Duvalier, who he opposed.

Brazil 1, Uruguay 2 (World Cup, 1950)

The 1950 World Cup was the only staging of the tournament not to have a final. Instead, there was a final pool, a minileague containing four teams — Spain, Sweden, Uruguay, and hosts Brazil — who all played each other, the table-toppers taking the pot. But as it turned out, the final game in the pool was effectively the final to all intents and purposes. To secure the title, Brazil, who'd won its first two games (scoring 13 goals in doing so!), only had to draw with Uruguay, who'd struggled to win one and draw the other. The Uruguayans could themselves still take the trophy home if they won, but few gave them a chance of beating the pre-tournament favorites on their own turf.

Nobody in Brazil did, anyway. On the morning of the game, one Brazilian newspaper printed a photograph of Brazil's national team on the front page, with the headline CHAMPIONS!. The mayor of Rio, not to be outdone, took to the field before kickoff and gave a congratulatory address: "You who in less than a few hours will be hailed as champions by millions of compatriots! You who will overcome any other competitor! You who I already salute as victors!" Meanwhile the Brazilian Football Association minted personally engraved gold medals for each member of the roster and commissioned a celebratory samba to be performed at the final whistle.

All seemed to be going to plan. Brazil dominated the first half, though it was scoreless at the break. Just after the restart, Friaca put the hosts one up. With Uruguay having been nonexistent as an attacking force up until then and now needing two goals to win, the game looked to be over. But with a world-record crowd of over 200,000 in the Maracanã stadium, Brazil became jittery. And when Juan Schiaffino equalized midway through the second half, the home fans became nervous. It was too much for their team, who crumbled with 11 minutes to go, the fullback Bigode allowing Alcide Ghiggia to skate past him and beat the despairing keeper Moacyr Barbosa at his near post. At the final whistle, the crowd fell into almost total silence. FIFA bigwig Jules Rimet handed over the trophy that bore his name and then observed that the atmosphere was "morbid" and "too difficult to bear."

Brazil played that day in its first-choice white jerseys for the very final time; now considered unlucky, the South Americans have not played in white since, and within three years had adopted a trademark yellow, green, and blue uniform.

England 3, Hungary 6 (Friendly, 1953)

People often cite this game as the first time a non-British team beat the English national team on home soil. But that's not actually true: Four years earlier the Republic of Ireland beat England 2-0 in an exhibition at Everton's

Goodison Park home. Even so, you can't underestimate the cataclysmic effect of Hungary's famous thrashing of England in 1953.

Hungary had won the 1952 Olympic title, bursting onto the international scene with a whole new way of playing. At the time, teams played with five men up front with the central striker farthest upfield leading the line. Hungary dispensed with that idea, allowing their nominal center-forward, Nándor Hidegkuti, to drop deep into space. England, stuck in a tactical rut, found Hidegkuti's movement impossible to counter.

Before the start of the game, the English players took one look at their opponents — the Hungarians were going through a complex warming-up routine, they wore lightweight cleats, and one of their forwards, Ferenc Puskás, was slightly overweight — and blithely told each other they'd steamroller a team who 'didn't even have proper kit' (uniforms) and fielded "a little fat chap." They were soon disabused of this notion.

Within a minute Hidegkuti — whom nobody had bothered to follow into the space behind the front men — went on a run and smashed in Hungary's first goal. England equalized but Hidegkuti soon added a second goal for Hungary, before Puskás scored a third, sending England's captain sliding off the field with an embarrassed look on his face as he did so. After 63 minutes Hungary had scored six times to England's two, and eased off the gas. Alf Ramsey scored a consolation goal from a penalty right at the death, but England's humiliation had long been complete.

Real Madrid 7, Eintracht Frankfurt 3 (European Cup, 1960)

For a while, it looked like Glasgow belonged to Eintracht Frankfurt in the spring of 1960. First the German team beat the Rangers 6-3 at Ibrox in the second leg of the European Cup semifinal, completing a 12-4 aggregate win over the Glaswegian giants. The victory saw Frankfurt return to Glasgow for the final, held at Hampden Park, where the Germans played reigning European champion Real Madrid. After 18 minutes of the game, having looked thoroughly composed, Frankfurt went a goal ahead through Richard Kress. And then the Clydeside sky fell in on them.

Madrid had won all four European Cups held to date, and was about to make it five in a row with a display that would go down in history as the team's signature performance — and perhaps the best of all time. A huge Hampden crowd of 135,000 oohed and aahed as Francisco Gento tore down the left wing time and again at breathtaking speed, while Alfredo di Stefano began to dictate play from the center of the field. Di Stefano scored twice in three minutes to put Real ahead before the half-hour mark, and then Ferenc Puskás took over. He added Real's third just before half-time, crashing in an unstoppable shot into the roof of the net from an impossible angle, and scored two more to complete his hat trick before the hour.

Puskás added Real's sixth and his personal fourth before a stunning team effort from Real sandwiched two late Erwin Stein consolation goals, di Stefano finishing a flowing five-pass move straight from the restart. On the final whistle Puskás picked the ball up. His four goals meant it was his, though he didn't keep it, shoving it into Stein's chest after the German striker had the audacity to pester him for the souvenir. Stein may have made off with the ball but Puskás took the plaudits — he's still the only player to score four in a European Cup final.

England 4, West Germany 2 (World Cup, 1966)

Alf Ramsey had promised from the outset that England would "most certainly" win the World Cup. "I'm certain of success," the England coach said on the eve of the tournament, though he did add one caveat: "We have deficiencies, and one is finishing." Just a minor problem with scoring goals, then — but one that the team would solve in spectacular fashion by the end of the tournament.

Star striker Jimmy Greaves hadn't found the net in England's first round group games, and even worse, his leg had been badly cut open against the French. He was to be out for the quarter-final.

Geoff Hurst took Greaves's place and seized his opportunity, scoring the winner against Argentina then setting up the clinching goal in the semifinal against Portugal. Greaves had recovered by the morning of the final, but in the days before substitutes Ramsey didn't name him for the team. Hurst, controversially, kept his place.

Ramsey's choice of Hurst over Greaves wasn't the final controversial decision of the day, either. The 1966 World Cup final between England and West Germany was the most contentious of all time. The Germans went ahead early on through Helmut Haller, only for Hurst to justify his selection with an equalizer. With 12 minutes to go Martin Peters poked home what looked like the winner — until Wolfgang Weber scrambled a last-gasp equalizer for West Germany.

"You've won it once, now go and win it again," Ramsey told his men before extra time began. And win it England did, though the host nation needed a large slice of luck when Hurst's shot came down off the crossbar and landed on the line. It wasn't a goal, but the Azerbaijani linesman gave it anyway. In the dying seconds of the game, Hurst became the first — and still only — man to complete a hat trick in a World Cup final. BBC announcer Kenneth Wolstenholme soundtracked the goal with the immortal words: "They think it's all over — it is now!"

Manchester United 4, Benfica 1 (European Cup, 1968)

This was the happy ending to the most bittersweet of soccer odysseys. Manchester United had been the first English team to compete in Europe, coach Matt Busby ignoring a Football League decree ordering United not to play in the new European Cup, a trophy the small-minded bureaucrats considered beneath English clubs. His young team reached the semifinals that year, 1956–1957, and were expected to go all the way the following season. Fate intervened, though, and tragically so: On February 6, 1958, a plane transporting the Busby Babes, as they were known, back home after a quarter-final win against Red Star Belgrade crashed on a snowy Munich runway. Seven members of the team were immediately killed and United's star man Duncan Edwards died in hospital 15 days later. Red Star asked the Union of European Football Associations (UEFA) to name United as Honorary Champions that year, but they denied the request.

Busby himself was at death's door for a while, but pulled through and within seven years had built his second great United team. That team, built around George Best, Scottish striker Denis Law, and Munich survivor Bobby Charlton, reached the 1968 European Cup final where the Manchester club faced Euesbio's Benfica. Law missed the final with a knee injury, but Best and Charlton provided the decisive blows.

After a goal-less first half, Charlton opened the scoring with a very rare header. Benfica equalized with 12 minutes to go through Jaime Graça. Eusebio was clean through right at the death and arrowed a shot goalwards, but United keeper Alex Stepney somehow smothered it. Eusebio could do nothing but stand and applaud Stepney for his amazing save.

The final went into extra time, and within eight minutes United had sewn it up. First Best scored what was effectively the winner by rounding the Benfica keeper and walking the ball into the net. Nineteen-year-old Brian Kidd — on his birthday — added another, before Charlton scored his second and United's fourth. Busby and Charlton had reached their holy grail ten seasons after the Busby Babes had perished.

Brazil 4, Italy 1 (World Cup, 1970)

Many consider the Brazilian team that won the 1970 World Cup to be the greatest ever in the history of the game, boasting the attacking quintet of Pelé, Gerson, Tostão, Rivelino, and Jairzinho. So amazing is this team's story that even the South Americans' qualifying campaign was the stuff of legend.

Brazil's national team had been struggling in 1968 and was under intense pressure from the media. So to shut the newspapers up, the Brazilian Football Association appointed a journalist as coach! João Saldanha was an instant success, gathering what would become the 1970 team together and winning all six of the country's qualifiers, scoring 23 goals along the way.

Saldanha didn't take the team to the World Cup finals in Mexico, though — having threatened a newspaper critic with a loaded gun, he was replaced by Mario Zagallo, who led the team to ultimate glory. In Mexico, Brazil won every game; the only team who didn't let in at least three goals to the Brazilians was the reigning champion England, who conceded a solitary effort in a 1-0 defeat.

Brazil faced Italy in the final, with the team's attacking verve up against the meanest defense in world soccer. Under a scorching sun, the Brazilians danced through the Italian backline time and again; their *pièce de résistance* was captain Carlos Alberto's sublime strike to seal a 4-1 win. Pelé had opened the scoring, marking his last international game with a goal, while Jairzinho became the only man to score in every game of the World Cup finals.

Nigeria 3, Argentina 2 (Olympics, 1996)

Nigeria claimed Africa's first global prize at the 1996 Atlanta Olympics' soccer tournament. The Nigerians' star man was Nwankwo Kanu, who'd won the 1995 Champions League with Ajax and was now playing at Italian giants Internazionale, but the African team's roster also boasted the likes of Jay Jay Okocha, Daniel Amokachi, and Celestine Babayaro.

Even so, people expected Nigeria to lose a semifinal against reigning world champion Brazil, whose team contained World Cup winners Bebeto, Ronaldo, Rivaldo, and Roberto Carlos. But in an amazing game, which saw Brazil 3-1 up with 12 minutes to go, Nigeria turned it around in the most dramatic manner. Victor Ikpeba pulled one back before Kanu scored twice in the final minute to pull off a stunning 4-3 win.

Could lightning strike twice in the final against an Argentina team featuring stars Hernán Crespo, Ariel Ortega, Claudio López, and Diego Simeone? It certainly could: Once again, Nigeria trailed with the clock against them. But from 2-1 down with 16 minutes left, Amokachi equalized before Emmanuel Amunike scored another last-minute winner. Nigeria won the gold medal, Africa its first major title.

United States 0, China 0 (World Cup, 1999)

Many people have argued soccer won't become as big as other sports in America as long as it allows ties, especially ones without goals. That argument should have been put to rest by the 1999 Women's World Cup final, watched by over 90,000 at the Rose Bowl in Southern California and a record television audience in the United States of over 40 million viewers, then the largest ever for any broadcast on network television.

The final itself did not lack for action even in a scoreless game — in extra time following 90 minutes of tied action, American midfielder Kristine Lilly leapt to keep out a goalbound header and ensure the game headed to a nerve-wracking penalty shootout to decide the result. Penalties may not be the ideal way to settle games, but there can be no doubting the high drama they entail — on this occasion, the Americans came out on top on home soil as goalkeeper Brianna Scurry saved China's third shot, with Brandi Chastain burying the winning kick.

Chastain's kick and the ecstatic response became an indelible moment in American sports history, and not because Brandi immediately ripped off her jersey to appear on national television in her sports bra. It was the first time the United States had won a global soccer title, and it was a landmark moment for women's sports in America.

Appendix A

Roll of Honor

The first soccer game between two clubs was played in 1860, whereas the first game contested by two countries was in 1872. Were I to list every single major trophy win, at both club and international level, I'd need to publish at least another 173 volumes of this book. Try carrying *those* home from the store!

Instead, here are a select few of the most significant results in soccer history.

For those of you interested in delving deep into the record books, may I recommend the peerless website of the Rec Sport Soccer Statistics Foundation: www.rsssf.com. It has absolutely *everything,* even the winner of the 1956 Guatemalan league (that was Comunicaciones, since you ask).

World Cup

The World Cup is the biggest soccer tournament in the world. All of FIFA's (that's Fédération Internationale de Football Association, or International Federation of Association Football) 209 member countries are eligible to enter. It's held every four years, with the winners earning the right to call themselves champions of the world.

World Cup Finals (1930–2010)

Year	Hosts	Winner	Runner-up	Score
1930	Uruguay	Uruguay	Argentina	4-2
1934	Italy	Italy	Czechoslovakia	2-1 after extra time
1938	France	Italy	Hungary	4-2
1950	Brazil	Uruguay	Brazil	2-1*
1954	Switzerland	West Germany	Hungary	3-2
1958	Sweden	Brazil	Sweden	5-2
1962	Chile	Brazil	Czechoslovakia	3-1
1966	England	England	West Germany	4-2 after extra time
1970	Mexico	Brazil	Italy	4-1
1974	West Germany	West Germany	Netherlands	2-1
1978	Argentina	Argentina	Netherlands	3-1 after extra time
1982	Spain	Italy	West Germany	3-1
1986	Mexico	Argentina	West Germany	3-2
1990	Italy	West Germany	Argentina	1-0
1994	United States	Brazil	Italy	0-0 after extra time (Brazil won 3-2 on penalties)
1998	France	France	Brazil	3-0
2002	South Korea and Japan	Brazil	Germany	2-0
2006	Germany	Italy	France	1-1 after extra time (Italy won 5-3 on penalties)
2010	South Africa	Spain	Netherlands	1-0
2014	Brazil			

The 1950 tournament had no official final, instead a final pool involving four teams: Uruguay, Brazil, Spain, and Sweden. However, the final game between Uruguay and Brazil was effectively a "final," because it was the decisive game.

Total World Cup Wins (1930–2010)

Wins	Team	Years
5	Brazil	1958, 1962, 1970, 1994, 2002
4	Italy	1934, 1938, 1982, 2006
3	(West) Germany	1954, 1974, 1990
2	Uruguay	1930, 1950
2	Argentina	1978, 1986
1	England	1966
1	France	1998
1	Spain	2010

CONCACAF Gold Cup

CONCACAF is a long acronym that stands for Confederation of North, Central American and Caribbean Association Football — of which the United States is a member. Their regional championship is known as the Gold Cup, and has been held since 1991 (before that, it was the CONCACAF Championship). It's now held every two years and usually hosted by the United States.

CONCACAF Gold Cup Games (1991–2012)

Year	Hosts	Winner	Runner-up	Score
1991	United States	United States	Honduras	0-0 (USA won 4-3 on penalties)
1993	United States and Mexico	Mexico	United States	4-0
1996	United States	Mexico	Brazil*	2-0
1998	United States	Mexico	United States	1-0
2000	United States	Canada	Colombia*	2-0
2002	United States	United States	Costa Rica	2-0
2003	United States and Mexico	Mexico	Brazil	1-0 (after sudden death extra time)
2005	United States	United States	Panama	0-0 (USA won 3-1 on penalties)
2007	United States	United States	Mexico	2-1
2009	United States	Mexico	United States	5-0
2011	United States	Mexico	United States	4-2
2013	United States			

* Guest nations from outside the CONCACAF region are occasionally invited to play in the Gold Cup.

Total CONCACAF Gold Cup Wins (1991–2012)

Wins	Team	Years
6	Mexico	1993, 1996, 1998, 2003, 2009, 2011
4	United States	1991, 2002, 2005, 2007
1	Canada	2000

European Championship

The European Championship — or Euros, as they're colloquially known — is held every four years, midway between World Cups. It was known as the European Nations Cup until 1968. The winners have the right to call themselves European champions.

European Championship Finals (1960–2012)

Year	Hosts	Winner	Runner-up	Score
1960	France	Soviet Union	Yugoslavia	2-1 after extra time
1964	Spain	Spain	Soviet Union	2-1
1968	Italy	Italy	Yugoslavia	2-0 (replay after 1-1 draw)
1972	Belgium	West Germany	Soviet Union	3-0
1976	Yugoslavia	Czechoslovakia	West Germany	2-2 (Czechoslovakia won 5-3 on penalties)
1980	Italy	West Germany	Belgium	2-1
1984	France	France	Spain	2-0
1988	West Germany	Netherlands	Soviet Union	2-0
1992	Sweden	Denmark	Germany	2-0
1996	England	Germany	Czech Republic	2-1 after extra time *

Year	Hosts	Winner	Runner-up	Score
2000	Belgium and Netherlands	France	Italy	2-1 after extra time *
2004	Portugal	Greece	Portugal	1-0
2008	Austria and Switzerland	Spain	Germany	1-0
2012	Ukraine and Poland	Spain	Italy	4-0
2016	France			

* Both the 1996 and 2000 finals were settled by a Golden Goal in sudden-death extra time.

Total European Championship Wins (1960–2012)

Wins	Team	Years
3	(West) Germany	1972, 1980, 1996
3	Spain	1964, 2008, 2012
2	France	1984, 2000
1	Soviet Union	1960
1	Italy	1968
1	Czechoslovakia	1976
1	Netherlands	1988
1	Denmark	1992
1	Greece	2004

Copa America

The Copa America is the oldest international tournament in the world. It decides the champions of South America. It has had a checkered history, being played irregularly and structured erratically since the first official staging in 1916. But since 1987 it's taken the same format, an entire tournament staged in one country. It's now held every four years.

Recent Copa America Finals (1987–2011)

Year	Hosts	Winner	Runner-up	Score
1987	Argentina	Uruguay	Chile	1-0
1989	Brazil	Brazil	Uruguay	1-0
1991	Chile	Argentina	Brazil	3-2
1993	Ecuador	Argentina	Mexico	2-1
1995	Uruguay	Uruguay	Brazil	1-1 (Uruguay won 5-3 on penalties)
1997	Bolivia	Brazil	Bolivia	3-1
1999	Paraguay	Brazil	Uruguay	3-0
2001	Colombia	Colombia	Mexico	1-0
2004	Peru	Brazil	Argentina	2-2 (Brazil won 4-2 on penalties)
2007	Venezuela	Brazil	Argentina	3-0
2011	Argentina	Uruguay	Paraguay	3-0
2015	Chile			

Total Copa America Wins (1916–2007)

Wins	Team	Years
15	Uruguay	1916, 1917, 1920, 1923, 1924, 1926, 1935, 1942, 1956, 1959, 1967, 1983, 1987, 1995, 2011
14	Argentina	1921, 1925, 1927, 1929, 1937, 1941, 1945, 1946, 1947, 1955, 1957, 1959, 1991, 1993
8	Brazil	1919, 1922, 1949, 1989, 1997, 1999, 2004, 2007
2	Paraguay	1953, 1979
2	Peru	1939, 1975
1	Colombia	2001
1	Bolivia	1963

Africa Cup of Nations

This is the pinnacle of African soccer, with the winners earning the right to name themselves African champions. The tournament has been held on a regular basis since 1957, and is now held every two years. It's scheduled in successive years in 2012 and 2013, because the tournament shifts so it no longer coincides with the Olympic Games held in the same years.

Africa Cup of Nations Finals (1957–2012)

Year	Hosts	Winner	Runner-up	Score
1957	Sudan	Egypt	Ethiopia	4-0
1959	Egypt	Egypt	Sudan	after final group
1962	Ethiopia	Ethiopia	Egypt	4-2
1963	Ghana	Ghana	Sudan	3-0
1965	Tunisia	Ghana	Tunisia	3-2
1968	Ethiopia	Congo Kinshasa	Ghana	1-0
1970	Sudan	Sudan	Ghana	1-0
1972	Cameroon	Congo	Mali	3-2
1974	Egypt	Zaire	Zambia	2-0 (replay after 2-2 draw)
1976	Ethiopia	Morocco	Guinea	after final group
1978	Ghana	Ghana	Uganda	2-0
1980	Nigeria	Nigeria	Algeria	3-0
1982	Libya	Ghana	Libya	1-1 (Ghana won 7-6 on penalties)
1984	Ivory Coast	Cameroon	Nigeria	3-0
1986	Egypt	Egypt	Cameroon	0-0 (Egypt won 5-4 on penalties)
1988	Morocco	Cameroon	Nigeria	1-0
1990	Algeria	Algeria	Nigeria	1-0
1992	Senegal	Ghana	Ivory Coast	0-0 (Ghana won 11-10 on penalties)
1994	Tunisia	Nigeria	Zambia	2-1
1996	South Africa	South Africa	Tunisia	2-0
1998	Burkina Faso	Egypt	South Africa	2-0
2000	Ghana and Nigeria	Cameroon	Nigeria	2-2 (Cameroon won 4-3 on penalties)
2002	Mali	Cameroon	Senegal	0-0 (Cameroon won 3-2 on penalties)
2004	Tunisia	Tunisia	Morocco	2-1
2006	Egypt	Egypt	Ivory Coast	0-0 (Egypt won 4-2 on penalties)

(continued)

Africa Cup of Nations Finals (1957–2008) *(continued)*

Year	Hosts	Winner	Runner-up	Score
2008	Ghana	Egypt	Cameroon	1-0
2010	Angola	Egypt	Ghana	1-0
2012	Gabon and Equatorial Guinea	Zambia	Ivory Coast	0-0 (Zambia won 7-8 on penalties)
2013	South Africa			
2014	Libya			

Confederations Cup

This is contested by the champions of all six FIFA confederations — Europe, South America, North and Central America, Africa, Asia, and Oceania — plus the World Cup winners and the host nation. It is yet to be considered a truly prestigious tournament, though its profile is rising sharply.

Confederations Cup Finals (1993–2009)

Year	Hosts	Winner	Runner-up	Score
1993	Saudi Arabia	Argentina	Saudi Arabia	3-1
1995	Saudi Arabia	Denmark	Argentina	2-0
1997	Saudi Arabia	Brazil	Australia	6-0
1999	Mexico	Mexico	Brazil	4-3
2001	South Korea and Japan	France	Japan	1-0
2003	France	France	Cameroon	1-0 after extra time
2005	Germany	Brazil	Argentina	4-1
2009	South Africa	Brazil	United States	3-2
2013	Brazil			

Note: *The 1993 and 1995 tournaments were called the King Fahd Cup and staged by Saudi Arabia. FIFA took over the tournament in 1997 and renamed it.*

Olympic Games

The Olympic soccer tournament was, up until 1980, an amateur tournament, fitting in with the Olympic ideal. After several tweaks, professionals have since been admitted, though only players under 23 years old can play, with the exception of an allowance for two players over 23 on each roster. It's now a de facto Under-23 World Cup.

Olympic Games Soccer Finals (1908–2012)

Year	Hosts	Winner	Runner-up	Score
1908	London	England	Denmark	2-0
1912	Stockholm	England	Denmark	4-2
1920	Antwerp	Belgium	Czechoslovakia	2-0
1924	Paris	Uruguay	Switzerland	3-0
1928	Amsterdam	Uruguay	Argentina	2-1 (after 1-1 draw)
1936	Berlin	Italy	Austria	2-1
1948	London	Sweden	Yugoslavia	3-1
1952	Helsinki	Hungary	Yugoslavia	2-0
1956	Melbourne	Soviet Union	Yugoslavia	1-0
1960	Rome	Yugoslavia	Denmark	3-1
1964	Tokyo	Hungary	Czechoslovakia	2-1
1968	Mexico City	Hungary	Bulgaria	4-1
1972	Munich	Poland	Hungary	2-1
1976	Montreal	East Germany	Poland	3-1
1980	Moscow	Czechoslovakia	East Germany	1-0
1984	Los Angeles	France	Brazil	2-0
1988	Seoul	Soviet Union	Brazil	2-1
1992	Barcelona	Spain	Poland	3-2
1996	Atlanta	Nigeria	Argentina	2-0
2000	Sydney	Cameroon	Spain	2-2 (Cameroon won 5-3 on penalties)
2004	Athens	Argentina	Paraguay	1-0
2008	Beijing	Argentina	Nigeria	1-0
2012	London	Mexico	Brazil	2-1
2016	Rio de Janeiro			

Women's World Cup

The Women's World Cup was founded in 1991, and has exploded in popularity over its brief life. The tournament is held every four years. The winners earn the right to call themselves champions of the world.

Women's World Cup Finals (1991–2011)

Year	Hosts	Winner	Runner-up	Score
1991	China	United States	Norway	2-1
1995	Sweden	Norway	Germany	2-0
1999	United States	United States	China	0-0 (USA won 5-4 on penalties)
2003	United States	Germany	Sweden	2-1 after extra time*
2007	China	Germany	Brazil	2-0
2011	Germany	Japan	United States	2-2 (Japan won 3-1 on penalties)
2015	Canada			

*Final decided by sudden-death golden goal

European Cup/Champions League

The Champions League — formerly the European Cup — is the biggest and most prestigious club championship in the world. The winners are crowned champions of Europe.

European Cup and Champions League Finals (1956–2012)

Year	Winner	Runner-up	Score	Stadium
1956	Real Madrid	Reims	4-3	Parc des Princes, Paris
1957	Real Madrid	Fiorentina	2-0	Santiago Bernabeu, Madrid
1958	Real Madrid	Milan	3-2	Heysel, Brussels

Year	Winner	Runner-up	Score	Stadium
1959	Real Madrid	Reims	2-0	Neckar, Stuttgart
1960	Real Madrid	Eintracht Frankfurt	7-3	Hampden, Glasgow
1961	Benfica	Barcelona	3-2	Wankdorf, Berne
1962	Benfica	Real Madrid	5-3	Olympic, Amsterdam
1963	Milan	Benfica	2-1	Wembley, London
1964	Internazionale	Real Madrid	3-1	Prater, Vienna
1965	Internazionale	Benfica	1-0	San Siro, Milan
1966	Real Madrid	Partizan Belgrade	2-1	Heysel, Brussels
1967	Celtic	Internazionale	2-1	Nacional, Lisbon
1968	Manchester United	Benfica	4-1 after extra time	Wembley, London
1969	Milan	Ajax	4-1	Santiago Bernabeu, Madrid
1970	Feyenoord	Celtic	2-1 after extra time	San Siro, Milan
1971	Ajax	Panathinaikos	2-0	Wembley, London
1972	Ajax	Internazionale	2-0	De Kuijp, Rotterdam
1973	Ajax	Juventus	1-0	Red Star, Belgrade
1974	Bayern Munich	Atletico Madrid	4-0 (after 1-1 draw)	Heysel, Brussels
1975	Bayern Munich	Leeds United	2-0	Parc des Princes, Paris
1976	Bayern Munich	St Etienne	1-0	Hampden, Glasgow
1977	Liverpool	Borussia Monchengladbach	3-1	Olimpico, Rome
1978	Liverpool	Bruges	1-0	Wembley, London
1979	Nottingham Forest	Malmo	1-0	Olympia, Munich

(continued)

European Cup and Champions League Finals (1956–2012) (continued)

Year	Winner	Runner-up	Score	Stadium
1980	Nottingham Forest	Hamburg	1-0	Santiago Bernabeu, Madrid
1981	Liverpool	Real Madrid	1-0	Parc des Princes, Paris
1982	Aston Villa	Bayern Munich	1-0	De Kuijp, Rotterdam
1983	Hamburg	Juventus	1-0	Olympic, Athens
1984	Liverpool	Roma	1-1 (Liverpool won 4-2 on penalties)	Olimpico, Rome
1985	Juventus	Liverpool	1-0	Heysel, Brussels
1986	Steaua Bucharest	Barcelona	0-0 (Steaua Bucharest won 2-0 on penalties)	Sanchez Pizjuan, Seville
1987	Porto	Bayern Munich	2-1	Prater, Vienna
1988	PSV Eindhoven	Benfica	0-0 (PSV won 6-5 on penalties)	Neckar, Stuttgart
1989	Milan	Steaua Bucharest	4-0	Nou Camp, Barcelona
1990	Milan	Benfica	1-0	Prater, Vienna
1991	Red Star Belgrade	Marseille	0-0 (Red Star won 5-3 on penalties)	San Nicola, Bari
1992	Barcelona	Sampdoria	1-0 after extra time	Wembley, London
1993	Marseille	Milan	1-0	Olympiastadion, Munich
1994	Milan	Barcelona	4-0	Olympic, Athens
1995	Ajax	Milan	1-0	Ernst-Happel, Vienna
1996	Juventus	Ajax	1-1 (Juventus won 4-2 on penalties)	Olimpico, Rome

Year	Winner	Runner-up	Score	Stadium
1997	Borussia Dortmund	Juventus	3-1	Olympiastadion, Munich
1998	Real Madrid	Juventus	1-0	Amsterdam Arena, Amsterdam
1999	Manchester United	Bayern Munich	2-1	Nou Camp, Barcelona
2000	Real Madrid	Valencia	3-0	Stade de France, Paris
2001	Bayern Munich	Valencia	1-1 (Bayern won 5-4 on penalties)	San Siro, Milan
2002	Real Madrid	Bayer Leverkusen	2-1	Hampden, Glasgow
2003	Milan	Juventus	0-0 (Milan won 3-2 on penalties)	Old Trafford, Manchester
2004	Porto	Monaco	3-0	AufSchalke, Gelsenkirchen
2005	Liverpool	Milan	3-3 (Liverpool won 3-2 on penalties)	Ataturk, Istanbul
2006	Barcelona	Arsenal	2-1	Stade de France, Paris
2007	Milan	Liverpool	2-1	Olympic, Athens
2008	Manchester United	Chelsea	1-1 (United won 6-5 on penalties)	Luzhniki, Moscow
2009	Barcelona	Manchester United	2-0	Olimpico, Rome
2010	Internazionale	Bayern Munich	2-0	Santiago Bernabeu, Madrid
2011	Barcelona	Manchester United	3-1	Wembley, London
2012	Chelsea	Bayern Munich	1-1 (Chelsea won 4-3 on penalties)	Allianz Arena, Munich

Total European Cup / Champions League Wins (1956–2012)

Wins	Team	Years
9	Real Madrid	1956, 1957, 1958, 1959, 1960, 1966, 1998, 2000, 2002
7	Milan	1963, 1969, 1989, 1990, 1994, 2003, 2007
5	Liverpool	1977, 1978, 1981, 1984, 2005
4	Ajax	1971, 1972, 1973, 1995
4	Bayern Munich	1974, 1975, 1976, 2001
4	Barcelona	1992, 2006, 2009, 2011
3	Manchester United	1968, 1999, 2008
3	Internazionale	1964, 1965, 2010
2	Benfica	1961, 1962
2	Nottingham Forest	1979, 1980
2	Juventus	1985, 1996
2	Porto	1987, 2004
1	Celtic	1967
1	Feyenoord	1970
1	Aston Villa	1982
1	Hamburg	1983
1	Steaua Bucharest	1986
1	PSV Eindhoven	1988
1	Red Star Belgrade	1991
1	Marseille	1993
1	Borussia Dortmund	1997
1	Chelsea	2012

Appendix B

Glossary

Advantage: When the referee decides to let play continue after a foul has been committed, as stopping play would benefit the team which has committed the foul.

Amateur: A player who plays without being paid.

Assistant coach: The second-in-command of a soccer team, after the head coach (or manager). Does not pick the team, but assists the team boss in whatever way is seen fit. Often a friend to the players, bridging the gap between the head coach and the team.

Assistant referee: Formerly known as *linesmen* or *lineswomen,* the assistant referees run along the sideline, helping the referee officiate the game. Their main responsibilities are determining if a ball has gone out of play, who touched the ball last, and whether a player is offside, though they also act as a second pair of eyes to any incident on the field, and advise the referee wherever necessary.

Back heel: Playing the ball with the heel, usually sending it in a backwards direction. The move can be utilized as either a pass or a shot.

Bench: Substitutes, coaches, physio, and whoever else is associated with the team but not currently playing. So called because they are usually sitting on a bench on the sidelines.

Bicycle kick: A difficult maneuver where the player jumps, leans backwards, and moves his legs as though pedaling a bicycle to kick the ball. The ball is sent over the head of the kicker, in a backwards direction.

Booking: A caution for foul play. The player is shown a yellow card. Two yellow cards result in a sending off.

Box: The penalty area, or penalty box.

Captain: The on-field leader of the team, as designated by the team coach. They are responsible for keeping up morale, communicating with the referee, and making minor tactical changes as the game progresses. (Captains are only permitted to make on-the-spot tactical changes if the coach has given them the authority.)

Caution: Punishment for foul play. The player is shown a yellow card. Two yellow cards will result in a sending off.

Center spot: The mark directly in the center of the pitch, used to position the ball for kickoffs.

Chip: A delicate pass, clipped up into the air and dropped towards a precise spot.

Clean sheet: A final score of no goals conceded. If a team lets in no goals during a match, the goalkeeper is said to have "kept a clean sheet."

Clearance: A ball being kicked or headed away from any particular danger zone. A clearance can be made to avert an immediate goal threat — a ball hoofed off the goal line by a defender is a *goal line clearance.*

Club: An organization that exists to put out soccer teams for the purposes of competition. Many clubs will have at least a basic setup of a first team, reserve team, and youth teams.

Corner: A kick taken by the attacking side, after the ball has been put out behind the goal line by the defending side. It's taken from the left or right corner of the pitch, on the side of the field the ball went out of play. It's usually sent straight into the penalty area, in the hope that an attacking player can get a shot or header on target.

Cross: A ball sent into the penalty area by an attacking player, from either the left or right side of the field.

Dead ball: The ball is considered *dead* when it's not in play, but still on the field. This means it has been positioned for a free kick, a corner, or a penalty.

Defender: One of the players whose first responsibility to his team is to ensure goals are not scored against them. They play in a formation at the back of the team, hoping to nullify the threat of the opposition attackers. They may be asked to follow a particular opponent around — man-to-man marking — or take care of a certain area of the field — zonal defending.

Direct free kick: A free kick from which a player can take a direct shot at goal.

Dissent: The act of arguing with the referee or the referee's assistants. Dissent is often punished with a yellow card. Extreme cases of dissent can see a player sent off, usually for swearing or aggressive behavior.

Dribble: Keeping control of the ball with the feet, and retaining possession, while running.

Drop ball: A method of restarting a game if the referee has had to stop it without the ball having gone out of play. This is usually for an injury. The ball is dropped to the ground by the referee, at which point players on both sides can touch the ball and get on with the game.

Dummy: Faking to kick the ball, or move in a particular direction, but not doing so, confusing the opposition in the process.

Equalizer: A goal that levels the score of a game. If a team was losing 1-0, and scores to make it 1-1, they have scored an equalizer.

Extra time: Two 15-minute periods of play contested when teams finish the 90 minutes drawn, but a winner on the day is required. (This usually occurs in cup competitions, where a replay would be impossible — or unfair — to stage.)

Fair play: Sportsmanship. Both teams and players can win "fair play" awards for good behavior.

Far post: The goalpost farthest from the ball.

Field: The playing area; sometimes referred to as the *pitch*.

Final whistle: The referee's blast on the whistle that signals the end of the game.

Final: The last tie in a knockout tournament between the two teams yet to be knocked out. The decisive game.

Formation: The tactical arrangement a manager or coach sets his team in. A formation is a numbered combination of the ten outfield players, reading from the back to the front of the pitch. So the classic 4-4-2 formation has four players at the back, four in midfield, and two up front.

Forward: A primarily attacking player. A forward's job is to score goals, or create them by combining with another forward player. They are also known as goalscorers, or strikers. Forwards can also play on the wings, or as attacking midfielders, but this is a much looser definition of the term.

Foul: An infringement of the Laws of the Game.

Fourth official: An official whose task is to help the referee and his two assistants, usually from the stand or the technical area. They oversee substitutions, keep the two benches in line, and announce the amount of stoppage time at the end of a match.

Free kick: A dead-ball kick taken by an attacking team, after a player has been fouled.

Friendly: A match which is not part of an official competition, counting for nothing in particular. Usually an exhibition game, either between clubs which rarely play each other, or two countries.

Fullback: Either a left back or right back; that is, a defender who plays on either the left or right wing of the pitch.

General manager: An administrator who assists the coach in transfers and other club-related business. Often a former professional player or coach.

Goal: 1. The ultimate aim of soccer. A goal is scored when the entire ball crosses the entire goal line, under the crossbar and between the goalposts. 2. The area where the goal is scored.

Goal kick: Method of restarting the game when the attacking team put the ball out of play over the goal line (but not in the goal). Usually taken by the goalkeepers, but occasionally by one of their team mates.

Goal line: The lines that run between each touchline at either end of the field. The goal is situated in the middle of the goal line.

Goal mouth: The area directly in front of the goal.

Goalkeeper: The only players on the pitch allowed to use their hands — but only in the penalty area — the goalkeeper's job is to ensure the opposing team does not score.

Golden goal: A sudden-death goal, scored in extra time, which wins the match immediately.

Ground: 1. The surface of the field. 2. In England, a stadium.

Half volley: A kick or shot made immediately after a dropping ball hits the ground.

Halftime: The period between the first and second halves, lasting 15 minutes.

Hand ball: A foul by a player who handles the ball with his arm or hand on purpose. Goalkeepers can only be called for this foul outside the penalty box.

Hat trick: Three goals in a game by the same player. A perfect hat trick is a trio of goals, one scored by a left-footed shot, another by a right-footed shot, and a third with a header.

Head coach: The person who runs the team, picks the players, chooses the tactical approach, and makes in-game decisions such as tactical rethinks and substitutions. They also determine which players to buy and sell. Known in England as the *manager*.

Header: Propelling the ball using one's head.

Indirect free kick: A free kick from which a player cannot take a direct shot (it must touch another player) at goal.

Injury time: Time added on by the referee at the end of each half, to account for any stoppages in play. Also known as *stoppage time*.

Inswinger: A shot, pass, or usually a cross that curves in towards the goal from wherever it has been hit.

Interval: Another word for halftime.

Keeper: A colloquialism for *goalkeeper*.

Kickoff: A kick from the center spot, which starts the game or the half or restarts the game after a goal.

Linesman: The old-school term for *assistant referee*. It was changed to become gender neutral in the early 2000s.

Manager: The head coach.

Man-to-man marking: A system where each defender tracks a specific opponent and stays with them all game, usually following their every move around the field.

Match: A game.

Midfielder: A player who spends most of their time in the center of the field. They are usually the most influential players in the side, contributing to both attack and defense, and dictating the speed and direction of play.

Near post: The goalpost nearest to the ball.

Nutmeg: A move in which a player kicks the ball between the legs of an opponent. The kick can be a pass to another team mate, or a "pass" to themselves.

Obstruction: Deliberately getting in the way of another player with no intention of playing the ball. Should result in an indirect free kick.

Officials: 1. The referee, the referee's assistant, and the fourth official. 2. Representatives of a club. For example, newspaper reports may say "officials of DC United were talking to Player X about a trade."

Offside: Players are offside when they are nearer to their opponents' goal than the second-to-last opponent — *at the time the ball is played forward by a team mate*.

Offside trap: A defensive tactic used to lure opponents into being caught offside. All defenders move up the field at the same time, leaving opponents stranded.

One touch: A kick or pass made using the player's first touch upon receiving the ball.

Outswinger: A shot, pass, or usually a cross which curves away from the goal from wherever it has been hit.

Overlap: When a defender runs down either wing, past their midfield, or attacking players, to become part of the attack.

Own goal: A goal accidentally scored by a player into his own net. The own goal counts as a goal for the opposition.

Pass: How a player moves the ball to another, using either his feet or head.

Penalty: A free shot from 12 yards in the penalty area, upon the award of a direct free kick in the box. Also known as a *penalty kick*.

Penalty area: The 18-x-44 yard area around each goal, in which the goalkeeper is allowed to handle the ball, and fouls by the defending team are punished with a penalty kick.

Physio: The physiotherapist, team doctor, or man carrying a bucket of water and sponge.

Playmaker: A player — usually a midfielder — whose job it is to dictate the way the entire team plays, and at what tempo. This is usually meant in a creative sense, with the player influencing the game through clever passing.

Professional: A player who is paid and earns his living from playing soccer.

Red card: A card shown by a referee to a player who has committed a serious offense, usually violent or cynical. The player is sent off and no longer able to take part in the game. The player cannot be replaced. He is also banned from a following game (or more games).

Referee: The official who is in charge of the game and makes decisions according to the Laws of the Game.

Restart: Another word for *kickoff.* A restart happens after any dead ball situation.

Save: A shot or header blocked, caught, or parried by the goalkeeper, which otherwise would have been a goal.

Semiprofessional: A player who is employed by a club on a part-time basis, but must also hold down a day job to make ends meet. Semipros are usually found in the lower leagues at small clubs which can't afford full-time salaries.

Set piece: A free kick, corner, throw-in, or goal kick pre-organized and practiced by a team.

Shot: A kick towards the goal. A shot at goal is off target; a shot on goal is on target.

Side: A team.

Sidelines: The lines running down both sides of the field, from each goal line. Also called the touchlines.

Soccer: Shorthand for Association Football. Often erroneously claimed to be an Americanism, when in fact the word was coined by British university students in the late 1800s.

Square pass: A pass played to a team mate standing alongside — rather than ahead, or behind — that player. Often used pejoratively, to suggest a lack of creativity or attacking gung-ho on the part of the passer.

Stoppage time: Time added on at the end of the game for injuries, arguments, substitutions, and so on.

Striker: Another word for forward. Often used for a player whose sole purpose is to score goals.

Substitute: A replacement player who can be swapped for a player on the field.

Tackle: A defensive motion in which a player uses his foot to take the ball off an opposing player, or block their progress.

Target player: A forward, usually a tall or bulky one, who is the target of passes and crosses — usually of the long variety. The target player is usually an adept header of the ball, and very strong.

Through pass: A pass that goes between and past the last line of defense, allowing an attacker to run into space and receive the ball.

Throw-in: The method by which a ball that has gone out of play over the touchline is deposited back into play, a player throwing it in over his head using both hands.

Tie: 1. If two teams end the game with the same amount of goals, the result is a tie, sometimes called a *draw*. 2. The name given to two teams in a competition who play each other in a specified round of a tournament.

Time wasting: Deliberately taking unnecessary amounts of time to restart the game from dead-ball situations in order to run down the clock. This is only ever done by teams which are winning the game, and are looking to close out the match. This is technically an offense, but is not always punished by the referee because it can be very subjective.

Trainer: 1. A team's medical expert. 2. A manager or coach, usually specializing in tactics or fitness.

Transfer: The method by which players change the teams and clubs they play for.

Unsportsmanlike behavior: Conduct that brings disgrace to the game.

Volley: Kicking the ball when it has been sent flying through the air, before it has hit the ground again.

Wing: Either side, or flank, of the field. Wingers are the attacking players who are positioned on either side of the field.

Yellow card: A card shown by a referee to a player who has committed an offence that requires them to be put on a warning. A second yellow card results in the player being sent off.

Zonal defense: A tactic where defenders look after a designated section of the field, or penalty area, rather than concentrating on a particular opponent.

Index

● *F* ●

• G •

• N •

Notes

Notes

Notes

Notes

Apple & Mac

iPad 2 For Dummies,
3rd Edition
978-1-118-17679-5

iPhone 4S For Dummies,
5th Edition
978-1-118-03671-6

iPod touch For Dummies,
3rd Edition
978-1-118-12960-9

Mac OS X Lion
For Dummies
978-1-118-02205-4

Blogging & Social Media

CityVille For Dummies
978-1-118-08337-6

Facebook For Dummies,
4th Edition
978-1-118-09562-1

Mom Blogging
For Dummies
978-1-118-03843-7

Twitter For Dummies,
2nd Edition
978-0-470-76879-2

WordPress For Dummies,
4th Edition
978-1-118-07342-1

Business

Cash Flow For Dummies
978-1-118-01850-7

Investing For Dummies,
6th Edition
978-0-470-90545-6

Job Searching with Social
Media For Dummies
978-0-470-93072-4

QuickBooks 2012
For Dummies
978-1-118-09120-3

Resumes For Dummies,
6th Edition
978-0-470-87361-8

Starting an Etsy Business
For Dummies
978-0-470-93067-0

Cooking & Entertaining

Cooking Basics
For Dummies, 4th Edition
978-0-470-91388-8

Wine For Dummies,
4th Edition
978-0-470-04579-4

Diet & Nutrition

Kettlebells For Dummies
978-0-470-59929-7

Nutrition For Dummies,
5th Edition
978-0-470-93231-5

Restaurant Calorie Counter
For Dummies,
2nd Edition
978-0-470-64405-8

Digital Photography

Digital SLR Cameras &
Photography For Dummies,
4th Edition
978-1-118-14489-3

Digital SLR Settings
& Shortcuts
For Dummies
978-0-470-91763-3

Photoshop Elements 10
For Dummies
978-1-118-10742-3

Gardening

Gardening Basics
For Dummies
978-0-470-03749-2

Vegetable Gardening
For Dummies,
2nd Edition
978-0-470-49870-5

Green/Sustainable

Raising Chickens
For Dummies
978-0-470-46544-8

Green Cleaning
For Dummies
978-0-470-39106-8

Health

Diabetes For Dummies,
3rd Edition
978-0-470-27086-8

Food Allergies
For Dummies
978-0-470-09584-3

Living Gluten-Free
For Dummies,
2nd Edition
978-0-470-58589-4

Hobbies

Beekeeping
For Dummies,
2nd Edition
978-0-470-43065-1

Chess For Dummies,
3rd Edition
978-1-118-01695-4

Drawing For Dummies,
2nd Edition
978-0-470-61842-4

eBay For Dummies,
7th Edition
978-1-118-09806-6

Knitting For Dummies,
2nd Edition
978-0-470-28747-7

Language &
Foreign Language

English Grammar
For Dummies,
2nd Edition
978-0-470-54664-2

French For Dummies,
2nd Edition
978-1-118-00464-7

German For Dummies,
2nd Edition
978-0-470-90101-4

Spanish Essentials
For Dummies
978-0-470-63751-7

Spanish For Dummies,
2nd Edition
978-0-470-87855-2

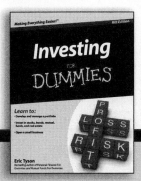

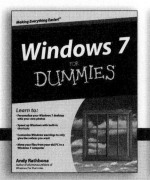

Math & Science

Algebra I For Dummies,
2nd Edition
978-0-470-55964-2

Biology For Dummies,
2nd Edition
978-0-470-59875-7

Chemistry For Dummies,
2nd Edition
978-1-1180-0730-3

Geometry For Dummies,
2nd Edition
978-0-470-08946-0

Pre-Algebra Essentials
For Dummies
978-0-470-61838-7

Microsoft Office

Excel 2010 For Dummies
978-0-470-48953-6

Office 2010 All-in-One
For Dummies
978-0-470-49748-7

Office 2011 for Mac
For Dummies
978-0-470-87869-9

Word 2010
For Dummies
978-0-470-48772-3

Music

Guitar For Dummies,
2nd Edition
978-0-7645-9904-0

Clarinet For Dummies
978-0-470-58477-4

iPod & iTunes
For Dummies,
9th Edition
978-1-118-13060-5

Pets

Cats For Dummies,
2nd Edition
978-0-7645-5275-5

Dogs All-in One
For Dummies
978-0470-52978-2

Saltwater Aquariums
For Dummies
978-0-470-06805-2

Religion & Inspiration

The Bible For Dummies
978-0-7645-5296-0

Catholicism For Dummies,
2nd Edition
978-1-118-07778-8

Spirituality For Dummies,
2nd Edition
978-0-470-19142-2

Self-Help & Relationships

Happiness For Dummies
978-0-470-28171-0

Overcoming Anxiety
For Dummies,
2nd Edition
978-0-470-57441-6

Seniors

Crosswords For Seniors
For Dummies
978-0-470-49157-7

iPad 2 For Seniors
For Dummies, 3rd Edition
978-1-118-17678-8

Laptops & Tablets
For Seniors For Dummies,
2nd Edition
978-1-118-09596-6

Smartphones & Tablets

BlackBerry For Dummies,
5th Edition
978-1-118-10035-6

Droid X2 For Dummies
978-1-118-14864-8

HTC ThunderBolt
For Dummies
978-1-118-07601-9

MOTOROLA XOOM
For Dummies
978-1-118-08835-7

Sports

Basketball For Dummies,
3rd Edition
978-1-118-07374-2

Football For Dummies,
2nd Edition
978-1-118-01261-1

Golf For Dummies,
4th Edition
978-0-470-88279-5

Test Prep

ACT For Dummies,
5th Edition
978-1-118-01259-8

ASVAB For Dummies,
3rd Edition
978-0-470-63760-9

The GRE Test For
Dummies, 7th Edition
978-0-470-00919-2

Police Officer Exam
For Dummies
978-0-470-88724-0

Series 7 Exam
For Dummies
978-0-470-09932-2

Web Development

HTML, CSS, & XHTML
For Dummies, 7th Edition
978-0-470-91659-9

Drupal For Dummies,
2nd Edition
978-1-118-08348-2

Windows 7

Windows 7
For Dummies
978-0-470-49743-2

Windows 7
For Dummies,
Book + DVD Bundle
978-0-470-52398-8

Windows 7 All-in-One
For Dummies
978-0-470-48763-1